QUIET FIRE

The Spiritual Life of Abraham Lincoln

"As to his religious nature, it seems to me to have certainly been of the amplest, deepest-rooted, loftiest kind." - Walt Whitman

DUNCAN D. NEWCOMER

Quiet Fire:
The Spiritual Life of Abraham Lincoln
by Rev. Dr. Duncan D. Newcomer

Cover photo by Susan Crysler
"Lincoln Standing" Painting by David K. Stone

Library of Congress Control Number: 2024949711
International Standard Book Number: 978-1-60126-976-8

SANTOS BOOKS

ENDORSEMENTS

"This truly is a magnum opus—clearly it is the product of many, many years of study and thought, drawing on a wide variety of sources and disciplines. Lincoln specialists will enjoy the allusions, references, and scholarly source material. The book will enrich their thinking and research with its depth and insights."
- Sheryl Fullerton

"This is a really interesting study of Lincoln, from an angle that is (as far as I know) unique. It's an interpretation of an aspect of Lincoln's psychology, which you call 'spirituality.' Maybe 'interpretation' is not the right word 'meditation' on Lincoln's spirituality is more accurate, because your reflections work in two ways: you're not only examining AL's spirituality, but reflecting on the nature of spirituality itself, and its possible roles in shaping character, values, behavior, world view...."
- Dr. Richard Slotkin, Olin Professor of American Studies Emeritus, Wesleyan University

"You get to the heart of how political values work. I love your sentence that "equality really means more equality," because it shows that we don't necessarily know what valuing equality will commit us to all the way down, but we do know what it commits us to here and now, and following out that commitment will make the next one more clear to us. I love also the wisdom this gives you about the limitations of historical figures, something I think we are in our too self-righteous moment too quick to forget. And best of all I like your notion of what the living God is."
- Dr. John Burt, Professor of English, Brandeis University

"I've read your book with a lot of pleasure. The main argument is very persuasive, and it is full of local insights. This book offers a new, non-dogmatic, non-denominational way to feel the power of religious themes (not really religious doctrines but religious themes) in politics and culture. I think you have a lot more to say about the religious quality of Lincoln's thinking than any one else I've read, even Wolf, even Niebuhr."
- Rev. Dr. John Philip Newell

DEDICATION

This book originated in my Master's Thesis at Union Theological Seminary under the guidance of Dr. Robert C. Handy and the inspiration of Dr. Robert Wood Lynn and Dr. Dwayne Huebner.

Students at the Loomis Chaffee School and church members at the Old Lyme Congregational Church often heard me read chapters of that original work.

Students at Belfast (Maine) Senior College more recently welcomed my course "The Spiritual Life of Abraham Lincoln." Dr. George Siscoe and the Old Professor's Book Store in Belfast sponsored the Shop Talk that gave me the outline for the material. WERU community radio in mid-coast Maine has sponsored my weekly short features "Quiet Fire, a program about the spiritual life of Abraham Lincoln and its relevance to us today."

Friends have read and encouraged chapters of the book. Rev. Dr. Eileen Sypher, William Boone Bonvillian, Peter Stevens, Thomas Jefferson Byrum, David Edgerton, Robert Rackmales. My sister Beclee Wilson, and her husband John Oliver Wilson, have read and heard parts of the book and encouraged me.

First Readers have provided major help and encouragement, including, Dr. John Burt, Dr. Richard Slotkin, Brian "Fox" Ellis, and Dr. Wayne Baker. Editor David Crumm at Readthespirit along with Dr. Baker offered me my first venue for widespread sharing of these ideas.

The Writers' Residency Program at The Poet's House in New Harmony, Indiana and the sponsorship of Docey Lewis, The Blaffer Foundation and the Workingmen's Institute gave me a home to finish the book.

No one has been a stronger believer in me and this work than Rebecca Phelps Jessup, my life love and partner, to whom the book is dedicated.

CONTENTS

FOREWORD

There was a full moon on the hot nights of the battle at Gettysburg, the nights of July first, second and third, 1863. Eighty years later, on July third, I was born. On the night of my fiftieth birthday, from the steps of the Lincoln Memorial, I watched a full orange moon rise over the long dark reflecting pool. The moon slowly changed to silver, and I felt the white moon on Lincoln looming behind me.

In that moonlight, 130 years after the sultry nights at Gettysburg, I thought about that battleground. Those fields and trees on the night before the final battle on the third would have held oddly moon-bathed warriors, and grotesque corpses already everywhere. The horses, cannon, wagons, the gathered equipment of several hundred thousand soldiers, all there in moonlight. I pondered: what star-courses had placed me in this history? I thought of his words, and the man himself, Abraham Lincoln.

It was hot, too, I've been told, in Morrilton, Arkansas, where I was born on July third of 1943. So I also thought, that night when I turned fifty, of what Lincoln called the mystic chords of memory. I felt them binding me and letting me go. I felt how the moon changes, changes everything it lights, and how I have changed. I thought of how Lincoln changed and what those changes mean to us today. But the moon white Memorial seemed constant behind me.

The irony of the Lincoln Memorial is that nothing seems more Lincolnesque than the constantly white Greek temple, its inner sanctum, and his iconic seated self. Nothing says "Lincoln" to us more than the Memorial, except perhaps for his miniature face on copper pennies everywhere. Yet it is really a most un-Lincolnesque thing. Lincoln was full of noises, laughter, soft slipper-footed shufflings, hand-shaking greetings, definitive instructions, long and short speeches, as well as silences. The statue itself is only still and silent.

Lincoln was as awkward as he might be majestic. He was often as homely as he was occasionally stately. He was abundant with profound words and prolific with wise actions. Lincoln was, in a word, dynamic. The Memorial, in eyesight, is static. But inside our own minds and hearts he continues to be dynamic.

The list of opposites in his character is almost endless. He was a rollicking melancholic, as comic as he was tragic. He was a leader who seemed to drift. Yet his spiritual life was not just a bundle of paradoxes, it changed within a direction. Ultimately it is his spiritual resolution of so many paradoxes that explains his way of leading, his way of thinking. But his spiritual being is also full of contradictions, especially between the secular and the religious. Still his thinking, as it emerged, about God, history, and justice, moved him in a direction of a certain kind of leadership, to a language of prophecy, to a teaching of mercy.

It is a misnomer to say that Lincoln was an autodidact, as if only schools teach, and only academic information is teaching. We are not entirely left on our own if we do not have schools, especially in terms of spirituality. Lincoln was educated without schools by spiritual forces that are historically definable in religious traditions, cultural heritages and by huge unconscious archetypal and conscious psychological forces. The spiritual life of Abraham Lincoln does not, however, fit the cultural form of religion the way his age or our own understands religion. Of the multitude of paradoxes in Lincoln none is greater or more relevant than his combination of spiritual formation and religious rejections. His is both a sacred and a secular journey. His spiritual formation was unique for his time and is instructive to our own. His religious rejections grew more and more characteristic of his time and are increasingly so in our own. Yet he had what Walt Whitman saw as a superlative religious nature, ample, deep-rooted, and lofty.

Lincoln was a man of values, and values hold, as John Burt argues in *Lincoln's Tragic Pragmatism*, a certain implicitness. He means that when values are lived in historical action they reveal further developments. Moonlight is a good light for seeing Lincoln. In shadows we see what Burt calls the "penumbra of implications." These were implications Lincoln looked at from the dark, like moonlight on the waters of the Lincoln Memorial reflecting pool.

The first time I walked the land of Lincoln's boyhood home in southern Indiana, a place called Pigeon Creek, I had the intense feeling that his sheer personal goodness was in still in the air. The spirit, or poetry, of that perception was, in a way, mundane and material, with no great apparitions or images. I just felt that, in the air, around the leaves of the trees, and hidden in the rough bushes, there was a vestige of his personal goodness. I had the passing hope that this spirit-in-the-air might rub off on me, but mainly I felt convinced that it followed him wherever, yes wherever, he went throughout his life. From my own religious tradition I thought of Jesus being baptized in the Jordan River and the Holy Spirit, a dove, and the voice of his Father, descending on him in deep blessing. I felt then a theological, mystical, conclusion: certain people carry with them a concentration of some spirit that actually affects people around them and lasts beyond their life. I thought too of Gandhi and the Buddha. That was my experience that summer day.

I have been carrying Lincoln around with me for decades, as many people do. As a teacher I have had a professional interest in his education. As a psychotherapist and family counselor, my work and my view of my own development have been informed by his psychological development. As a minister and preacher, I have been intellectually challenged by his theology and his nearly sermonic speeches, which reveal to me the meaning of personal and national history. His literary achievements and interests have inspired me as a poet and writer.

A person who likes Lincoln needs to be humble because so many people like him, even love him. Each of us takes our interest intensely and also personally, as if he is somehow our own. I have read that Marilyn Monroe told Carl Sandburg that she wished Abraham Lincoln had been her father. Leo Tolstoy knew enough about Lincoln that he esteemed him as the greatest of leaders because of his Christ-like nature in teaching love for the enemy.

Lincoln has been with me through my four careers: teacher, therapist, preacher, and writer. I have also brought him with me through my life in a large painting of Lincoln that I had commissioned in 1970, to be done by the well-known David K. Stone, eventually President of the American Society of Illustrators. It is one of the few paintings or pictures of Lincoln standing. His right face, not his so-called weak left side, is featured as well. Its mysterious oil image has the haunting look of his face those last few months before his death.

Mystery is the final concept in understanding Lincoln's advent, development, and changes. No one can fully explain how he came to be who he was. As John Philip Newell says introducing his study *Shakespeare and The Human Mystery*, "What cannot be said about each of us is always greater than anything that can be said."

Or as Shakespeare himself said "For what you see is but the smallest part/…were the whole frame here, / It is of such a spacious lofty pitch/Your roof were not sufficient to contain't." (1 Henry VI).

No field of investigation can explain sufficiently why Lincoln was able to do what he did, how it was possible for him to do what seemed so fundamentally impossible, much less how he ended up in a position to do all those things. I thank my partner, Rebecca Jessup, Latin teacher and poet, for the insight that Lincoln reminds her of Joan of Arc. How, in other words, do we explain that such unlikely persons, in all ways, could have come into existence and have done, in real history, what they did?

Mark Twain took twelve years to write his biography of Joan of Arc. He thought it was his best and also his favorite book. In his massive research and his many pages he never gets beyond his original astonishment at her very being, and he is almost worshipful at the end. What came to me in my first walk on the Indiana Boyhood Home grounds was my original astonishment at Lincoln's palpable and good presence, a worshipful feeling that he came to be what he became and, moreover, that he came to be at all.

INTRODUCTION

This book names six aspects of Lincoln's spiritual life and organizes them into two categories. The first category includes three ways of defining his spiritual cast of mind: his use of language, his sense of vision and mystery, and his poise. The second category includes three ways of defining his archetypal psychology: his spiritual life defined as Warrior, as King, and as Grail King.

How he used language and what language meant to him is the place to begin. If his reportedly distant-looking eyes were the windows to his soul, his words are the doorway to his spirit. Second to his language is a cast of mind that is unique to Lincoln. The best term of art for his sense of vision and mystery is Carl Sandburg's word, "Yonder." If, as some anthropologists tell us, the human mind was originally shaped by its view of the plains and savannahs of Africa, so too Lincoln's mind was spiritually shaped by the frontier and prairie he viewed. Rabindranath Tagore, the Indian poet, saw the forests of India as the sanctuary for ancient sages, giving them a view of wholeness and a vital link to the infinite. So Lincoln's mind was as immersed in frontier and prairie landscapes as well as in the religious and national hopes implicit in his early communities. Yonder also includes a sense of hope that comes from both his mother and his stepmother. Along with language and Yonder, Lincoln's spiritual life bears a striking resemblance to that attitude of poise in the face of uncertainty described by the poet John Keats. His odd term for such inner balance is "Negative Capability." The Keats scholar Walter Jackson Bate correlates this capability with the Taoist principle of non-action, called wu-wei. Lincoln's many unpredictable actions, and non-actions, are understandable from this view, a spiritual orientation to all of life. Negative Capability is a secular name for a stance that others might call faith, a religious stance that Lincoln came too late and then only ambivalently.

While all three of these aspects of Lincoln's spiritual life could be capitalized to clarify their objective value, "language" is left in lower case because it is a common human function. Lincoln read aloud most of his life, and his view of language is closely correlated to how we define speech. His use of language in his public addresses fits the oral traditions of prophecy and revelation. His is often a secular sacred poetry.

Yonder is capitalized because it is used here in the same way that other spiritual categories are used, such as Grace, Holy Spirit, and Thou. Words like these mean a spiritual place or aspect. Lincoln's unique way of blending secular and sacred traditions also means that a word like Yonder becomes an elevated and definable spiritual quality. Yonder is not a word he used, but is the right word to name his far vision and, as we shall see, his near hopes.

Negative Capability is usually capitalized by literary scholars and by Lincoln scholars who use the term, such as John Burt and David Herbert Donald. Keats, of course, usually capitalized it as well. It is a strange enough category, and it helps to understand Negative Capability to contrast it with what we usually think of as the positive capability to be pro-active and ideologically informed in a decisive way. Students of theology who know the term Negative Theology will recognize that the odd use of the word "negative" can mean something valuable, such as the mystery and unknowability of God in the Via Negativa.

In addition to this epistemology of Lincoln's spiritual life there are three psychological archetypes that reveal the spiritual life of Lincoln acting in history. These terms, from Jungian psychology, give us ways to interpret Lincoln's spirit. Jung's well-known word for these unconscious instincts that he believed governed our common behaviors and meanings is Archetype. They are patterns that emerge independently of history but are deeply formative of history. In Lincoln's case the Warrior and the King are the primary archetypes that reveal his spiritual as well as his secular value. They help us see where he fits into the dichotomy of Caesar and Christ, making that paradox understandable. Warrior and King, as well as the unfinished myths of the Grail King (12th and 13th century European stories of quest and healing) give us revealing ways to see Lincoln. The Grail King helps us see him as the so-called innocent country fool. He emerges as the one who knows how to ask and answer the mythic question, "Whom does the Grail serve?" That question's answer defines the purposes of both the sword and the chalice, which were essential issues for Lincoln's Civil War leadership. He was the Warrior in Chief and he was the one who restored the national authority, and, as he said, with a "King's cure," ended the evil of slavery with the Thirteenth Amendment banning slavery. The spiritual aspects of Lincoln as Warrior and King are fulfilled in the Grail Myth.

These six terms then, language, Yonder, and Negative Capability, Warrior, King, and Grail King, mark our turns into the labyrinth of Abraham Lincoln. As spiritual capacities they did not develop in Lincoln in sequence. We use them to look at Lincoln's relevance to our time. These themes are woven through various crucial times and events in his life to reveal his spiritual life.

PREFACE

"Catastrophe has imposed on America a profound unmooring sense of the unknown, and at this particular time we have to protect not just our external world but our internal one. This requires vigilance, an insistence on living with ambiguity, on thinking against received opinion, and mastering anxiety."

- John Lahr, *The New Yorker* November, 2001 (following 9/11)

We come to Abraham Lincoln divided against ourselves in many ways. One of his most remarkable abilities was how well he housed things divided. He was liberal in his goals but conservative in his methods. He was secular in his intellect yet often religious in his language.

Lincoln, however, did not sacrifice his passion in order to accommodate the divisive wars going on inside him and 'round about him. Rather with his own quiet fire and intense concentration he found a bright point of transcendence, a third alternative, to many of the darkly irreconcilable conflicts of his era.

We study Lincoln, his intellect and his spirit, hoping to understand more how to hold our house together, spiritually and politically. As he became President many Americans were talking past each other in languages that deepened division. Christian piety was strong in the country and yet some preachers increasingly mined the Bible for an ore to forge into steel for war. The self-righteous used religious language, North and South.

Not an orthodox Christian in any traditional sense, Lincoln's own fiery furnace yielded a nearly Biblical theological language that we hold as almost sacred and certainly unifying. We have wide religious differences and wonder what sacred canopy covers us. Much of his language can hold us.

As he grew to become one of our more literate and eloquent presidents, much of the educated elite was leaving Evangelical religion for the modern fields of science and rational enlightenment. Science fueled industry, reason seemed to erode the religious moral core, and educational and economic divisions grew.

Poor and formerly uneducated Lincoln learned practical science and enlightened reason well. But he could, in fact he did, see a religious moral vision beyond them. We have trusted technical progress and higher education and can wonder if religion holds any practical or moral vision for our time.

Lincoln had two points of reference that stood outside of the liberal-conservative, secular-religious, views of his time. One point of reference was that he saw the American experiment as a beacon to the peoples of the world. In that sense he shared in a secular way the original Puritan vision of an experiment set like a beacon on a hill. In fact, unknown to him, six generations back, in the late 1630's, his ancestors had moved from Hingham, England, a hot bed of Puritan revolt, to Hingham, Massachusetts in the Bay Colony. Throughout Lincoln's struggle to hold the American proposition together, to prove itself to a doubting world, he had in mind a light for the common peoples of the world, especially old Europe and benighted Russia. He felt deeply that America was crucial to the world.

His second point of reference was simply this: He felt that American was important to God and that God was crucial to America. He didn't go into his life believing things like that. In fact it was only fate and necessity that he first believed in. But fate—from the view of the fiery trial he lived in his last five years—took on the face of God, and necessity took on the hand of God's justice and judgment, calling for God's mercy.

With these two perspectives Lincoln could take a political stand greater than that held by either side in the war, and he had a moral means for the goal of union. The defeat of the Southern rebellion was a win for America in his mind, and a win for American was a win for the real freedom of the world's peoples who had been ruled by despots for years. The eventual moral means of conducting the war—emancipation—became his theological stand and a necessary response to the demands of God's justice. Not only was the world watching him and the American experiment, but God was as well. Lincoln would say in his Second Inaugural, sounding like a Biblical Prophet, that God could compel justice by imposing suffering for the mutual evil of slavery.

The things that divided the house he presided over did not divide him because he had these two greater points of view, the world and God. Opposing forces, however, seemed to settle on Lincoln's shoulders like gigantic birds of prey.

But, as historian Allen Guelzo says in his book *Redeemer President*, Lincoln actually had an increasingly Calvinistic notion of God's providence. It led him to stay with a war policy that extended the war. "Lincoln had to step outside liberalism and surrender himself to the direction of an overruling divine providence whose conclusions he had by no means prejudged." What unified Lincoln more and more in the end was his conviction of divine providence as the just cause of the extended suffering. Guelzo attributes Lincoln's depth and resiliency, his "great resources," to this cohesion. He followed neither bird of prey, abolitionist nor unionist, on either of his stooped shoulders. Yet he ended up fulfilling the abolitionist and the unionist hopes, despite them not because of them. He had this third way, and in anyone less skeptical and thoughtful it would have seemed like religious fanaticism.

Part I

CHAPTER ONE

The Origins of Lincoln's Spiritual Life, Land and Language

When Walt Whitman stood watching the mounted Lincoln ride by his street corner he wrote of him as a "Westerner." He, like most of the nation, saw the dark-skinned and rustic Lincoln as someone from the edges of American civilization. There is a long tradition of spiritual figures emerging from the liminal spaces of wilderness. One such tradition is that of the ancient sages of India that the mystic poet Tagore writes about. Whitman, the poet, was able to see the comfortable inner quiet of Lincoln, as well as his fire, as spiritual qualities of his religious nature.

Lincoln's spirituality emerges in his language but originated in his experience of place, the land. Those places, frontier and prairie, defined his visual and then mental picture of the world. His spirituality is rooted in how he saw those places, literally in his vision.

The bird-noisy, thick forests and human-scarce, open prairies had their spiritual impact on the growing Lincoln. Those places of his original sounds and sights are primary to understanding him, and for that understanding we use that significant word for his spirituality, Yonder.

The knobby hills, clear streams, and open small-farm lands in Kentucky, where he was born, were most likely bucolic for the very young Lincoln. But the millions of acres of former Indian territory, newly made into the State of Indiana, were largely virgin primeval forests when he moved there with his family at the age of seven. Trees were over a hundred feet high and the never-seen-before trunks were impossibly close together. That is what greeted the little Lincoln family of four as they hacked their way through the dozen or so miles from the Ohio River to the blazed markers of their new home. To expand what eventually became a site of more than one hundred acres, trees would be girdled one year and set afire as giant torches the next. The Lincolns then were back to the rudiments of civilization and survival, with a rifle, an axe, and a few other tools. On Thomas Lincoln's original exploratory journey he had lost his tools overboard in the Ohio River crossing.

This Indiana experience has significant parallels to the origins of the spiritual sages of ancient India. Compare the Lincoln's 1816 frontier America with the geographical and spiritual situation described by Rabindranath Tagore in *Sadhana. The Realization of Life*. He writes, "The first (Aryan) invasion of India has its exact parallel in the invasion of America by the European settlers. They also were confronted with primeval forests and a fierce struggle with aboriginal races."

But Tagore observes that the Americans followed a different fate from the invaders of India and never "came to any terms" with the land and the people. He does not note the Romantic and Transcendentalists coming to terms with the land in American civilization, but only the more dominant narrative of economic and political manifest destiny. "In India the forest … became the sanctuary of sages, but in America these great living cathedrals of nature had no deeper significance to man." Except, he imagines, for a solitary poet, and perhaps the Romantics and Transcendentalists, the Americans did not come to the same sort of spiritual awareness as did these ancient Indian sages.

"They (the forests) never acquired a sacred association in the hearts of men as the site of some great spiritual reconcilement where man's soul's had its meeting-place with the soul of the world." The story of the American move west is not a story of seeing mountains as sanctuaries for sages and forests as cathedrals of nature. Except, that is, for Lincoln. He was that solitary poet. For all his eventual promotion of the expansion of American civilization Lincoln did come to a spiritual reconciliation with land and nature. To him the austere and awesome land was different than it was to most all those around him. The forested places and open lands nurtured his spiritual life. He stood out from his cohorts when it came to what land and animals were all about and what his relationship to them was.

Benjamin Thomas, in his classic biography, quotes a student of Lincoln who noted how odd Lincoln felt himself to be, and how that sense of being odd led him to his strength and his independent self. He was odd and he was independent. As William Lee Miller points out in his book on Lincoln's virtue, the young man Lincoln said "no" to almost everything his contemporaries said "yes" to. He said "no" to hunting, even fishing, as well as alcohol, swearing, and cruelty against nature and each other.

Lincoln's spirit then was oddly closer to those unknown and ancient Indian sages. Those were people who reconciled themselves into a place of union and accommodation with the natural environment, not a mode of exploitation and domination. While Lincoln was a proponent of the advance of American civilization, railroads and all, he consistently shows in his language and his actions, his spirit, a mode of irenic acceptance with the natural world and with a larger, inclusive, view. His constant use of homely metaphors, his return to rustic rough-hewn simple speech, his clear-eyed perception of physical and moral realities, all show him to be that odd "Western" man that Whitman called him. Whitman sensed how Lincoln was comfortable in the real world, within himself, and like the iconic, unpretentious Westerner, did not make artificial separations of himself from others. That was his spiritual sense of connection, his deep sense of communion with the people and the country. This was his visceral spirituality.

Lincoln was able to see with a clarity that feels almost physical, as if his mind made something happen. He reaches a depth of understanding about the issues facing the country that escaped almost everyone else. His mythologized image as a rail-splitter suggests how his calm, incisive mind worked. Recalling the metaphor of a razor-sharp mind, Lincoln's mind was sharp and weighty like an axe. The issues at stake in the country, manacled as it was by slavery and self-righteousness on both sides, could appear tangled and impossibly complex. It was not just Euclid's logic, or lawyerly analysis, or even moral courage that drove Lincoln to clarity, it was an original and primitive clarity of vision and a fundamental sense of oneness. Lincoln's mind literally was formed, frontier and prairie, by seeing the forest and the trees.

Lincoln's first major address show us just what he might make of the forest and the trees, trees being a theme from nature he returns to often. In 1838 to the Young Men's Lyceum in Springfield, Illinois, the somewhat bombastic young lawyer Lincoln is lamenting the falling away of patriotic passions as the generation of the founding American revolutionaries is passing away. The memory of those fathers and sons and brothers has been a "living history." Their wounds and scars were authentic reminders of their revolutionary passion. Lincoln calls for a "political religion" to continue their fight. He gives his listeners images. He poeticizes that "the silent artillery of time" has leveled the walls of the fortress lives these men lived. But he has also imaged their living sacrifice as witnessed by their "limbs mangled." That image takes his mind and rhetoric to the forest memories of his youth, much more of Indiana than the flat prairies of the Illinois in which he is speaking. These revolutionary men were a fortress, but they were also "a forest of giant oaks, but the all –resistless hurricane has swept over them and left only, here and there, a lonely trunk, despoiled of its verdure, shorn of its foliage, unshading and unshaded, to murmur in a few more gentle breezes, and to combat with its mutilated limbs, a few more ruder storms, and then to sink, and be no more."

His poetic mind has gone from men with "limbs mangled" to trees with "mutilated limbs." This is more than language to him, this is memory. When Lincoln was seven and first in Indiana he would have seen in the Pigeon Creek area huge swaths of the primeval forests that had been leveled by a gigantic and historic earlier hurricane. With the size of the trees and the extent of the clearances the boy Lincoln would have been mightily impacted by the devastation. Only, he proclaims, against such natural temporal forces could a political religion based on cold and unimpassioned reason raise up new men as pillars for the temple of liberty. But it would be a fight against "the artillery of time," which was everyman's fate.

The mystic Indian sages' accommodation with natural reality is spiritually akin to Lincoln. For him accommodation was a Calvinistic fatalism, as well as a naturalistic belief in fate. His was an oddly passive nature at times, with an inner quiet. He was also learning from the Transcendentalist Emerson about joining the powers of the natural world. He had read and maybe even heard Emerson talk of joining the forces of nature. Water, in river images and in his famous ode to Niagara Falls in 1848, were his way of seeing the power of history. That was his version of what Tagore saw in the old sages. Those sages were the ones who knew, said Tagore, that one could "use the forces of nature for his own purpose only because his power is in harmony with the power which is universal…." That spirit of wisdom that Tagore finds in the old sages is the spirit we will find again and again in Lincoln. "Man must," says Tagore, "realize the wholeness of his existence, his place in the infinite; he must know that hard as he may strive he can never create his honey with the cells of his hive."

That is the kind of homely image and thought that we find in Lincoln. For Lincoln the honey of democracy was the will of the people, and not something he could create. This spirit of basic trust, natural harmony, and union—so prevalent in Lincoln's generous spirit and inclusive world-view—is not something he learned from a mystic vision passed on from India. Lincoln learned accommodation by seeing natural reality. He incorporated that vision into his own spacious nature. He was willing to live his place in nature and history as his response to a fate, a fate he came to see eventually as from God. For most of his life he was much more likely to speak of nature than of God. The detailed image that Tagore expresses of bees and honey and hives could easily have been Lincoln himself writing. Often little details from the natural world clinched his point. In a military telegram he wired General McClellan, "You must know that major-generalships in the regular army are not as plenty as blackberries." To find just the right word was an obsession with Lincoln. His mind would have sifted down through layers of reading and thinking to arrive upon "blackberries" as just the right way to talk of the scarcity of generals. There were layers to Lincoln's mind, language built up with the Bible, with Shakespeare, with the poetry of Burns—a naturalistic source—and then the law and political documents and arguments. But in the clear bedrock—like those visible pebbles in Knob Creek in his boyhood Kentucky—there were images from his close life with the natural world. He could easily turn to Stephen A. Douglas in their debate and point out how important it was to know the difference between horse chestnuts and a chestnut horse.

Lincoln was odd and rustic but gentle, he was contrary without being negative, austere in his thinking without being cold-hearted, and he was far-sighted without being vague or fuzzyheaded. All these are nature-bound traits that Americans, like Whitman, associate with the Westerner. And like other Westerners, such as Mark Twain, he was a profound thinker, an intellectual, a master of words written and spoken, but he had most of his book-learning from the books themselves, not from schools, just as his spiritual life was less from churches than from books and people and the land itself.

The lack of a school-building education is crucial to the spiritual life of Lincoln. Tagore begins his book contrasting the Greek City State's learning environment—a city with a wall, "cradles of brick and mortar" he calls them. This is compared with being open to the mountains and the forests as the learning place, the place of the ancient cave-living sages. "These (brick) walls leave their mark deep in the minds of men," says Tagore.

> They set up a principle of "divide and rule" in our mental outlook, which begets in us a habit of securing all our conquests by fortifying them and separating them from one another. We divide nation and nation, knowledge and knowledge, man and nature. It breeds in us a strong suspicion of whatever is beyond the barriers we have built…[1]

One could hardly describe better the culture and society of the country and its paranoia and conspiracy theories in the decades prior to the Civil War. It is, as we shall see, not a mind-set we find much in Lincoln. A school without walls, like a roofless church, is a different kind of place in which to learn the world or the spirit. One can easily see that Lincoln learned from the forests and the prairies to have an openness of view and spirit that a walled campus would not have fostered. As Melville says in *Moby Dick* of Ishmael, the sea was his Harvard and his Yale. So Lincoln could have claimed the forest

---

[1]   Tagore, *Sadhana the Realization of Life,* 1916, pg. 3.

and then the prairies as his higher education. Tagore says the fruits of such learning are this, "…it was in the forests that our civilization had its birth, and it took a distinct character from this origin and environment. It was surrounded by the vast life of nature, was fed and clothed by her, and had the closest and most constant intercourse with her varying aspects."

Lincoln, like the ancient Indian sages of Tagore, had an accommodation to land itself. The spaciousness in Lincoln's own spirit mirrors the spaces he saw and knew in the land. He taught himself to be a surveyor, and was good at it. He knew maps and how to read both rivers and the land. In his annual message to Congress in 1862 he rallies the nation to a clear sense of purpose and cause, and his arguments are as solid as he felt the land to be. After quoting the Bible on the passing and the coming of generations, he introduces the earth, "but the earth abideth forever." So he said that first we must look at "this ever-enduring part." And he states, "That portion of the earth's surface which is owned and inhabited by the people of the United States, is well adapted to be the home of one national family; and it is not well adapted for two, or more." To him the union was matter of fact, and as he said in his First Inaugural disunion was just an inadequate idea. This is more than just nationalistic manifest destiny talk; this is a grounded vision of reality with a mystic purpose. It brings him to a piercing point. After going through all the legal and social impossibilities of a divided nation trying to co-exist side by side, with slavery as well, he just says this: "There is not a line, straight or crooked, suitable for a national boundary upon which to divide."

This is a spiritual principle of accommodation to the natural world that Tagore features for the ancient sages of his land. For Lincoln the land holds a powerful eternal spiritual principle. He concludes:

> Our national strife springs not from our permanent part; not from the land we inhabit: not from our national homestead.

There is no possible severing of this but would multiply and not mitigate evils among us. In all its adaptations and aptitudes it demands union and abhors separation. In fact, it would ere long force reunion, however much of blood and treasure the separation might have cost. [2]

This is also a different kind of nationalism than the "blood and iron" of Bismarck's Germany. This is not about domination by the Fatherland so much as it is about the holding mother country, the national "homestead."

In his biography, Thomas writes about Lincoln's education what we also see as his spiritual formation:

> "In a manner, the frontier environment of the place had been his school, amplifying what he learned from books. Rural living developed a talent for inventiveness....The Westerner, primarily a realist, was speculative too. In Lincoln's case, the conditions of rural living intensified a natural bent for philosophical thinking. The vastness of the country gave him breadth of outlook....The traits of birds, and farmyard animals, the majesty of forests, plains, and rivers, the beauty, the mystery, the bounty, and the dreadfulness of nature quickened his imagination, bestirred his reflections, and increasingly adorned his speech....So Lincoln drew into himself the raw, rich strength of the frontier." [3]

Benjamin Thomas is writing about Lincoln's spirituality.

People said of Lincoln that no matter how attentive he could be to you personally in a conversation, he also seemed not to lose a dreamy far-away look in his hazel eyes, as if he was also seeing

---

[2]   Annual Message to Congress, December 1862.
[3]   Benjamin Thomas, *Abraham Lincoln—A Biography*. New York, Barnes & Noble Books, 1994, Pg. 65.

beyond you and beyond the moment to something grander, deeper, bigger, more beautiful and sustaining. Perhaps it was a vestige view of the prairie or, perhaps it was some spirit, some providence, some source of judgment and mercy, even some God.

Lincoln's accommodation to nature was in visions minute and distant, a theme he shows repeatedly, detail and scope.

Language Becoming Deeds

A spiritual person is a person of word and deed. Language and action become one in Lincoln's spiritual life. Lincoln did things with words, and his words did things. He is the nation's Chief Priest when he decrees, in 1863, a third National Holiday. Thanksgiving is to be added to the Fourth of July and Washington's Birthday. In rhetoric this is called performative speech, as when a judge declares the accused "Guilty" or a minister says, "You are husband and wife"—things made actual with words. Biblical revelation is such speech. God said "light" and there was light. Jesus Christ, according to John, is God's Word.

We see this, and more, when Helen Keller's teacher Anne Sullivan writes with her finger the letters "w-a-t-e-r" on Helen Keller's one hand and holding her other under pump water. She made something happen with a word. A word was literally made into a deed that then transformed a mind and a life.

Helen Keller described this event in her autobiography *The Story of My Life*:

> I stood still, my whole attention fixed upon the motion of her fingers. Suddenly I felt a misty consciousness as of something forgotten—a thrill of returning thought; and somehow the mystery of language was revealed to me....the living word awakened my soul, gave it light, hope, joy, set it free!

This is the story that Walker Percy, the novelist and essayist on language, tells to show how language symbolically transforms a person's mind. Anne Sullivan was the artist and her words, to Percy, were the virtual creation of the form that symbolizes not just information but actual feelings and value in the receiver. Such forms of feeling are more than emotions, they are organs of reality and the concepts of truth that, Percy says, St. Thomas Aquinas wrote about.

Lincoln was the artist of the *Gettysburg Address*, and with his words he transformed the American mind. He took and takes our hands and puts words that take us out of our own misty vagueness about equality and the idea of America. The *Gettysburg Address* is a symbolic transformation of Americans. The movie *Lincoln* opens with him asking soldiers, some black and some white, why they are fighting. They say that they had heard his *Gettysburg Address* and that this is why. They walk off camera as one black solider recites his Address back to Lincoln. They are living the symbolic transformation that his language created. This inner change made outward is what theologians like H. Richard Niebuhr mean by Biblical revelation.

There is often a spirit of reverence that surrounds Lincoln and his words. In his seminal work on American history Daniel Boorstin talks about the Western States' influence on American language and what is called Tall Talk. He notes the influence of Indian speech not just on vocabulary but also on our respected ways of language. In short this is what we learned from movies: that the white man speaks with "forked tongue." This straight talk then is what the cowboys picked up from Indian culture, what we now know of as "walking the talk" deeds that fit the words. Robert Persig asserts the same source of honest language in his novels *Zen and the Art of Motorcycle Maintenance* and *Lila*. This is the heartfelt sorrow and withheld rage we associate, stereotypically, with the tight-lipped Indian Chief. It is a rhetorical seriousness, real gravity. Lincoln spoke, as John Burt ably illustrates in his long essay on *Collective Guilt in the Second Inaugural Address*, with such sober reticence, especially in his Second Inaugural Address. Silence, the tacit dimension of knowing, so essential to Yonder, is deeply present in Lincoln's speeches. He gave roughly only one hundred addresses in his public career.

Lincoln was also deep within the other aspect of Western forms of language: Tall Talk. These were big tales such as those of Paul Bunyan and Pecos Bill. Lincoln loved the humorists that featured such rollicking exaggeration, and in his less serious moments filled the air with such exaggerated prose, often to the political befuddlement of his opponents.

Lincoln spoke and was also silent, acted and also did not act as the fate of history rolled over all Americans. Millions of Americans acted and reacted to the catastrophic challenge of the American Civil War. In his years following the war, Captain Oliver Wendell Holmes, Jr., Supreme Court Justice, who was wounded severely, said," I think that, as life is action and passion, it is required of a man that he should share the passion and action of his time at peril of being judged not to have lived."

But not everyone rose to the occasion of the Civil War. Many men of letters stand out in both their inaction and in their lack of writing about this most important event in the history of the country. It is part of the definition of Lincoln's spiritual life that he was a person of both words and deeds. It is a spiritual achievement.

Among the best of contemporary Civil War literature are Herman Melville's few poems. He was in his forties, traveled to the battle sites, but did not fight. Only two of Henry James Sr.'s sons fought in the war. The most famous ones, Henry Jr., the novelist, and William, the founder of pragmatism and American psychology, did not. Mark Twain fought foolishly for a few weeks on the Confederate side in Missouri before going west. His moral actions and words on the issues of slavery and the American imperial spirit mainly came later. There were significant and unique women of action and words. Julia Ward Howe, Harriet Beecher Stowe, and Emily Dickinson wrote little about the war but, as Rosanna Warren points out in *Fables of the Self*, they acquired a rhythm, diction, and syntax that reflected the hard new realities of the world-changing war. The life's work, letters, and speeches of Clara Barton rise to the level of actions and words. (Her words, through no fault of her own, have not risen in our national, patriarchal consciousness.) But of all the elite literary giants of the age none rose to the level of heroic action and heroic words like Lincoln.

Lincoln was of course an ethical man. Actions were essential to him as a politician, and being a politician was his proud calling, as William Lee Miller so well tells us in his book on Lincoln's virtues. He does all that the Knight of Faith in Soren Kierkegaard's thought would do. He leaves behind the imaginative detached illusions of what Kierkegaard called the Aesthetic Way. He rises above the Ethical Stage that the Danish theologian defined, to be willing, like Father Abraham in the Biblical story, to sacrifice his American sons and then himself, for the absolute relation to the absolute as he saw it. Lincoln, in the end, went beyond the ethical life to what Kierkegaard called the Religious life, the life of an absolute leap of faith. We see that when he makes of the Emancipation Proclamation a personal covenant with God. We see it again in his drive for the Thirteenth Amendment outlawing slavery.

We read his spirit in his thoughts, just as we see his spirit in his deeds. Language as a driving force in his spirituality is fused with his deeds. But he is so unique in his words, so powerful in his actions, that we must try to understand first the inner life of this man, and we can. Lincoln's spirit is actually available. He wore it on his sleeve. People saw it in his eyes. Lincoln's spirit is visible, even translucent.

With some knowledge of the inner Lincoln we can look at the world the way he did. We can see, as if with his vision, what he saw, both near and far.

We see his spirit formed and expressed in his actions. Increasingly in his life his best words create new life. In the Bible the fundamental concept of divine revelation is the union of word and deed. This is a familiar spirituality.

CHAPTER TWO

Language: A Case Study

Lincoln's language, seen in speeches, addresses, poems, and personal conversation, is the bedrock of his spiritual life. Lincoln did not build his spiritual house on sand. He built his verbal dwellings carefully knowing that he, and perhaps we, would reside in them a long time.

He takes the spiritual knowing of Yonder and the partial knowledge of Negative Capability and expresses reasoned ideas and ideals in words as earthy as they are lofty. Most importantly, he secularizes the language of the evangelical Christian religion that he grew up with. That religion was a backbone to the Whig and Republican parties of his political life.

We see this secularization in the way he edits what Secretary of State William Seward, a more conventional man of faith, offered Lincoln as editions to his First Inaugural Address. But, even more remarkably, Lincoln finds a living, expanded spirit within the Enlightenment language of Thomas Jefferson's Declaration of Independence. While he secularizes the religious language of Secretary Seward he sanctifies the Enlightenment words of Jefferson. He makes sacred and immediate the distant divine machinery of Jefferson's Laws of Nature. Nature's God comes down to earth in a living issue, a "proposition," in the *Gettysburg Address*.

The nation, Lincoln will assert in that short speech, has been since 1776 dedicated to the Creator-endowed truth that all men are created equal. This is a truth that may have been "self-evident" to

Jefferson at his desk. It is of course ironic to assert as true a self-evident truth. But, by Lincoln's hand, it has become a proposition to be tested in a great civil war.

Lincoln rewrites two great writing men, Seward and Jefferson. Jefferson was perhaps the greatest writer of his era. Lincoln wields a pen now as he did an axe as a boy—with mastery. Yet Lincoln could be gracefully humble about almost everything, including his writing.

For his First Inaugural Address Lincoln willingly sought opinions and revisions. While always sensitive to the slights, rebuffs, or praise of others, his egoless regard for the advice and admonishments of others is exceptional. He received forty-nine notations for changes from Secretary of State Seward, accepting twenty-seven of them. Looking to understand Lincoln's spiritual life through language we will interpret several spiritual ideas as they differ in the secular wording of two drafts—Lincoln's and Seward's—of Lincoln's First Inaugural Address. Lincoln shared his speech with his new Secretary of State William Seward and then Lincoln worked with and changed some of his speech.

The images of spiritual life that Seward used picture a traditional three-story Biblical world. Lincoln's word-images, however, are more in keeping with 19th century science, but are not always secular. He is more humanistic and his world is not one of heaven and hell with earth in the middle.

The main spiritual idea that Seward offered in his editing was the idea of inspiration. His image was largely one of music. His words for this musical inspiration were "mystic chords." Now Seward doesn't say where exactly these mystic chords come from. They are almost like lines, or ropes or cables, but that is not clear. They become musical. He does not say they come from God, but they are, indeed, mystic. They will eventually be acted upon by the breath of the guardian angel of the nation.

The nation, in Seward's religious world, which is not necessarily ecclesiastical, has a guardian angel. The mystic chords arise from battlefields and patriots' graves. They are the musical voices of dead soldiers. This is the stuff of Seward's spiritual imagination and language.

What do these musical voices do? We don't so much hear them as they "pass through" our hearts and they "pass through" our hearths, our home fireplaces. For Seward, they are not a church choir and they do not sing in our sanctuaries. They also don't even have words. They don't bring a divine message or a scriptural truth. Seward may sound more traditionally religious than Lincoln will, but he is not preaching a sermon.

The musical voices in Seward's version do change. They also go through the hearts and hearths of the whole broad continent, "our" continent. They are bringing one main spiritual thing, inspiration. They are going to harmonize, and they will be harmonized. They bring the spirit of harmony, of union. We can presume that with their harmonizing we will also be able to be in harmony. The music, in Seward's spiritual imagination, is ancient as well as mystic, and relevant.

What, we can ask, will bring about this spiritual effect, this harmonizing of battlefield grave voices? The chords, the mystic chords, will be "breathed upon by the guardian angel of the nation." That is what will change them and us. The voices of these ghostly former soldiers will undergo a musical transformation into an ancient harmony, a pre-existing harmony. They can do this because the country has a, only one, guardian angel. Seward's imagery flows. We are adding the poetic and literal ramifications to his spiritual ideas.

As a religious image the spiritual idea of the breathing guardian angel echoes the Genesis story of God's creation, of God breathing upon Adam and giving life to humans. This image could also echo in people's minds the angels who bring glad tidings to all men in the Christian Nativity story. While it is not God that Seward asserts, that will breathe on these chords of sound, it is through the inspiration of an extra-terrestrial being, the angel of the nation, that this harmonic inspiration will happen. The rhetorical effort on Seward's part is somewhat religious, it is not church-bound, and it is also fairly secular. His idea is of an angelic inspiration, in ancient chords. This inspiration will have come through us, and will harmonize the whole country. This is not exactly Christian. It is somewhat Biblical. It has the mythology of a heavenly angel. And it has, for Seward, a national secular political impact.

Now Lincoln accepted and used a good part of this rhetorical creation of Seward, although John Burt says the original idea of a closing with the inspiration of friends with sacred ties of affection was Lincoln's. But Lincoln offers his own version of spiritual inspiration. It is decidedly humanistic and earthy and not at all heavenly. He made significant changes, if subtly less religious, are still spiritually inspiring. Lincoln brings the imagery down to earth. The mystic chords are not disembodied sounds from battlefields and graves. He moves away from the 19th century maudlin, almost spooky, poetics around death to a more modern and psychological image.

These mystic chords are not sounds of an ancient music. They are in fact the chords of memory. They are more clearly sounds, not ropes, and they are humanized and embodied as memories. It is the sounds of our memories that we hear, and they are not ancient, they are not harmonized, nor are they breathed upon. They swell. They breathe themselves. They swell into a chorus.

There is never any location to the sounds in Seward's version. In Lincoln's world the sounds show up in a choir, even a chorus, which belongs to the Union. It is the chorus of the Union that will be swelling. Why? Have they been breathed upon by the national guardian angel? No. These choral chords, which are memories, and are becoming a chorus of Union music, have been touched. What has touched them?

God? No, says Lincoln. What has touched them? What "will yet touch them"? Not the single guardian angel of the nation, says Lincoln. No, we don't know, in Lincoln's spiritual world, that there is such an angel being. This touch will come, Lincoln implores, only in, or as, an invocation, in a "Let It Be So," a rhetorical Amen. This change in us, in Lincoln's spiritual view, is not a predestined prediction as in Seward, but rather a heartfelt human plea from the new President.

Lincoln's final image here is his antiphonal response to what he has just said about the breaking strain of passion that must not break our common bonds of affection. These mystic chords of memory swelling in a chorus will yet swell when they again have been touched, as they will be, by something inside them. This is a human function, something psychological and spiritual. This something Lincoln will call—and he had seen words with this image in his boyhood school Readers—the better angels, plural, angels of our nature. We have good, as well as not-better, angels in our nature. They can touch us and we can sing together. Our human sounds, then, can be transformed by our human, not altogether-sinful, nature.

In Lincoln's religion the nation does not have a single guardian angel. We are, to him, only God's "almost chosen people." He has said this before. In fact the angels that exist, like his "sweet angel mother," are just the better parts of our human natures. It is earthbound images Lincoln uses. Heaven, or wherever in Seward's spiritual imagination it might be that an angel might breathe upon a mystic chord, that place does not exist in Lincoln's language here.

Lincoln cleaned up Seward's language. As Ronald C. White says in his biography of Lincoln, "Lincoln pared away all superfluous words." He points out Lincoln's use of assonance, placing words together that had sound and related syllables, "Battlefield and patriot grave," "heart and hearthstone," and including consonances like "break, bonds, battlefield, broad, better."

Lincoln did not just light upon the words of a "chorus swelling into a union," he had a deep notion of what, John Burt says, was his concept of "the public mind." The public mind can be vulnerable, but here it is durable. It can be reckless, but here it can be protective and holding against dangerous passions. The public mind swells up into song in Lincoln's earth-bound spiritual image. Lincoln wants something more than just mystic sounds or harp strings; he wants the public sounds in a choir of mystic memory. He wants "we the people" to sing. Burt says that Lincoln set Seward's words to music.

There is also in Lincoln's spiritual life a vulnerability that he is strong to claim. He says in his version of this closure not "I close." But "I am loath to close." He reveals his personal and longing heart and his fears that in closing the speech the war will begin. Lincoln's spirit includes open pathos. His is a high, but not a weak, voice. While, as Burt points out, Seward pleads with the people not to be enemies, Lincoln speaks in a commanding proposition saying, "We are not enemies, but friends. We must not be enemies." It is almost performative speech, that rhetorical category that makes true what is expressed. Lincoln, referring to our bonds of affection, uses the imperative "must not" be broken, which is both a strong claim and a humble imploring.

For both men the image of chords is a mixed metaphoric confusion, a weak pun says John Burt, in that these are chords like bonds and ropes and binding strings as well as choral sounds. In Lincoln's version they go "to" every human heart they don't just pass through. There is a personal, inter-personal, connectivity that is more humanistic and less ethereal than Seward's more idealistic imagery and language. Burt says that for Seward the chords are actually more like the strings in an Aeolian harp that make music when breathed upon. But in Lincoln's version the spiritual action is from within the human heart, in our better natures. We inspire as we breathe not as we are breathed upon. This is a very different kind of religious stance. The spiritual action in Seward is from outside coming down and touching. Doris Kearns Godwin also has noted this. The better angels of our nature, John Burt calls our "divine second thoughts."

The inspiration that Seward hopes to engender is from a weaker spiritual nature than the one Lincoln appeals to. Seward hopes that the breathing guardian angel will be a soothing influence on the disharmony people are feeling. His is a pleading, almost a "Can't we all just get along?" appeal for the bonds of affection, which he assures us won't be broken, but we hardly feel assured. To Lincoln there is more than feeling at stake. The nation does not just need to feel better and be soothed by angel-given feelings; it needs to think more clearly. The better angels of our nature, because we are now talking about ourselves and not angels, include our reason as well as our hearts. Later, in a speech to Congress, he will say, "we must disenthrall ourselves." He means we must wake up and free our hearts and minds so we can act to save our country. Lincoln's is a thinking person's religion, spirituality of the head and of the heart. A youth movement that supported Lincoln's election was called The Wide Awakes.

The texts:

Seward's Draft	Lincoln's Delivered Version
I close.	I am loath to close.
We are not, we must not be, aliens or enemies, but fellow-countrymen and brethren.	We are not enemies, but friends. We must not be enemies.
Although passion has strained our bonds of affection too hardly, they must not, I am sure they will not, be broken.	Though passion may have strained, it must not break our bonds of affection.

| The mystic chords which proceeding from so many battle fields and so many patriot graves pass through all the hearts and all the hearths in this broad continent of ours will yet again harmonize in their ancient music when breathed upon by the guardian angel of the nation. | The mystic chords of memory, stretching from every battle-field, and patriot grave, to every living heart and hearthstone, all over this broad land, will yet swell the chords of the Union, when again touched, as surely they will be, by the better angels of our nature. |

Language: A Reflection

F ollowing his Second Inaugural Address Lincoln confessed pri-
vately that people did not, at first, like hearing that "the Almighty" had purposes that differed from their own. That had been
the crux of his message. He recognized the role of the Prophet, both
Biblical and secular.

We still see and seek his prophetic wisdom. In our time we
need to hear from him again even if we don't like at first what we
hear. America is poised to become a mature leader among the nations of the world, to shake off our heady adolescence, if we can learn
from our sufferings and see the tragic implications even within our
highest values.

Lincoln, through personal suffering and a willing identification with the sacrifices of the whole country, could and did forge the
words that speak to our potential maturity, words that define a power
beyond our righteousness, truths beyond absoluteness, and a compassion beyond familiar boundaries. Lincoln drew upon a Yonder
vision where tragedy speaks of life, to life and for life.

Not only does Lincoln belong to the ages, he belongs to each
age differently. There is enough in Abraham Lincoln for each era to
find in him the character, thought, and historical record to satisfy
our ongoing needs for guidance and inspiration. This is not unlike
the religious task of interpreting sacred texts and figures of faith. It
is also a secular task. For example, the philosopher and psychiatrist

Jonathan Lear says that each age must find their own Freud. These two quests for reinterpretation, the religious and the secular, fit our time's need for Lincoln. In a word, Lincoln was a spiritual and a secular figure in our history. It is another step in the unique tradition of civil religion in America to see the spiritual robes that invisibly shrouded this visibly secular man.

Not only does our era need to know the Lincoln that speaks to us, but each one of us who reads and thinks about Lincoln feels he or she has a true, even intimate, connection to the real Lincoln. He is like a story telling doll, in the Southwest Native American traditions, covered with the listening children. His giant figure at the Lincoln Memorial almost asks for us to climb up and take our place. We may also want to join him like a Huckleberry ruffian on a raft down the Mississippi or stand in awe in the March Inaugural Day sunlight listening as he makes Biblical pronouncements and asks for Christ-like charity in his last Address. It is not only history that owns Lincoln, but many feel owned by him. This book tells of his profound secular religious historical significance, but it tells it personally as well. Writers and readers about Lincoln feel in the presence of a Lincoln who calls to us.

Change is a key to understanding Lincoln. He was himself like that Father of all Rivers, the Mississippi. Not only, as Heraclitus said, can you not stand in the same river twice, but Lincoln, as did Mark Twain, knew that in navigating the river the topography of the river itself is never the same. Lincoln is intellectually and politically as huge as the Mississippi and he was, like that river, always changing boundaries, angles of direction, and flow. Always one, always many.

These dynamics of change make Lincoln relevant to our spiritual and our secular life, and to their intersection. He was the product, not the master, of his own changes. His ability to tolerate ambiguity and yet act was his stance, both as a deeply religious thinker and a powerful political actor. Without ideology or dogma he held himself, and the country, to a few absolute ideals. He made war like a Samurai warrior, with blood but not hate. He made peace like a figure in a Christian parable, all mercy and charity. He understood history like a Biblical prophet, all justice and redeeming retribution. Our most theological President was never baptized, was not a professing Christian, and yet had a glory in his bosom that transfigures you and me. His was, we shall see, a religion without religion, a secular religious truth for our changing ambiguous times.

CHAPTER FOUR

Yonder

There he is rolled up in a ball on the un-scrubbed wooden floor hugging his knees, a significant lawyer in Springfield. In their offices at Sixth and Adams streets overlooking the State Capital, his partner, Billy Herndon, realizes Lincoln's been there for quite a while and asks what on earth this could all be about. Out of his bony muscular knot Lincoln explains he was looking for the right word.

We now can walk the stepping-stones of his fewer than 100 speeches, or the fewer than 300 words of the *Gettysburg Address*, and see how each word has been properly found. Lincoln was the kind of writer who would find the word "disenthralled" for his idea: to think anew. He later would have the Congress realize that they must rise "with" the occasion not "to" the occasion, because they were all in the same boat, bound on the river of history, and boats rise with the water not to the water. Lincoln, of course, had rafted down the Mississippi. "No personal significance nor insignificance can spare one or another of us" was his idea and context.

If Mark Twain had not illustrated the point of finding the right word in the difference between "lightening" and "lightening bug," Lincoln himself might well have hit upon that apt joke. He certainly would have rollicked hearing Twain. In thinking about Lincoln, especially if we are to consider Lincoln in any way as a spiritual source, we will need to untie the knot of Lincoln and language, a knot he tied so tightly. There is a Yonder in his words.

It is puzzling that it took so long in the endless writings about Lincoln for books to emerge about Lincoln not just as the source of a new declamatory literature, as Daniel Boorstin once asserted, but Lincoln simply as a writer. In 1900 the remarkable founding chair of the University of Illinois English Department, Professor Daniel Kilham Dodge wrote a slim volume entitled, *Abraham Lincoln, The Evolution of His Literary Style*. It was reprinted by the University to mark it as the first scholarly publication issued under the auspices of the University of Illinois. Professor Dodge confessed his obsession with Lincoln to be like that of Mr. Dick's obsession with Charles the First in Dickens's *David Copperfield*. Professor Dodge published again, in 1929, a second volume entitled *Abraham Lincoln, Master of Words*. More recently however Fred Kaplan has done so in his thrilling book, *Lincoln: The Biography of a Writer*. Kaplan asserts in his first sentence, "For Lincoln, words, mattered immensely." Kaplan reverses the famous ploy of William Dean Howells, "The Atlantic" founder and 19th century novelist, who claimed of his friend Mark Twain that he was, "The Lincoln of our literature." Kaplan makes the equal claim, "Lincoln was the Twain of our politics." It could also be said that both Lincoln and Twain are similarly dark theological strugglers, two God-haunted, word-drenched, hard-boiled former riverboat pilots. Lincoln, Mark Twain and Herman Melville, can be seen as 19th century theological Calvinists, haunted by the idea of the sovereignty of God, and yet rational, maybe cynical and heart-broken, over the apparent chasm between God and human history, especially on the most personal level. All three men lived an openhearted agony over a hope for a faith they could not feel. Only Lincoln had the courage to fully act in history within the bounds of doubt. Ronald C. White has now also traced Lincoln's spiritual odyssey, and his remarkable language as an orator, with equal relish and perception in his books *The Eloquent President* and in his thoroughly refreshing biography *A. Lincoln*.

We don't, however, need only to refer to great and deep thinkers to grasp our own elementary sense of the importance of words and our shared questions about the role of language in life, and life's ultimate concerns. As children we play with the power of language with our first games. "Simon Says" gives the speaker the power to control the movements of friends. "Blind man's Bluff" guides the seeker-in-the-dark with the clues of words, "warmer", "warmer", and we are not bluffing. Young friends will pose this profound proposition about language: What if a thousand monkeys had a thousand years to type on a thousand typewriters? Could they, would they, come up with Shakespeare? It is a question rooted in science, statistics, and probability theory. The question now begs for a computer, but it came from some wonder, some notion, that the language of Shakespeare is special. It asks, is language a matter of an alphabet soup of cosmic size? Could random letters be complied in a Shakespearean way if we had time enough and typewriters, and only monkey brains? In other words, is the brain of a Shakespeare different from a thousand monkeys over a thousand years, or is his writing a matter not ultimately of the quantity of word choice but the quality of mind, even spirit. Whether we are scholar, child, or just being thoughtful, to us the very nature of language, language as a spiritual dynamic, is a part of understanding the spiritual life of Abraham Lincoln.

Lincoln's first childhood experience of language came to him in a frontier world that was barely defined by calculative science. His experience of language was however as a tool for logic and for mechanical invention. It was a source for information and culture. Most unusually it was an instrument for meditative reflection, poetry and eventually theology. Language on the new frontier tried to get the world into a human frame of reference, from naming places to discovering rocks and minerals. It was language that bridged, but did not close, people's relation to the opening world around them.

For Lincoln, in addition to solving the problems of survival, picking up the news and history, he enjoyed language. Books, sermons, courthouse speeches, poetry filled his days and mind. But Lincoln, also and unusually, lived in that gap between life and language. Some would call it the Buddhist place of Nothingness. Sandburg just said that the element of silence in Lincoln was immense. The frontier world as he found it would also have been tacit, filled with silence.

For the son of a subsistence farmer, a hunter-gatherer in an emerging nation, Lincoln also came to language through his mother's voice and Bible words. What followed were a small number of significant books on grammar, rhetoric and history, and then live speech from some lawyers, some preachers, and something called Blab school, where everyone vocalized their independent lessons. For the rest of his life Lincoln read almost everything to himself out-loud.

But he was also immersed in nature and in a world of plants and animals and his unschooled friends. It took the oft-criticized poet-historian Carl Sandburg to name what emerged as the quality of Lincoln's childhood mind. He says Lincoln inherited and possessed a sense of Yonder. Historians and biographers since have shied away from such a poetical, even metaphysical category of explanation. Yet the idea of a Yonder sensibility describes, if not explains, much of Lincoln's way and his way with words. It fills in the blank left by so many Lincoln scholars. John Burt comes the closest, as does David Herbert Donald, when they use the John Keats category of "Negative Capability" to describe how Lincoln positions himself in terms of human understanding and expression, both as a speaker and a writer. Yonder is a category that allows for that critical distance from events that gives both the passive poise of Negative Capability and an opening for the prophetic voice and transcendent view behind that voice. Yonder is aware of fate with openness to participation. Yonder includes Necessity. Lincoln always believed in a Doctrine of Necessity, but, paradoxically, with both a sense of abandonment and a sense of belonging. Yonder is a holding mystery that uplifts and does not dismiss. Yonder is a heart-concept as much as a mind-category, and so it leads to mercy, compassion and empathy. Yonder is the one place, because it is dwells in silence first, that allows a politician to compromise, settle differences between ideologies, respect opponents and not go wild with fellow partisans. This is because, in a sense, in Yonder one is in the world but not of it. It allows space for neutrality and for the Other. People said of Lincoln's eyes that he had a dreamy look, a look of distance, about him. It's an atmosphere of Yonder. He spent long, long periods of time gazing into empty distances.

Yonder is, of course, what we see last in the face of Lincoln. In those haunting photographs we see the face of a very fragile and distant spirit, a gentleness that is almost heart-breaking, a sense that his face, like that once cracked-looking photographic frame itself, could shatter, or that we could reach out and break off that large parchment-like ear of his, as if he were a tea-cup, translucent, yet warm and inviting ready to twinkle into nothing less than love. He is the commander, the victor of the greatest military campaign our history had then known. Yet nothing about him in those final photographs shows the aspect of a conqueror. His task was to save not to subdue, and so we see values that transcend the history he so powerfully influenced. He was all along in some sense outside of history as well.

There is an agnosticism in Yonder that allows for all of this. His words ring true to us now in the ways that other great expressions of that age do not. For example, the hero of Gettysburg's battle for Little Round Top, Joshua Lawrence Chamberlain, was faith-filled and full of the history of rhetoric. But he does not move us with his words like "splendid valor, heart's blood, the great day of revelation and recompense...these heights shall flame again with transfigured light—they, too, have part in that adoption, which is the manifestation of the sons of God!" Those are his words ending his book, *Through Blood and Fire at Gettysburg*. Or, for example, Oliver Wendell Holmes, Jr., another Civil War hero, whose renown "Life is action and passion..." speech, calls us to join in that action and passion, but offers a faith in nothing more than action and passion itself, a kind of hyper-existentialism. We may, from within a community of faith, understand the sources of Chamberlain's words. As modern existentialists we may resonate with Holmes. Yet we have in our time a certain sense of the darkness of history. Chamberlain's words just do not speak to us of felt meanings that include for us what we now know. Our minds are darker than Chamberlain might allow. The austere existentialism of Holmes, certainly hard-earned by him, guides us not at all now. There is passion in his brave assertion to action, but it is all everywhere or nowhere. In Lincoln's cast of mind there are not so much definitive conclusions but rather deep gazes with certain end points and vanishing points. In other words, in Lincoln's mind he held great room for what he did not know, couldn't know, or did not yet know. That is what is meant by agnosticism.

Yonder allows for a gap between the world and ourselves. Lincoln first found, he said, so little poetry there in southern Indiana. The application of English words to the land and to experience would have been new and tenuous, not habitual and accepted. The gap between life and death was wide and constant. It is in the loss of his mother at the age of nine that we can believe Lincoln began to know Yonder as an ultimate category of life experience. Never again to see or hear her, she who gave him the sounds of words so dear to his heart. No conception could overcome the gap of her loss, and then all the other losses, his sister at 19, his Anne Rutledge a few years later, and then his sons, and then the sons of America. No love could close the gap between the world out there and the heart's hopes inside. Yonder is a safeguard from false faith, from bad faith, and yet is also a living place away from nihilism and despair.

In the Bible Yonder would be in the darkness that covered the face of the deep, in the Genesis creation story. Yonder would be that pre-existing expanse. The Hebrew poets of scripture saw God as the rushing wind, a breath, filling that Yonder place, and filling it with words that created light and then life. In the Gospel of John that Word is God. How life is brought forth out of Yonder into words that name things, that is a primary metaphor in the Bible. The Bible is a book for frontier spirituality.

Here are some of the times and the places where Lincoln learned language and Yonder.

When Lincoln was seven his family moved to Indiana, to a place referred to as Gentryville. It was called that because James Gentry had a store there. But it is also said that the Lincolns settled at Pigeon Creek. One area had many names. The county name eventually changed. The community was called the Little Pigeon community. Why "Little" Pigeon? We can understand why Gentryville was named as it was. Historian Daniel Boorstin has estimated that in the settling of the frontier between one and three million things needed naming. Among the 40 families within a five-mile radius of the Lincolns who would dare contest Mr. Gentry's entitlement to Gentryville?

But why Pigeon Creek, or Little Pigeon community? Why not Carolina Parakeet Creek, after the big multi-colored birds that flocked in the area? Maybe it was because John James Audubon, who lived at the same time and roamed the same area, had once noted 163 flocks of pigeons within a 21-minute time span. They literally blocked out the sky. In his novel "Abe" historian Richard Slotkin has a dramatic scene where gatherings of neighbors plunge into descending flocks of pigeons and simply club the air to fell them, gathering the resources that so many dead pigeons would offer a frontier people. Would it seem strange then to name a creek Little Pigeon Creek? Was there Big Pigeon Creek? And when the newly built church, which Lincoln's father, Thomas, most likely helped to build, was called Little Pigeon Church did people feel it strange to name a church after such a bird, and not, say, the dove or eagle, the more Biblical birds?

The Lincolns' open-faced lean-to, and then first cabin, in the winter of 1816, was in an area that had been known as Perry Country in the Illinois territory. But in that year the area to be known as Indiana separated from Illinois and became a state. The Indians, however, had lived in this three million acre area for thousands of years. Surely they did not call it Indiana. When their last great Chief, Tecumseh, "He who walks across the sky," was defeated on November 7, of 1811 at Tippecanoe by William Henry Harrison, the Indians lost claim to the vast and ancient wilderness. Why then was the state named after them?

All this naming was the first application of language, at least the English language, to the realities of life for the people who spoke English. Lincoln had already gotten his name from his grandfather, Captain Abraham Lincoln, who had been shot by a small party of Indians while tending his cornfield in Kentucky in 1786.

We can ask about the relation between language and reality in these contexts. What would be the heady experience of naming, even proclaiming, that this is to be called that? To take vast millions of acres land and to call them what you will, to settle in a small spot of that land and to call that place what you will, to receive the name of a murdered grandfather, what known or unknown depths would be experienced in all these language events? What community of agreement would need to be felt in order for there to be some continuity of meaning?

These would not be foreign musing to Abraham Lincoln. Carl Sandburg, as do others, reports the young Abe was caught in the mystery of his own name, his own name in written letters. He liked best hearing his whole first name. A friend once said, of his written name, it "'peared to mean a heap to Abe." Lincoln's musing was,

"That stands fur me. Don't look a blamed bit like me." Words and reality, separate, and then together.

Two of the first entries in *The Collected Works of Lincoln*, Volume one, page one, have to do with his reflecting on his name and on his relations to words in general. "Abraham Lincoln is my name/ And with my pen I wrote the same/I wrote in both hast and speed/ and left it here for fools to read." Posterity off-handedly proclaimed, through language.

Also this, "Abraham Lincoln his hand and pen/he will be good but god knows When." The spelling and capitalization are his.

The thought is: What is it like to know, through sensations first, the reality of land and place and bodies. To know the past, for example, your mother's dead body for whom you helped build the box, and then to know land, place, and bodies, through words themselves? Especially what is it like to be the giver of those words? In the case of Lincoln's oratorical legacy to America, and the world, this is not just a question for philosophy. Lincoln was the word-giver to the most important experiences Americans have had as a nation struggling to fulfill its promise. We live inside much of what Lincoln named.

In 1844 at the age of 35 and a hard-working politician, Lincoln returned on a speaking tour to his boyhood home in southern Indiana, this area he once called the most un-poetical of places. Yet he writes one of his most profound poems based on this moving return visit. It is a long poem of four Cantos about death and memory, loss and grief. He opens with a Wordsworth-like line, "My childhood home I see again, /And sadden with the view;/"

He concludes the poem with a deeper reflection on the relation between himself, his body and the land. To that reflection he writes these words, "The very spot where grew the bread/ That formed my bones, I see/ How strange, old field, on thee to tread, / And feel I'm part of thee!"

Language, his poem, names a link between himself and this place. He personally addresses the land as "thee." His words honor the duration, as well as the evaporation, of that link. It is also in that field that I walked when I felt a palpable sense of his goodness and his presence. He tells us that he feels the mystical link of wheat and bread and bone, a oneness of himself, that he and this field are part of each other, a place he can address, personally. Lincoln was learning to speak, to write, about what was not there except in memory and feelings, and to what was not really knowable except within a sense of that something else, some mystic chords, found in memory and language, known in Yonder.

The philosophy of Martin Buber tells about the relationship between language and reality in his two categories: The I-It relationship, and the I-Thou relationship. Clearly Lincoln is having an I-Thou relationship with this land, this old field, and all the life and the memory of life that comes to him, mind and heart, as he sees it again. The field is Thou to him.

We can expand upon his reflection. We know that the next field over, on a hill, is the buried body of his mother, Nancy Hanks Lincoln, his "sweet angel mother" as he called her to distinguish her later from his also beloved stepmother, Sarah Bush Lincoln. A quarter of a century earlier the little boy, Abe, helped his father to build her casket. From her, even more than from the wheat of the field, his bones were bred, and his mind was seeded with words.

This is a spiritual relationship with the land that Lincoln has, and it leads, as noted, to a deeper knowing. We see his spiritual wisdom about the land, the earth itself, in his most mature years in his Second Annual Address to Congress. Just a month before the issuing of the Emancipation Proclamation Lincoln is defining the central themes of the war. While Union and slavery have been the political issues, Lincoln has a deeper imagination and a real knowing from the land. The land itself helps him know what to think about the Union and slavery. He has studied maps. He was a surveyor. He has walked and worked the land as a boy and traveled it almost endlessly as a circuit lawyer. He cannot, then, he says in his speech, see where a line could be drawn across the country that could settle the issue. The line would just produce a border of conflict over which he understands slavery would try to extend itself and free-soilers and abolitionists would try to intrude. As much as the Constitution and equality dictate the stage on which they all are acting, so also does, he says, the land itself. His language is both down to earth and in the heavens. Yonder is a place of land and words. He writes,

"A nation may be said to consist of its territory, its people, and its laws. The territory is the only part of which is certain durability. 'One generation passeth away, and another generation cometh, but the earth abideth forever.' It is of the first importance to duly consider and estimate this ever enduring part. That portion of the earth's surface which is owned and inhabited by the people of the United States is well adapted to be the home of one national family, and it is not well adapted for two or more." He credits steam, telegraphs and intelligence to have brought about this advantageous combination for one united people, rooted in one land.

His point of view is profound in reality and inspired in image. The land is one and it is holding all of us, he says. But it is for the people of each generation to settle the strife between them, and that is done with language and with a certain spirit. "Our national strife springs not from our permanent part, not from the land we inhabit, not from our national homestead. There is no possible severing of this; it would multiply, and not mitigate, evils among us…. Our strife pertains to ourselves—to the passing generations of men; and it can without convulsion be hushed forever with the passing of one generation." These passages of that Address to Congress have been explicated by Daniel Kilham Dodge, in his 1924 book, "Abraham Lincoln: Master of Words."

The land also was in the vision of Ralph Waldo Emerson in his poem for January 1st, 1863, the day of the new year of Lincoln's Emancipation Proclamation. Emerson's own secular-sacred vision in that poem is that the "word of the Lord" comes again to the Pilgrims, filing their hearts with flame and announcing—as Lincoln so deeply felt—that God was tired of kings. Emerson's vision goes on to include the God-heard outrages of the poor, that the weak and poor regain the purposes of the ball, earth, and God's angel, "Freedom" is offered as the new king. Freedom will cut a pathway "east and west" (not, we note, north and south) and "Lo! I uncover the land/Which I hid of old time in the West, /As the sculptor uncovers the statue/ When he has wrought his best[.]" The land, the land, it is what God, the sculptor, has hidden and is now his best revelation. This is, of course, the same kind of revelation as the Biblical one of the Promised Land. It becomes the deep image of America's problematic and adopted belief in a manifesting destiny. It is a secular-sacred vision perhaps now filling hearts with flames as this ball earth itself is endangered. Emerson and Lincoln knew each other. Emerson visited with him in the White House. Fred Kaplan in his biography asserts that Lincoln had read and maybe heard Emerson's visionary words on the power of Nature. They shared a similar coherent vision of land and promise.

CHAPTER FIVE

Language and the Wilderness

Wilderness is a place where religious figures go to be close in time to the spiritual origins of life. A spiritual figure, such as Lincoln, will find a place, a gap, between the former history and the history to come where it is possible to have spiritual experience. Wilderness allows the spirit what we have called Yonder. Yonder, as a cast of mind, is a spiritual person's ability to hold aspects of wilderness in their mind—emptiness and silence, hardship and temptations, openness to a vision. It is time out of time, a gap between history and eternity. Wilderness is a liminal space between secular and sacred realities. Yonder is what you see when silence is what you hear.

In the Exodus from Egypt the Hebrew slaves had a symbolic forty years of wilderness between enslavement and the Promised Land. Jesus marked the transition from his meager origins to his inspired ministry in an ordeal of temptation in the wilderness. The wilderness is a crucial place for the traditional initiation rituals of young men. He is to be cast out into a silent, motherless, wild place so as to connect to the deeper self, and to receive a newly named spiritual identity.

Lincoln grew up in the American wilderness with the nation only 33 years old when he was born. He lived with the history of the Old World clearly more and more behind. Ahead, across a gap, the unknown future for the experimental Americans was waiting. As Lincoln came of age both geography and history were teaching the same lesson: the future, in space as well as in time, is open. The wide-open spaces of land, the frontier prairies, were before him. The known histories of the European past were, hopefully, over. Open to the future, moving from the past, Lincoln faced in space and time the unknown but promised possibilities of America. We cannot over-estimate the excitement that lived and breathed within the thousands of families that moved west from the Eastern seaboard in the 1800s, having had families that had already moved west from the Old World. It was an excitement that all three regions of the country originally shared—North, South and West.

The visions and ideas that Lincoln read and heard about, such as Daniel Webster's words "Liberty and Union forever," were like scripture to him. Political information, news and history, was defining the New World. His sense of the Promised Land to come was a strong vision for him, more than the Gospel's promise of salvation. The Biblical idea of the Promised Land embodied a spiritual meaning for history. The New American World was a secular vision, a political creation, and a spiritual vision. It embodied the transcendent and innate values of freedom and equality. The Bible was a founding language for the culture out of which he and America came and into which he went. It bridged the gap between the Old World and the New. Surrounded by the wilderness these political and religious languages of freedom would shape Lincoln as he emerged.

When Lincoln was a young and intense visionary, in 1838, he called for, in his words, a "political religion" to stand against evil, violence and lawless passions, not unlike, he said, the way that the church was thought to stand. Lincoln's Lyceum Speech of 1838, in a full-blown style he would later foreswear but worthy of a preacher then, does nothing less than worship Reason as the governor of wild and violent passions and Law as the nearly divine enforcer and hand-maiden of Reason. Lincoln preached this and, four years later, also a tolerance for drunkards, in the face of a strong Presbyterian cohort of town leaders in Springfield, to whom he did not subscribe. He did this without much overt language about God, and clearly without a direct appeal to Christianity. Yet these speeches had a spiritual and moral tone. Moral improvement was in the air as the upshot of the Second Great Awakening, and he used the moral tone of Biblical language. Biblical righteousness was a part of the language of settling the West. Lincoln was speaking his Yonder visions, with clearly secular accents, but well within the religious rhetoric of Christian Old Testament preaching. His secular language can be seen, like Martin Luther's as well, as a secular reformation and not a rejection of the dominant sacred traditions of Christianity.

Language, especially in the wilderness, is a source of revelation. Language was Lincoln's Jacob's Ladder, angel-words ascending from the real earth and descending from the lofty heavens. When Jacob slept on a rock in the wilderness, before his ladder dream, he did not know that God was in that place, that it was a holy place. Lincoln also did not begin by knowing where God was or that he was in God's holy place. But there was a theological dimension to the world that Lincoln grew up in. The grammars he read as a boy had as much reference to God and Biblical virtues as anything he would hear in church. The prairie schooners and Conestoga wagons bringing pioneers west were like so many rolling Mayflowers. They carried people with Bibles and the belief that a free community could be virtuous, and that holy communities could raise virtuous children. These were also Lincoln's beliefs. Not everyone was religious on the Mayflower or on the prairie. The Mayflower Compact of the Puritan pilgrims was a political not a religious document. But in this new world people believed that God was being brought into the wilderness.

Lincoln learned from the frontier, most historians agree. Usually they mean the qualities of frontier community and society. But the spiritual lessons from the wilderness differ from the lessons of civilization. The sea for Ishmael in *Moby Dick*, as we have noted, was his watery college and not just the society of his whaling ship, *The Pequod*. The wild water was everywhere. So too the wilderness of Lincoln's early years surrounded him, oceans of empty land. He island hopped from Gentryville to New Salem, to the little growing town of Springfield. For years later he rode the judicial circuit covering prairie land the size of Connecticut. One of the lessons of the wilderness is silence. As silence surrounds language, music and art, so the wilderness enveloped Lincoln and his devotion to language.

It was also the drama of Lincoln's frontier and prairie town life that shaped what he learned from books and from people. There was a freethinking cast to life in New Salem, Illinois when young Lincoln arrived there—his first home away from home. He joined an elite debaters club by invitation. That must have been thrilling to him compared to the church-based ethos of Pigeon Creek and Gentryville, Indiana. New Salem was a miniature model of American progressive culture for a short while. The Post Office even got the speeches from Congress in the Congressional Globe. But in Pigeon Creek he had gravitated not to church so much (although he was a candle-counting sexton at the Baptist church) as to law offices and court hearings for modern talk and thought.

Hundreds of covered wagons brought to the western borders of the new country a religion that informed practical life and the meaning of their great adventure. The promises of religion are on two levels, the big picture and the personal picture. As the plains ebbed away from the eastern seaboard, the messages of religion condensed into two versions of the religious promise of the Kingdom of God in America, one big and one personal. In the big picture the Kingdom of God meant the sovereignty of God. Both Christianity and Judaism understood that to mean God's rule over history. On the personal level the growing evangelical movements and awakenings from the East meant that the Kingdom of God in American was the rule of Christ in a person's life.

Thinking about Lincoln as a religious figure it is clear that he never came to good terms with the second version of those religious promises and hopes, even while he actually lived the personally righteous and sober life that Christian morality would dictate. It is highly doubtful that he was a virgin upon marriage, however. But he lived willingly, by and large, as a rational and responsible, simply good, person, and a member of the Whig Party. He had no emotional taste for personal salvation. Indeed he accepted the sovereignty of God to such an honest degree that he confessed that in the great Election of God for salvation, the Calvinist view, he believed that God had not chosen him for that salvation. There is something stark and honest about such a confession. While many Calvinists then struggled to appear modest about God and their Election, as if they knew what they could not really know, Lincoln allowed for just the opposite: God's choosing rule, and his exclusion from the company of believers.

Such a deterministic view of his life was a part of what he did believe. He was, we might say, a secular Calvinist. He believed in the determination of all things in life, but he first only called it Fate, not God, and he used the term, a Doctrine of Necessity. He came to this belief through the revelations of language itself; in this case, Shakespeare. From *Hamlet* he took his favorite quote, "There's a divinity that shapes our ends, rough hew them though we will." The rule of God then, this divinity, was as big and overarching as it was also particular and personal. As a man who had rough-hewn thousands of logs for cabins, and rails for fences, he knew the precise particularity of what humans do to build our world, as well as the fate and futility he would feel at not really being the master of the building. Fate, like wilderness, constrained what language could and could not do.

CHAPTER SIX

Indiana and Illinois

B uilding a nation was like building a cabin. That would have been an easy thought for Lincoln. His boyhood grammar books included Aesop's morals about a house divided against itself not standing. He knew also the New Testament reference about that as well. These were secular and sacred sources for him. The fate of the big picture, as well as the importance of human effort, was implicit in both sources. The role of fate told that cabins and nations stood or fell for reasons beyond human control. A huge hurricane had leveled a five-mile swath of land in Indiana, in 1810, near the spot where his family built their first home in 1811. He would have seen the power of such things beyond human power. Yet he would also know the practical role of human handiwork. It might be a theological mystery that God rules and yet humans must do their part, but on the frontier that was just how things looked to be.

A cabin in those days was usually 18 feet by 20 feet and nine logs high with space between them for a kind of stucco filling. To rough-hew the ends of nine longs for each of the four walls would have given Abe 72 ends to shape. They had no window but if you put in a doorway you would have maybe four score ends to shape, with a chimney maybe then four score and a few more. But it would need to be an even number. In his cabin days Lincoln was not talking in the Christian language of the Kingdom of God in America nor of his own personal salvation. But the levels of national and personal history were embodied and would have been evident to him in the work of his daily subsistence.

Lincoln was naturally good with the ambiguity of two levels of thought, whether it was God or fate as well as individual human effort. The paradox between human effort and human history was reality to him. As a political issue Lincoln would eventually struggle with the ideas of liberty, freedom, and union. The political issue of the Civil War was how to settle the competing claims of several levels of thinking, personal, state, and national. As a theological issue, increasingly haunting and intense to Lincoln, was the role of Providence in the continuing of the war and the issue of human freedom and responsibility.

On the personal level, much like his spiritual cousin Mark Twain, Lincoln was never very absolutist or hidebound about the righteousness of individual conduct. Unlike Twain, we've noted, Lincoln actually lived a smoke-free, liquor-free, straight arrow life. Although with people like his law partner Herndon, he seemed to gravitate, not unlike Jesus, toward being close to those who did not toe the line. Herndon was a drinker. But Lincoln did not adopt, nor did Twain, a personal piety or much less a Christian piety for understanding his life. He was not trying to be a good person for God or Christ. He did want to be a good person as a Whig, and to be worthy of the esteem of others. Despite his passionate faith in reason and the law Lincoln was somewhat superstitious, believing in curing stones and portents and even things in the dark. He once, we are told, refused a boat ride because the party was made up of thirteen people. He did not outgrow this aspect of his wilderness childhood. He was personally intuitive about dreams and prescient about fate as well as the character of other people.

Also on a personal level Lincoln was deeply ambitious to become someone who would make a mark in history, to be remembered, and he was desperately trying to be worthy of the esteem of his fellow citizens. He had a democratic role for the greater power, the Super Ego, over his personal life. For him it was The People. This makes him the perfect President for a government of, by and for the people. For him the will of the people functioned as guideline for individual behavior. That, and the Constitution. He did not think that God was the same thing as the will of the people, but he cared religiously what the people thought and felt about him and what he did. He was then politically ethical and responsible. But he was theologically humble and even contrite. He did not think he knew clearly the will of God enough to think he could be doing it, except perhaps for one shining moment when he signed the Emancipation Proclamation that he had hand-written. He began to discern the Will of God as he looked at the consequences and limits and justice of human actions. Certainly the story of the people and their larger moral purposes in history was paramount to him. He never wanted to go far from the world of their approval. After a crucial defeat in the war he was to remark, "What will the people say?" For him that was both a political remark and homage to a higher, democratic, value.

There were, however, more than private cabin homes that needed to stand, more than individual dwellings on which to muse. In Pigeon Creek and the surrounds, there was Gentry's store, there were law offices and courthouses, a post office and a schoolhouse for Blab School, and finally the Free Baptist church. Further, in Vincennes, there were patent title offices where Thomas Lincoln finally got a secure tile to his land, government buildings, a printing office where Abe first saw a printing press, and in Princeton, on the way, places to have your grain ground and weighed, and fabrics measured and sold. Down the road not far was New Harmony, Indiana, with its mysterious German utopian believers. In New Salem, Illinois, there were taverns, home churches, trading places also for learned debates, food stores that could hardly make a profit, and a river dock of sorts. People worshiped in several gathered communities in various homes. By the time he got to Springfield there were the rudiments of a real town, almost a city, eventually with a Capital building, churches, and, crucial to him, a State Library. There were also very muddy and/ or dusty streets with pigs running free. One question in the air was: What did this all have to do with those original notions from back East, Biblical religion and Enlightenment, a free community being virtuous and a holy community raising virtuous children?

Back East? There had been six generations of Lincolns backing up Abraham Lincoln. Three Lincoln brothers from Hingham in East Anglia, England, came in 1637 as part of the Great Migration of thousands of East Anglicans to Massachusetts. Economic depression among linen weavers and growing persecution of Puritan religious dissenters were the reasons. The Pilgrims had hit First Encounter Beach on Cape Cod in 1620. The ship the *Arabella* and Massachusetts Bay Colony with Governor John Winthrop landed in 1630. They were a heavy mix of introspective, soul searching, righteous Puritans freely reading their own Bibles and thinking outside the box about the King and the Bishops. They formed a dominant but not entirely homogeneous ethos of these early communities.

While certainly all peoples in villages and towns everywhere have a notion of their virtue and value, even a larger picture of their destiny, these intensely Calvinist Protestant Puritans with their Congregational method of self-governance were a particular and earnest brand of people. Through the six migrations of Lincolns that outline of social and religious values was not lost.

Young Abe Lincoln emerges in Indiana and then Illinois as a minted version of the ideas that a community can and must be good and virtuous, and that individual people must find a good way to be free from the King and the Bishop, as well as a good way to bond with each other. Lincoln worked out these issues even as a boy in Indiana among his neighborhood gang of friends. The seemingly paradoxical values of God's Providence and hard-working human responsibility produced, in Lincoln's secular version, the same traditional religious and human values that had been borne to and reborn in America, Providence and freedom.

CHAPTER SEVEN

The Soaring Eagle & The Melon Thieves Parable

I t is 1822. Can you see a young eagle soaring off in the cloud-banks near the Ohio River?

Can you see young Abe Lincoln, thirteen years old, already almost six feet tall, glance up at the eagle while he is hiding behind a thick tree ready to spring out and shock his so-called friends?

Can you think, what did he think of that soaring eagle?

Can you imagine, as did his longtime true friend Joshua Speed, that such an eagle would be a metaphor of Lincoln's "unfathomable achievements" as historian Kenneth J. Winkle called them in his volume, *The Young Eagle*?

This is a good metaphor. It balances the well accepted, near-myth, of the lone hero, the single bird, emerging from a frontier nowhere. The metaphor of the eagle for Lincoln also works because of the supporting atmosphere of America. His story merges, not from a frontier nowhere, but within the unique cultural and political winds of his time. What was emerging in America as Lincoln grew to manhood was as astonishing as what he did.

The interaction of these two dynamic and unique forces, Lincoln and America, is what Joshua Speed captures in his words, "For me to have lived to see such a man rise from point to point seems to me more like fiction than fact. (Like) a young eagle…. None but a genius like his could have accomplished so much, and none but a government like ours could produce such a man…. It gave the young eagle scope for his wing."

We, in our time, may not like the idea, as Speed terms it, of something external like a government producing a man. We might gravitate toward psychological biography versus social history as the cause of personal greatness, especially spiritual greatness. But without a sense of what was then valued as America it may be hard for us to understand the reasons why so many men would willingly fight in the Civil War. There were reasons, such as we heard from Ken Burns' Civil War series in the words of Sullivan Ballou from Rhode Island. He told his beloved wife, "I know how strongly American civilization now leans on the triumph of the government—and I am willing—perfectly willing—to lay down all my joys in this life, to help maintain this government." He is willing to die for this new American civilization.

We may wonder also, looking at Southern social history, at the quaintness of Robert E. Lee or George Pickett's devotion to the state of Virginia. This is another version of a greater-than-personal history, even if it is only a tribal history with ancient associations and a certain kind of culture. It too functions as a larger force for the deepest individual devotions, however we might think of the meaning of Virginia.

These are the winds that eagles fly into. These are the larger currents that give rise to individual lives. The winds that blew through America in the first half of the 1800's were as unique as was Lincoln's flight into them. To focus on him is not to lose the sense that both winds and wings together make flight. The flight of Lincoln into America's headwinds has proven to be of a value different than Lee's flight into the winds of his Virginia.

When Ralph Waldo Emerson, in the 1830s, invoked his appeal for individuals to join in the dynamic nature of the world, Lincoln, we are told by biographer Fred Kaplan, deeply wanted to do so and by the 1850s was ready to answer that call. It is hard for us to imagine that Lincoln was fully able and equipped to match his wings with the fast currents of history that were swirling around and about him. But the mystery of Lincoln's story is not just his meteoric rise and his astonishing ability to grow and change. His is also the story of the dynamism of a country that could grow and expand. In May of 1862 Lincoln established the Department of Agriculture and signed into law the first of several Homestead Acts granting 160 acres of land for men, women and former slaves. In July he established the Pacific Railway Act for the transcontinental rail link, and the Morrill Act establishing land grant colleges. In February he had established the Legal Tender Act for paper currency, and the next February the National Bank Act. His *Thanksgiving Day Proclamation* of 1863 shows that even as America fought a total and horrendous war, the dynamic nation grew in size, wealth, science, industry, and commerce. What was emerging was both more and less than the new birth of freedom Lincoln had called for. The changes in both Lincoln and America at the mid-point of the 19th century are almost unimaginable, and by sheer intellectual, physical, and spiritual energy Lincoln bent America in many ways to his own inspired will.

To tell the story of Lincoln and America in his time requires both realism and imagination. Historians gather around these twin poles. Lincoln scholars of the last century, like Albert Beveridge, thought that a lot of the imaginative had been written about Lincoln, that the prose needed to be fumigated of too much saintly poesy. The poet who wrote six volumes of Lincoln history, Carl Sandburg, was accused of creating a folk hero. But realism is not sufficient. Imagination has always been needed just to get to the truth of the story. In our time the historian Richard Slotkin needed to write a novel, *Abe*, about Lincoln's youth, to get to the real essence of much of Lincoln's life.

The following story here is of young Lincoln and his melon-stealing friends. It is realistic and most likely it was not imagined. In this early story Lincoln enters a social situation outside of his family. We know he went to Blab school. We know he imitated the preachers from the church service he attended. But in this story he has what may be his first known encounter with a social problem. This is a freewheeling moment in his unfolding community. It reads like a parable of Jesus, or a fable by Aesop. Recorded by William Herndon, Lincoln's law partner, from an interview in 1865, it is reported by Louis A. Warren who gets most if not everything correctly. As John Burt says, sounding like Mark Twain, if this story isn't true it should be.

Here is young Abe Lincoln, in his one suspendered, too short, pants breathing heavily having run to this large hickory tree knowing his friends will be coming this way.

And here's how I told the story in the online journal *Readthespirit*:

> Big and strong as he was—he'd been wielding an axe for years—13 year old Abe Lincoln told himself that he would do something about this soon! Summer produce was necessary for winter survival. Melons in this new state, Indiana, were fine big ones, and he knew who'd been stealing them. There were only nine families within a mile of each other, about fifty young folk. He might have mused: I could beat them up. I'm the big buck of this lick and they know it. But mostly, he thought: We are friends.

Something he had read in his *Webster Speller* might stick in his mind like a seed in a crow's bill:

"Revenge—Q. Is this justifiable? A. Never, in any possible case."

Then the next preachment in the Speller:

"Justice—Q. Is it always easy to know what is just? A. Where there is any difficulty in determining, consult the Golden Rule."

And also, "Murray's Reader" said, "Revenge dwells in little minds."

If young Lincoln knew anything, he knew that his mind was big and free and full of Yonder—like the new country.

The issue of revenge, of course, would come back in the Civil War. Lincoln faced then what he called "The greatest question ever presented to practical statesmanship," in other words, how to be bring the state-stealing southerners back into the national community.

At a low point, as the war seemed to be ending, the Confederacy threated to shoot every captured Negro soldier. Lincoln, outraged at this breach of "the laws of war," issued an order of retaliation, a rebel soldier killed for every Union, even Black soldier executed, and for every re-enslaved Negro a rebel solder would be put to hard labor. Reportedly even Ralph Waldo Emerson supported this plan of an eye for an eye. Eventually, however, Lincoln rejected the idea of retaliation, writing his War Secretary, "blood can not restore blood, and government should not act for revenge."

One wonders if he remembered his *Webster Speller* and "Murray's Reader" or if it was, as we see with the melon thieves' story, just in his nature to reject revenge.

The young Lincoln must have wondered: How to do what is right, reclaim and keep the melons, and also claim and keep these boys as friends?

One of Aesop's Fables, which young Lincoln had read, concludes, "Nothing is more necessary towards completing and continuing the well-being of mankind than their entering into and preserving friendships and alliances. The safety of government depends chiefly upon this....A kingdom divided against itself is brought to desolation...."

Many years later, one of those melon-stealing boys told Herndon, how the story ended.

Joseph C. Richardson said, "We got the melons, went through the corn to the fence, got over. All at once, to our surprise and mortification, Lincoln came among us, on us, good naturedly said, 'Boys, now I've got you.' Sat down with us, cracked jokes, told stories, helped eat the melons."

Lincoln would have known another lesson from "Murray's Reader":

> "To have your enemy in your power and yet to do him good is
> the greatest heroism."

The character, thinking, and spirit of Abraham Lincoln are all in this story. Simply imagine one of the melon thieves to be South Carolina, another to be Georgia, and you see how the issues and the solutions parallel the greatest issues in Lincoln's life: individual, separate will and action verses the common good.

Not that he sat down and cracked jokes with a Senator from South Carolina, but he could have in certain circumstances, and he would have wanted to. In fact much earlier he often did share meals in his Congressional boarding house with the brilliant Alexander Stevens of Georgia who was to become the Confederate Vice-President. Stevens was to write long treatises that defended the institutions of slavery as a higher moral system. Lincoln was to meet him near the end of the war in a somewhat tense and fruitless diplomatic meeting. Lincoln, we know, had a personal quality of showing respect and humanity towards this man, and to most all men, as he did to his childhood buddies.

Lincoln, in this story clearly uses his physical power, as he did in the Civil War use power and might, to declare the terms of surrender: "I've got you now boys!" But he resorts to no ego-driven power needs to settle the matter. Neither does he humiliate his foe; he does not drive them to the wall, asking of them that fatal sacrifice that so kills political process.

They—his childhood friends, the later southerners—are not even enemies to Lincoln. He also preserves something for himself that he needs, the esteem of others. This is clearly "love your neighbor as yourself." He loves himself too in this event, keeping their esteem. He does not rise above the human family to flaunt a moral position. But one also doubts that his friends would ever try this again. Lincoln sets the pattern of conflict resolution that he will use in solving the most difficult of political issues. In terms of his eventual theology we re-read this way of being in Lincoln's Second Inaugural Address.

Note here however the mix and blend of book learning that would have been present in Lincoln's brain: a true mix of political and ethical conceptions from sources both secular and Biblical. Yet in the hands of Lincoln this turns into an almost Jesus-like event filled with a non-violent spirit and forgiving fellowship.

The young Lincoln shows a strong and engaging personal presence in this episode. It is an all-boy event and the melon field can been seen as an early battlefield for the traditional issues of male dominance. There would be others, usually involving his legendary power as a wrestler. However, one could imagine the powerful bull-like presence of his popular and respected father, Thomas Lincoln, walking up at the beginning of this "gotcha" event. But without Abe's spirit and the many lessons from book reading to inform his actions, his father assuredly would have made the boys drop the melons, and they would have run off with perhaps later parental consequences from the patriarchal system.

Rather than being how his father most likely would have been we can imagine that the joyful and companionable Lincoln revealed in this story had within him the spirit of goodness that was nurtured by his mothers' love. There was the physically capable, quietly loving, and potentially word-loving mother Nancy Hanks Lincoln. There was also the powerful protector of his sensitive nature, Sarah Bush Lincoln. She is the one who saved his reading from his impatient father. She is the one who tolerated the event in which he held some younger kids upside down and had them walk muddy footprints across the whitewashed cabin ceiling! He also, quickly, the story goes, took responsibility for his prank and washed the ceiling white again. It does not contradict history to imagine Sarah Lincoln laughing. This is a stepmother who has a legendary non-anxious presence. These mothers, then, can be felt in this Melon Thief Event, an event that turned out to be a parable for the future, as Lincoln would solve the problem of sovereignty among the States as he had among his friends, the melon thieves.

Where did this congenial power come from? Was it from the "divinity" of good mothers, the wisdom in remarkable early reading, or the stability of a good enough father whose cruelties and lacks were also strengthening to his son? His father is understandable in light of the trauma of his own father's murder, and the bitter hardships of a life on the frontier that lasted only if you could last.

Without believing that we can answer the mystery of how all these factors were parts of the making of Lincoln some concepts and values can help us understand the way such a person came to be. These concepts and values can be called "divinities."

CHAPTER EIGHT

Divinities and His Remarkable Mothers

Here are six clues that can partially explain the mystery of Lincoln's ultimately enigmatic spiritual life. These clues are found in what can be called secular divinities, that category of fate that *Hamlet* alluded to and Lincoln believed in. They offer us tools for the interpretation of Lincoln's spiritual life. Anyone of them could be the key; all of them are ways to see Lincoln.

One. Was the divinity that shaped his ends found within history itself? Was it geography, the new world, its people and its government? Is history itself the transcendent force shaping his life, all lives? Was it more the winds of history than the power of his wings?

When Lincoln quoted *Hamlet*, that "there is a divinity that shapes our ends rough-hew them though we will", as he so often did, was that for him an agnostic axiom? What did he think he was referring to? Was it merely history or was there a divinity within history? Was it history with a capital H?

He certainly had a sacred idea about history. "Four score and seven years ago" is not secular talk for 87 years, as H. Richard Niebuhr pointed out many years ago in *The Meaning of Revelation*. Was it space and time in the New World that was the open river, the dynamic life of Nature he heard about from Emerson? Was Nature the stage for history?

Two. Was the shaping divinity within Lincoln himself as his soul's code? Was there a generous and revealing collective unconscious "streaming clouds of glory" into his life? That is a possible conclusion to be drawn from the Melon Thief story, that he was just following some deep inner nature of his own. The soul's code is a general notion, advanced by the Jungian James Hillman, that the genius, talent, of a person is implanted prior to the conditions of birth and development. Lincoln, in this case, would be someone endowed with a generosity, even a conflict-resolution code, and a habit of heart. Is the soul's code from God, is God somehow voiced in the collective unconscious? M. Scott Peck wrote in *The Road Less Traveled*, that he believed that God just is the Collective Unconscious.

Three. Was the divinity that shaped him the love from his remarkable mothers? Was it something sacred and feminine found in his mother and stepmother that nurtured him? Was the love within their relationships the force that would sustain him throughout the fiery trials?

Four. Was it in language itself? The symbolic representation found in words takes outer history and the events that we value and gives them inner meaning. We take up these words in what Kant called the practical heart. H. Richard Niebuhr defines this as Revelation. He writes that the language that reveals inner meanings for the community becomes the religion of a culture. Revelation gives us an inner history of interpreted meaning that we share. When a person has this history, Niebuhr says, that person has a God. Language, it can be said, comes from Being Itself. Not just the Bible but great literature itself, like Shakespeare, can be a source for shaping his life. Language can be a place of secular and religious revelation. Lincoln's speeches can hold these gifts.

Five. Was the divinity that shaped him the wisdom and teachings of the books he read? Was it the content of the Bible and the secular Enlightenment thinkers and poets? Some of those sources are seen in the ethical precepts that guided him with the melon thieves.

Is wisdom itself the divinity that shaped Lincoln and was it mainly from the Bible? Or was Reason his main inspiration, the principles, especially of equality, that he knew through the Enlightenment thinkers quoted in his Blab school Readers?

Six. Was divinity a force ultimately revealed to him in grief? Was it in loss and the bottomless sorrow of an infinite Yonder that both grounded and inspired him? Was the tragic spirit what gave him dynamic life power? When everything is taken away in Yonder did that shape his wisdom, his humanity and insight? Was divinity for him the experience of Nothingness defined by certain mystics and the Buddhist traditions, or the wisdom of the Stoics? Was his a Tillichean version of the courage to be in the face of finitude and nothingness?

In this chapter we turn to one divinity in the above categories, the remarkable mothers that Lincoln had. How did what psychologists call the Feminine shape his life's ends, rough though he did? When Lincoln was seven, he came up with his family from Kentucky to Indiana. He also comes more into our view. There is simply more historical material about him in Indiana, including the death of his mother from Milk Sickness when he was nine.

In David Herbert Donald's keystone biography he writes that Lincoln at age eleven reminded his friends that "an ant's life was to it as sweet as ours to us." Donald admits that he is speculating here that such a sentiment was a part of the young boy finding terms for grief over the loss of his mother. Lincoln is also at that time protecting turtles from the hot coals on their backs that his friends find delight in. He is already averse to bloodshed after the shooting of a turkey brought him to tears. We have alluded to these stories as a part of his spiritual life with nature. Were his words, his tears, enabled by the legacy of his first mother and the protections of his stepmother?

Along with this extremely tender heart, Donald shows us the relentlessness of Lincoln's mind. Abe loved mathematics. He once scribbled these figures to find the sum of this complicated multiplication: 34,567,834 x 23,423! Why this mental love for infinite calculations?

His young mind, we know, would fiercely wonder why things are the way they are, why things turn out the way they do. Would he also ponder the death of his mother, and what role if any, do human beings have in shaping outcomes. Are there rational rules governing, shaping, the high number of possible outcomes? Even sums, even deaths?

We are also asking that question of the phenomena of Lincoln himself. How and why did he become what he became? What force—in this case what "divine" force—shaped him. Historians can be as reluctant to look into psychological origins as they are to look into theological interpretations. But the sheer devotion to Lincoln, evidenced by the enormous scholarship done about him, tells us that something more than objective history is on the table when an historian spends so much of his or her lifetime turning the crystal of Lincoln in hand looking at his life.

When Donald goes on to say that it is tempting to trace Lincoln's moodiness to the loss of his mother he as an historian wants, hesitantly, to say something psychological. A non-historian can do that. A professional psychotherapist can offer an interpretation of Lincoln's life. Disciplined and trained awareness, and common sense, can allow us to say some things about how Lincoln's mother and his stepmother shaped him, and his rough edges. Further reflection on the role of motherhood, and even the Feminine in life, can tell us about the shaping of Lincoln by these two women, and the many other older motherly women he sought out in his life.

If we are circumspect about our own "social location" our viewpoint can be useful, interesting, and truthful. Freud, as a German Jew promoting his own school of thought, was out of his field when he analyzed Woodrow Wilson. Psycho-bio-history got a bad name. The poet Carl Sandburg irritated less poetic historians when he turned to history to write six volumes on Lincoln. Yet his poetic Lincoln has as much value, or more, than the "Arrow collar Lincoln" we get from Albert Beveridge. An "Arrow collar Lincoln" was what Sandburg predicted we would get from the stiff-necked, Arrow brand white-collar wearing politician-historian Beveridge, who himself didn't think highly of Sandburg's folk-hero version, or his historical mistakes. Yet Sandburg's poetic musing and poetic language on the baby Abe and his mother tell us a great deal about who Lincoln was and how he become what he became. There is nothing wrong with trusting the wisdom of a poet to tell us something of a life in history. Think of Homer.

Here are some words the poet-turned-history writer Carl Sandburg wrote about Lincoln's mother, Nancy Hanks. First he knew there were several women with that name around Kentucky at the time of Thomas's marriage to her. He writes, "Tom Lincoln had seen this particular Nancy Hanks…and noticed she was shrewd and dark and lonesome." Well, was she shrewd? We have no reason to think she was feckless. That there was nothing careless about her is plausible from the direct quotes from people who knew. Was she dark? Lincoln was dark. His father was dark. We have, perhaps, his photograph. Some have suggested she had some Indian blood. It fits her life events as we know it that she was dark. But we don't know for sure. There are no photographs of her. Was she lonesome? If not, she became so in her trek into cabins and woods and newfound places. But she had relatives and extended family, and settlements were inter-woven communities.

"He had heard her tremulous voice" says the poet Sandburg, "and seen her shaken with sacred desires in church camp-meetings; he had seen her at preachings in cabins when her face stood out as a sort of picture in black against the firelights of the burning logs."

Well, fanciful as this is, we know that Thomas and Nancy were members of a Free Baptist church in Kentucky and left one and helped start another over the slavery preachings. They were serious about church. They were strongly anti-slavery. Thomas helped build a new church in Indiana, and even made the pulpit. Abe was the sexton and left a hand-written note in the cracks between the logs about the number of candles left. We know that religious fervor is often stoked by the woman in a family.

There is nothing counter to their lives here in Sandburg's words. We are establishing possibility and suggesting a probability, even as we acknowledge that poetry is not history. Here is the key paragraph from Volume One of Sandburg's six:

"She believed in God, in the Bible, in mankind, in the past and future, in babies, people, animals, flowers, fishes, in foundations and roofs, in time and the eternities outside of time; she was a believer, keeping in silence behind her gray eyes more beliefs than she spoke. She knew…so much of what she believed was yonder—always yonder. Every day came scrubbing, washing, patching, fixing. There was so little time to think or sing about the glory she believed in. It was always yonder…." The dots here are Sandburg's.

All that may be a little hard to take. Except when you are reading it for the first time, as I did as a youth, you would grant her that, living in three-faced lean-tos and then cabins, she could believe in foundations and roofs. Re-reading it after decades of studying Lincoln you can again feel felt moved and persuaded. Nothing contradicts anything we know about her, their life, or that frontier life. If that picture of her is not true, we know enough about Lincoln's spiritual life to see in him the imprint of this kind of spirituality: Secretive, silent, fundamental, not doctrinal, but hopeful, inspired and visionary. Knowing Lincoln now as we do we can see him in her. Knowing mother-son relationships we can see her in him. This isn't science, it is sensible.

Sandburg is accused of making Lincoln into a folk hero. But looking behind all the true stories that are folksy and heroic what you see is a folk hero. Lincoln was a folk hero before Carl Sandburg wrote about him. Lincoln became a fairly wealthy railroad lawyer in Springfield. That does not mean the nostalgic and heroic poem he wrote about wild animals in his Indiana boyhood was not true. His own musings were deep, authentic, and folksy, like a Sandburg poem, or Frost, or Wendell Berry.

Imagination in the hands of a professional historian can indeed tell us more about Lincoln and his mothers. The professional historian Richard Slotkin went deeply into his imagination to write a novel on young Abe. His opening vision of the baby Lincoln in the lap of his Bible-reading mother is historically defined, and also poetically imagined. It tells us a great deal about his mother, and how language and history came to Abe. All this was imagined—but is totally likely—in a story of the baby Lincoln hearing of Moses as Liberator of the slaves while wrapped in the lap of his loving mother. She brought Bible words to his ears and placed a book of Bible words before his infant eyes.

In his novel, *Abe: A Novel of Young Lincoln*, Slotkin opens by giving us imagined but realistic details of Nancy Hanks. She is bony, big knuckled and with a "telling voice." Lincoln once referred to his love of her voice, reading to him. In this opening scene he is an infant, one year and 10 months. The chapter heading and subheading both give us an accurate Biblical context and an apt Calvinistic doctrinal reference: "Book I: My Home Is over Jordan. Chapter 1, 'In Adam's Fall…'." It takes a good historian and a good imagination to pick those headings.

He is in her lap. She reads but we know from her words she is really telling the story of Moses freeing the slaves as she has heard it. She need not be literate, and maybe was not, to be showing him the Bible words and telling him this story. Some historians say she was not literate, others say she was. Slotkin has us imagine how the magic of letters on a page would enter an infant's mind. That is good psychology, but it is also good history, it is realistic, because we have quotes of Lincoln as a boy being very mysteriously interested in how letters form words and words form meanings. Slotkin poetically sees these Bible words that the baby would be gazing at as "black spots and squibbets…a flow of spots that made her voice come.…"

As we look for origins of some divinity in Lincoln's shaping we can allow for a mother's voice and Biblical words seen and heard. The story itself, about Moses, is historically realistic for a novel. We know that Lincoln would have known this story well, and it does figure largely in the freeing of slaves in his life. We can grant, then, the appropriateness of a novelist placing this story before the infant. This infant, Lincoln, will become like the infant Moses floating down the Nile in a basket to a new mother. This is suggestive of Lincoln who is going to have a new mother, not his birth mother. Lincoln, at the urgings of writers like Emerson, is going to enter into the river of his time and be carried along. Near the end of his life he has repeated dreams of rushing over water to a distant shore. He often referred to how he was drifting and being carried like driftwood in history. Good historian that Slotkin is, all those themes and images go into this fancy:

Abe leaned back in the warm swaddling, the bony curve of Mam's body home-solid behind him, the river flowing under them all, dark, and him drifting with it, yearning towards a dim shore that almost had a shape.

Lincoln here too has Yonder coming into his psyche.

Lincoln held both his mothers with precious respect. He made consistent reference to his long-deceased mother with the words, "my sweet angel mother." He honors her while also honoring his stepmother, whom he also dearly loved, calling her a different name,

"Mama." We see a man who can love two mothers, equally, deeply. Was it those sweet mothers themselves that shaped him?

When his mother was dying grotesquely from "the milk-sick," her final words to her children were to be good, and to be kind to their father, and to one another and to the world. How would those words dwell in his breaking heart and horrified mind?

Lincoln is a well-mothered man when, as an important adult, as President, he would write a letter to a young girl who was grieving her father to say, "in this sad world of ours, sorrow comes to all; and to the young it comes with bitterest agony, because it takes them unawares.… I have had experiences enough to know what I say." He was comforting her and encouraging to her that she would get beyond this sorrow in some way, because he knew he had.

Lincoln told his law partner that he owed everything he was to who his mother was. Some historians conclude that Lincoln was thinking about his genetics and the story of his mother having been conceived by a wealthy Virginia landowner. It is not clear why that context defines these words for them. But nonetheless, in terms of origins, he clearly attributes his value to sources through his mother. He is pointedly saying that it is not through his father. Lincoln's self-definition of what is positive in his origins is matrilineal, even as patriarchal as his actual childhood environment was.

Descriptions of Lincoln's mother, Nancy Hanks, vary widely, from tall to not so tall, to eye color and to weight. But there is great agreement as to her sweetness, her intelligence, and her strength. A potentially reliable source would be Dennis Hanks, her cousin and the adopted child of this blended family of Hankses, Sparrows and Lincolns who make up the family of young Abraham. Louis A. Warren reminds us that Dennis saw Nancy Hanks several times a day for several years. Dennis Hanks wrote,

Mrs. Lincoln…was 5-8 in high (t), spare made—affectionate—the most affectionate I ever saw—never knew her to be out of temper, and thought strong of it. She seemed to be unmovably calm; she was keen, shrewd, smart, & I do say highly intellectual by nature. Her memory was strong, her perception quick, her judgment was acute almost. She was spiritually and ideally inclined, not dull, not material, not heavy in thought feeling or action. Her hair was dark, eyes were bluish green—keen and loving. Her weight was one hundred and thirty…She was one of the very best women in the whole race known for kindness, tenderness, charity, and love to the world. Mrs. Lincoln always taught Abe goodness, kindness, read the good Bible to him, taught him to read and to spell, taught him sweetness and benevolence as well.

This is in an 1865 letter from Hanks to William Herndon. From what we know of Lincoln this would be the kind of mother he would have. From what we do know of mothering Lincoln would not fall far from this tree. While there are legitimate limits, historical methods need not exclude what we know from other disciplines and ways of thinking.

Imagination and fact go hand in hand in much Lincoln history. We learn from Warren, and hear again from Ronald C. White, that the fall leaves were brilliant that day in October when Lincoln's mother was buried in a coffin his father had made, and he had helped. The trees are variously named, walnut, maple, oak, and persimmon. Why doubt this history? If we can credit these details, can we not also know something of how his two mothers shaped him as well?

Of course objective historical data is important as we speculate. Whatever deep grief Lincoln felt, we know that in the context in which he grew up, parental death was far from uncommon. It did not separate him from the common lot of those all around him. In the nineteenth century one-half of American Presidents had suffered parental loss by the time they reached adulthood. Lincoln himself said that these deaths are not "an unlooked-for sorrow." It is also true that the role a mother played in a boy's life shifted, in his context, as soon as the boy was able to help with farm work. Abe had an axe in his hand even before his mother died two years later. A mother's orbit of influence was short-lived. His older sister too would have been a figure in his life, only adding to his later grief when she died in child-birth when Abe was twenty years old. We see here the importance of social history, the winds of history.

All this known and imagined history of Lincoln and his birth mother sets a stage for understanding his origins and his nature. We have a picture, it even could be a painting, of Lincoln and his mother. It could be entitled, in a nineteenth century way, "Heavenly touches from an Angel Mother."

The portrait of his stepmother only adds to the story of how these feminine figures in his life were a force, a divinity, in his with secular life. There is a sacred feminine force within the place we call secular religious.

Lincoln's Second Mother, Sarah Bush Lincoln, what do we know of her power to shape his life?

> "His mind and mine—what little I had—seemed to move to-gether—move in the same channel."

That is Sarah Bush Lincoln, his "Mama," being quoted in a late in life interview.

This, his truly loved step-mother, is as close to a God-send as Lincoln, or anyone, could hope for in life. Everything that was wrong and bad in his life was about to be made right and good as she arrived when he was ten years old. Thomas Lincoln, over the year that followed Nancy Lincoln's death, had barely been able to keep the little family alive. Hunting game with Dennis Hanks was about all he could manage. He reached back into this memory and into his Kentucky past to find what would be nothing less than the savior of the situation. He had a romantic interest in Sarah Bush earlier, and now, due to the death of his rival, her first husband, she was ready, willing and able to respond to his request that they make a new life together. It speaks well of him, as some historians remind us, that Tom Lincoln had the local reputation and the attractiveness in all ways to persuade this eminently sensible practical and herself attractive woman to leave her home in Elizabethtown, Kentucky, for the more radical challenges of frontier Indiana.

There were many faults in Thomas Lincoln, but among his strengths was his choice of Lincoln's mother and then his stepmother. Thomas Lincoln was sensible and had a humble heart. He, for example, named his firstborn son after his own murdered father not after himself. Whatever trauma he suffered as a young boy sitting next to his Indian-killed father, seconds away from being killed himself, he memorialized that moment and made his son his father's namesake with the entire legacy that comes from such "replacement" naming. Only his second son and third child would get his name, and that boy died as an infant. How would that have felt to him? There was more than tremendous physical strength in Thomas Lincoln; there was strength of purpose and heart.

The mother and the three new siblings that he brought back with him from Kentucky found Abraham and his older sister in a nearly savage condition. For months they had been largely alone. Their clothes were in such tatters as to render them almost naked. Abe had a head full of lice. The children had expected their father far sooner and had only long fears to tell them what might have happened.

What gratitude Lincoln must have immediately felt toward this woman who took him in hand, washed his head and body, got him into clothes, and made him real food! Perhaps most miraculous of all she brought with her *Webster's Speller*, *Robinson Crusoe*, and The *Arabian Nights*. A real floor, not hard dirt, was her first demand, and then some more furniture from her carpenter husband.

She brought more than just physical survival. Lincoln learned over the next few years that she understood just who he really was. His notion of his own mental power was protected by her. Without her Lincoln, the reader, would have been left to the patriarchal demands of a farmer-hunter father who had slight respect for the thinking and feelings that were his life-blood, his motivating power. Lincoln was a strange young boy. What does any boy, any child, want more than a mother who powerfully protects and deeply understands him? Psychologically it is call "mirroring" and is an essential factor in self-development. No wonder Sarah Lincoln reports the following, "Abe never gave me a cross word or look and never refused in fact, or even in appearance, to do anything I requested him…I never gave him a cross word in all my life…Abe was the best boy I ever saw or ever expect to see."

Significantly, she only was only willing to say that after both he and his stepbrother were dead. She made the point that she would never compare them in such a way were one still living, or both. This is a woman with a knowing heart, a powerful sense of fairness and boundaries. She was able to love two very different sons and hold them in fairness and equality in her family and in her heart. These two different sons, she reports, had only one fight or argument between them in all their decades of growing up together. We see Lincoln's heart here. This home life echoes the deep attitude Lincoln later had toward both the South and the North and their coming brother-to-brother fight.

Lincoln went by himself to see his beloved stepmother after he was elected President and before he left for Washington. He did not make that longish carriage ride to southern Illinois even when his father died. Of his stepmother Lincoln said, "She had been his best friend in this world." This acclamation is from a man who had collected a huge number of very good friends, people very loyal and loving towards him. Lincoln concluded, "....no man could love a mother more than he loved her." To have such a loved and close mother is a remarkable fact in Lincoln's life.

Even while blending a stepfamily of widely divergent origins, Sarah became extremely fond of Abe. His quality of absolute loyalty, gracious compliance and cheerful obedience is the definition of anyone's idea of a good son or even a supplicant in a religious life. Any monastery would love to have a novitiate such as this young man, and he would want a Superior like his mother.

Abe Lincoln reflected his real mother in some ways, her Yonder dreams in life were like his dreams of life, her love of the Bible and stories and words became his. We can assume that Lincoln received from his father physical endurance and a rational stubbornness that made both men rock-like. Thomas Lincoln may even have been a better rollicking storyteller than his famous spellbinder jokester son. But what Lincoln mainly received from him was Sarah Bush Lincoln, his stepmother. In her we have a large story. Where, in any larger sense, did she come from? How would his life have ever been without her? The magnitude of her mental, spiritual, understanding of him and his gratitude for her exceeds the best fiction we may recall.

Think of *David Copperfield*, an orphan who deeply loved his mystical mother and was totally enraptured with her nature. Think, then of Peggotty, his beloved and constant nurse, and then his powerful and wave-making Aunt Betsy Trotwood. When you think of the impact that Charles Dickens imagined these women had on young Davey, you can get a sense of the effect Lincoln's real mother and then his real step-mother, his Peggotty and his Aunt Trotwood, had on this very needy, very talented, and very unusual boy.

This boy remembered his "Mama" as he went off to Washington. Because her mind flowed in the same channels as his, she deeply worried some great harm would come to him, as he, too, wondered if he should ever return.

CHAPTER NINE

Yonder and Sandburg

Thomas Jefferson's agrarian dreams, rooted in images of early Saxons in the forests of Germany, were swept off the face of America in the nightmare of the Lincoln's Civil War. The tragic entailment of values, to use John Burt's phrase, is manifest in this awful turn of events. Because, ironically, it was Lincoln's devotion to Jefferson's Declaration of Independence, his natural law assertion that all men are created equal, that led to the end of the culture of Jefferson's vision, and the Southern devotion to that vision.

There may be a rebirth of Jefferson's agrarian yeoman dream. But Lincoln and the one hundred years of the "rebirth of freedom" what Orville Vernon Burton calls "The Age of Lincoln" was of a different kind of America than Jefferson's dream. What griped Lincoln led to a reformation of our political culture as revolutionary as the Reformation of Martin Luther. Lincoln's spiritual life was a secularization of America's Protestant religious spirit, Luther's a secularization of the Roman Catholic.

Carl Sandburg's word "yonder" becomes a concept to define the secularized religious consciousness of Lincoln. Yonder, we have asserted earlier, is a word for the cast to Lincoln's mind. Sandburg attributes it to the cast of his mother's mind, as we have seen. A look at Sandburg's rhetoric using the word helps us understand how it can become a definitive if not also purposefully vague and encompassing, secular concept. Yonder is a human term, not a scriptural term.

But Yonder is a word like other significant religious categories, such as the Tao, Enlightenment, Salvation, mystical union. It is also, we have noted, a word like many spiritually informed states, like bliss, peace, beatitude, grace. Yonder, while not a scriptural word, is a concept that can apply to the holy. It is not a word from traditions of revelations or even necessarily wisdom traditions. It is a word more at home with the secular and humanistic way we know things. It is then more of a philosophical notion than a dogmatic one. It has to do with epistemology, how we know what we know. Yonder also moves from a category of mental consciousness to a psychological category. When Shakespeare coined the terms "to think feelingly," he had moved mental thought into a hybrid with feelings. When Carl Jung said he didn't believe in God but that he knew God he moved religious language to an empirical level. Jung was a spiritual empiricist. This is a wonderful paradox. Yonder is known and unknown, and it is secular and religious.

Yonder, whether as a secular or as a religious term, is not directly involved in ethics, concepts of justice, or the political areas of freedom, or law. Yonder is a way religious and spiritual consciousness can be defined. Less ethically focused, it is inspirational and even generative of language.

There is a spaciousness of mind and action that comes with a Yonder way of mind. This open-minded vision is compatible with the slow to action quality of Keats' idea of Negative Capability. Both terms point to a connoisseurship of poise. There is a Buddhist kind of passionless action, a yogic form of balance. Such modes of being can be attributed to the archetypal idea of the Feminine. Lincoln's inaction was sometimes criticized as being passive or even feminine.

Harriet Beecher Stowe flat-out said in her newspaper column that Lincoln led from a passive feminine nature, that he stood strong not like a stone buttress wall, unmovable, but like a taut wire cable, swaying from one side to every influence, yielding as to the winds of change, but always holding, tenacious and bound. You can see in that image also not just change and motion, but also a relationship, a holding of something to and with something else. One of Lincoln's strengths as a leader was that he held together whatever and whomever he could—a family, a Cabinet, an army, a country.

There is, as we have noted, in Lincoln's spiritual life a third element, along with Yonder and Negative Capability. That is language itself. It is within this trinity of aspects, a Yonder consciousness and a Negatively Capable way of being, that language forms the base. In thinking about Yonder it is important to consider all three of these characteristics.

To think of Yonder it is also helpful to have a visual image of Lincoln's world, as we suggested in the introduction, seeing the distant views of the frontier and the western prairie where he grew up. To young Lincoln in Kentucky the world must have been naturally beautiful, and unremarkably so, as he knew nothing else. Historians have spoken of the rare beauty of Sinking Springs, Kentucky and the two knolls of Knob Creek, the area of his birth. In the clearness of the creek water, even in the early 20th century, you could see all the way down to the stones in the bottom of the creek. His home in southern Indiana, he said, was the most un-poetical of places. Yet he wrote a great poem re-visiting there. As one walks the fields of this triangle of land between the Wabash and the Ohio Rivers, the hills are like huge and peaceful ocean swells; they have folds and crinkles like a huge unmade bed. But the thick trees were a primeval forest when the Lincolns arrived. A few Indian-made fields would allow views. There was the hope of a view beyond. Where the hills open, the sense is of the same beyond, hills after hills. The horizon is hard to find, the hills being close and convoluted. When Lincoln arrived in south central Illinois he saw the land to be much flatter and the view falling out into a misty middle distance. The land extends, and you know it extends. But unlike seeing the Rocky Mountains from western Kansas, you can only guess at the expanse in Illinois. There is no clear border, and so it fades off into a nearly horizon-less horizon. These would have been the visual sensations of the large geography of Lincoln's formative years. Then as a circuit-riding lawyer he spent a third to a half of each year riding his horse, or a carriage, going from distant town to distant town on the prairie. Except when he was reading, he would be gazing out, out and away.

It is then easy to see how a fellow Illinoisan, Sandburg, born in Galesboro, would find the right word, "Yonder," for a sense of the consciousness of life that Lincoln would have had, and that his migrating mother, from Virginia to Kentucky to Indiana would have had.

It does not matter if Sandburg was reading from Lincoln back to the character of his mother's mind, or in an explanatory way from his mother to him. The point is that the minds of these two flowed in similar ways, as we also know about his stepmother. The words Sandburg gives, again, are, "She knew... so much of what she believed was yonder—always yonder."

What we see here is a transition, basic to all faith, from the verb, "knew," what she knew, to what she believed. Hers was a belief in Yonder. She knew, and then the three dots. In that gap, that hiatus, her mind shifts from knowledge to belief, and it is not a belief in knowledge, it is a belief in a boundary. Yonder is a place, the place of receding boundary; it is not a piece of knowledge. It is a place that lies beyond the hard work of everyday. It is a place of glory, known maybe in song, and it is a place of eternal continuity, at least in its yonderness, as it is eternally Yonder.

Sandburg makes use of his expansive idea of Yonder elsewhere in his poetry and stories. In the poem, "Hope is a Tattered Flag" he says that "Hope is an echo, hope ties itself yonder, yonder."

There is a dialogue with or to hope. The dialogue is in an echo, a voice that comes back to you. But also it starts out from you. It is a humanistic voice that has a return. We saw something of this human quality of voice in Lincoln's "chords of memory" in his First Inaugural Address. The echo that is hope has a return to its origin, at least a hitching place. The echo that is hope ties itself to "yonder" but it also ties itself back to you. Like the steel cable that Stowe describes in Lincoln's passive style of using power, hope also is tied to something at the other end, that something is called Yonder.

As we use this cast of mind to understand the rational mind and the spiritual mind of Lincoln we could assume that his hope is tied to something, even if it is something out of sight. But that is not the nature of the mind in Yonder, nor is it the nature of belief in Negative Capability. Jacques Derrida, the philosopher, talks of faith as being blind. He says only in blindness do we have faith. As soon as we see, it is no longer faith but fact. Yonder is to sound, the echo sound, as blindness is to sight. Echoes in the far reach of the human cry are tied to some hope that also has a point of return. Yonder is the point in vision where seeing becomes not the seeing of a thing, but only seeing itself. Yonder is the blinded line beyond what we cannot see. That is just where hope returns. Yonder, in sound, is the returning echo of our hope.

Sandburg uses Yonder in his famous Rutabaga stories. In these stories there are two talking, leaning, whispering, loving skyscrapers who say that "over there" where the mountains are, where the sea is, where the railroad goes, still goes, across the prairie, that is where Yonder is. That is how they talk with each other, these two skyscrapers. In the wild imagination of Sandburg it is toward Yonder that the offspring of these skyscrapers is going to go. The offspring of the twin towers is the railroad, and the train is called the Golden Spike Limited. Although it meets with tragedy, it is on its way to Yonder when it does. Twin towers. Tragedy. A predicting echo.

These images are particularly appropriate for understanding Lincoln and the spirit of the age he represented, the one hundred years of a new birth of a certain freedom. Lincoln and his whole political party were, of course, railroad people. Lincoln was a railroad lawyer. His son became a railroad executive, as did some Civil War generals including the inept and slow to fight McClellan. He did know how to organize. The railroad was the new life blood of the industrial technological America that was replacing the agrarian and slave society of the old south, Jefferson's south, and the hold it had on the whole country. The railroad was seen, as the 19th century historian Henry Adams would say, as an almost spiritual force in American history then. He called it the Dynamo and he contrasted it with the spiritual value of the Middle Ages and the reign of the Virgin.

There was then a vision of an expanding world with almost limitless horizons, a characteristic of the American mind since that time. No longer was the Kingdom of God in America just a City on a Hill sending back its true light, it was an idea of expanding life for its original values, including freedom and equality. All that expansion was tied to hope, and it is a gift of Yonder that Lincoln never let go of, even as he unknowingly dreamed of his fast approaching death and the landing in victory of the ship of state on the new far shore.

CHAPTER TEN

Yonder Near and Far

There is a near side to Yonder, an inner sense, a close focus and a presence, and a far side, a sense of beyond reach. When, for example, you stand at the Grand Canyon you are at once thrown back upon your near and immediate self. You feel your finite existence in an intimate and personal way as you see the expanse before you. But you are also aware of the miles over which you gaze. You try to imagine not just the reach across the cavernous depths between the rims, but also the far reaches up and down, both East and West.

Lincoln never saw the Grand Canyon. But in September of 1848 he stood in the mist and spray of that other great natural wonder and symbol of American expanse, Niagara Falls. Of course, even Lincoln was small next to the Falls. There is a nearly private feeling in being there. The cold wet on your face, the thundering sense of an ancient and huge force, this is nature near and yet beyond you. Lincoln was eloquent about the far side of Yonder in his viewing of the Falls, "But still there is more. It calls up the indefinite past. When Columbus first sought this continent—when Christ suffered the cross—when Moses led Israel through the Red-Sea—nay, even when Adam first came from the hand of his Maker—then as now, Niagara was roaring here." He goes on more as a Darwinian than a Biblicist. "The eyes of that species of extinct giants, whose bones filled the mounds of America, have gazed on Niagara, as ours do not....In that long—long time, never still for a single moment. Never dried, never froze, never slept, never rested."

The far Yonder reach of Lincoln's mind and words is also sensed in the close and keen scientific observation he was used to as a land surveyor, a river navigator. But nature, not God, and time's eternity not God's providence, were what filled Lincoln's mind. Yonder for him, in 1848, was a gateway to philosophical thought, not a stepping-stone to theological faith.

Reflecting on Niagara Falls was not the only time Lincoln's rangy mind had expressed itself in an essay about history and things. In 1859 he gave a lecture on "Discoveries, Inventions, and Improvements." He had also delivered a talk at the Wisconsin State Fair whose opening lines rival and pre-date Walt Whitman's "Specimen Days." Lincoln wrote, "Every blade of grass is a study; and to produce two, where there was but one, is both a profit and a pleasure. And not grass alone; but soils, seeds, and seasons—hedges, ditches, and fences…" until it ends with, "The thousand things of which these are specimens—each a world of study within itself." Lincoln's mind is close in and far reaching. This is the near and the far side of the Yonder. He had been immersed in both with the ocean-like swells of southern Indiana and the expansive vistas of the tall-grassed Illinois prairie. They were his first Niagara and his Grand Canyon.

This cast of mind, like his Niagara thoughts, is awakened by water as much as by land. Around the time of his lecture at the Wisconsin Fair, known sometimes as the "Milwaukee Address," Lincoln visited in Chicago. On the piazza of the home of his important supporters, Mr. and Mrs. N.B. Judd, overlooking Lake Michigan, Lincoln mused and Mrs. Judd wrote down her memory. "(He) seemed greatly impressed with the wondrous beauty of the scene, and carried by its impressiveness away from all thoughts of jars and turmoil on earth. In that mild pleasant voice, attuned to harmony with his surroundings, as was his wont when his soul was stirred by aught that was lovely or beautiful, Mr. Lincoln began to speak of the mystery which for ages enshrouded and shut out those distant worlds above us from our own; of the poetry and beauty which was seen and felt by seers of old when they contemplated Orion and the Arcturus as they wheeled seemingly around the earth, in their nightly course; of the discoveries since the invention of the telescope, which had thrown a flood of light and knowledge on what before was incomprehensible."

We hear his voice "attuned to harmony with his surrounding" and his words in this piece of history recorded by Daniel Kilham Dodge in his 1929 book *Abraham Lincoln, Master of Words*. Dodge goes on to comment on the Niagara reflections by saying, English professor though he was, "Nowhere else in Lincoln's writings do we find so fine an example of the historical imagination."

Lincoln's visit to Niagara Falls was at the end of his one term in Congress and he was on his way home. His ambitions would both be energized and dwarfed by this mighty waterfall and the river with its magnificent near ending, its place of momentous change. All this awakens a human sense of Yonder in him. While some of his references are Biblical they are placed alongside natural history references, and the God of creation is not mentioned in his romantic broken-sentenced near poem.

Not everyone knew of these romantic and philosophical musings. His partner Herndon asked him about the Falls and Lincoln said he wondered where all that water came from. Herndon did not know of these ponderings on the Falls. Even now there are students of Lincoln who focus only on the intricate logic of his speeches and not also the Yonder that his calculations approach. There are also those who look closely for religious, even Christian, meanings in his words and thoughts. The concept of Yonder with its finite and its infinite side bridges the space between logic and faith that Lincoln truly occupied. Yonder says little about God but it also says more than detailed logic might. If there is a religious word for Yonder it is the word Holy. The awe and fascination, the large and small of life, the fear and the attraction in the idea of the Holy is a part of what Yonder is.

Among the paradoxes contained within Lincoln, the finite and the infinite is one of the most profound. As a politician, the large version of America was his driving force. The legal idea of the Union, so persuasive to him, was that it was in perpetuity, it was timeless and extensive and held no clause for its own finite demise. The Lincolns had been in perpetual motion since the 1630s. He, unknown to himself, was the sixth in a flow of generations that had come to America for its original promise of opportunity and religious freedom. Each generation moved south and then west, from Massachusetts, to New Jersey, to Virginia, Kentucky, Indiana, Illinois. The American dynamo was in the blood of the Lincolns. The American story was in his Grammar books, his Readers. George Washington was a mythical hero to Lincoln. When, as newly elected President, he spoke to the Assembly of the New Jersey Legislature, he spoke of his boyhood thrill at reading about the New Jersey battle events of the Revolution. He also spoke of how he would put his foot down if need be, and some say he did, in that speech, let down his heel with force as he said so. (New Jersey was the only Free State he did not carry, he shared it with Douglas.) The boyhood thrill of being an American was still strong in him. More perhaps than the other youth of his generation in that original New Jersey Colony, the frontier Lincoln knew what it meant to have the country as a possibility. It had been immediately thrilling to him to read Webster's speeches on freedom and the Union.

The infinite grand side is most often what is emphasized in political history and biography. However, with thanks to Carl Sandburg, the close inner workings of the heart of Lincoln have become a field for inquiry. Before we turn more to that side it is important to show again that Lincoln was grand and huge in his Yonder sense. This is what he spoke to that New Jersey State Assembly,

If the relative grandeur of revolutions shall be estimated by the great amount of human misery they alleviate and the small amount they inflict, then, indeed, will this be the grandest the world shall ever have seen. Of our political revolution of '76 we all are justly proud. It has given us a degree of political freedom far exceeding that of any other of the nations of the earth. In it the world has found a solution of the long mooted problem as to the capability of man to govern himself. In it was the germ which was vegetated and still is to grow and expand into the universal liberty of mankind.

This is the great and infinite Yonder that we hear again in the *Gettysburg Address*. He says further in this New Jersey speech,

But with all these glorious results—past, present, and to come—it had its evils, too. It breathed forth famine, swam in blood, and rode on fire; and long, long after, the orphan's cry and the widow's wail continued to break the sad silence that ensued. These were the price, the inevitable price, paid for the blessings it brought.

Here Lincoln sees not only the grand reaches of an infinite hope, but the tragedy, the personal and intimate losses, the flow of blood. Knowing the intimate near side of finite, specific sorrow is a part of the complex and profound spirit of Lincoln. We also see his ability to have his eye on both the good and the evil of anything in history. One thinks of the insight of the poet Robert Penn Warren who famously states in his novel *All The King's Men*, fundamentally a novel about the Civil War, that "...what we students of history always learn is that the human being is a...contraption and that they are not good or bad but are good and bad and the good comes out of the bad..." Such is the tolerance for ambiguity that we also see defined in the concept of Negative Capability.

On the grand side it is clear that Yonder in Lincoln's mind is a bigger category than Virginia in the mind of Robert E. Lee. While Virginia, the home of Jefferson, takes on the life of the good tribe in Lee's mind, all of America, on the other hand, became the true home of Lincoln. His Yonder takes on the life of a grand ideal, the coming universal equality and liberty of humanity, housed in a uniquely formed government. It isn't clear that Lincoln's Yonder dream immediately survived the war—so like the war he describes in picturing of the Revolution of 1776—any more than Jefferson's agrarian utopia survived. Certainly the progressive reforms of Lincoln's government, the land grant colleges, the expanded rail and water ways, the increase in mineral science and in industrial technology all were building a new kind of freedom for a new version of America. While the seed was sown for the solution to the poison of slavery it was a hundred years before its roots could support anything close to the freedom of the Lincoln promise. Yet there is the Moses quality to Lincoln's grand side, the liberation of a people, the founding of a new land of promise. The excitement within the hearts of that generation is palpable upon reading their words, including Lincoln's.

It is in the tears of sorrow over the great sacrifice of the Civil War that we come more to see the near side of Yonder. The intimate inner life of this man reflects, in his spirit, a nation as tragic as it seemed victorious. This aspect of intimate sorrow is crucial to Lincoln's spirit, his view of himself and the country's turmoil. It is the tragic aspect that Walt Whitman conjures in his image of men at the opening of the next century, collected and talking of memories, when "some ancient soldier sitting in the background as the talk goes on, and betraying himself by emotion and moist eyes—like the journeying Ithacan at the banquet of King Alcinous, when the bard sings the contending warriors and their battles on the plains of Troy:

'So from the sluices of Ulysses' eyes
Fast fell the tears, and sighs succeeded sigh.'

I have fancied I say, (so writes Whitman in his *Memories of President Lincoln*) some such venerable relic of this time of ours, preserved to the next or still the next generation of America."

It is eerie then to read Lincoln's earlier words about the Revolution and its cost in blood, the widows and the orphans, all the costs of the freedoms won by war. It is a "predicting-echo" to raise the paradox of what was to come from the Civil War. The note of a tragedy to come was also struck in Carl Sandburg's children's story from Rootabaga County. There the great free child of the two city skyscrapers, the railroad train named The Golden Spike Limited, is speeding out to Yonder, to the mountains and to the sea, and it meets there with a catastrophic crash. The winds bring back the tale of sorrow for the animate twin towers to hear. It is eerie to read of the twin towers and their conversation over their tragedy.

Yonder ultimately becomes a word to connote, if not denote, the dynamics of a religionless spiritual consciousness. It is a spiritual mode of knowing, and in our time it knows the intimate side of Yonder better than the far and grand side. Lincoln's frontier was peopled by thousands of families in rolling Prairie Schooners bringing with them various versions of a hope for the Kingdom of God in America. That grand providence of God becomes the final definition for Lincoln of why the war is what it is—a suffering for divine justice. But his entry point into such grand awareness is as much through the nearly shut, tear-filled eyes of sorrow as it is through the wide and wild-eyed views of boundless hope. In Lincoln, as we heard from Sandburg's poem, hope is a tattered flag, and it is bound to a Yonder that is not yet to be.

CHAPTER ELEVEN

The Near Side of Yonder

P resident Lincoln was living at the Soldiers' Home, which was a
site for cooler weather in the summer time. Among the members of his party there one day a dispute arose as to whether a specimen of a green tree was a cedar or a spruce. Lincoln entered the fray, "Let me discourse on a theme I understand," he said. "I know all about trees in right of being a backwoodsman. I'll show you the difference between spruce, pine, and cedar, and this shred of green, which is neither one nor the other, but a kind of illegitimate cypress." He then proceeded to explain the difference and distinctive formation of the foliage belonging to different kinds of trees. He went on to philosophize that trees are as deceptive in their appearance as are certain types of men who are only recognizable to a trained eye, or until events develop and the moral features of a person become clearer. His Yonder vision did not mean that he didn't have clear sight of what was before his very eyes.

His close observations of nature had also led him, at another time, to a revealing talk with a friend as they rode through some Virginia woods. He noted that the vine that was wrapped around a certain tree was both decorating and ruining the tree. The next day in a conversation about certain people he turned to his riding friend and said, as if winking, that, yes, certain men were like trees and their reputations were like shadows. One needed to see the tree and not the shadow, not the vine. Knowing trees taught Lincoln a lot about how to know people.

In the near side of his Yonder-filled consciousness Lincoln was paying attention to detail, to what was right before him. His Yonder vision, such as his ideas on the Union and human equality, was of great value, wisdom and guiding truth. So too was his near vision, still with a certain dreaminess, but indelible and practical.

Lincoln's partner, Herndon, according to Edmund O. Wilson in his book *Patriotic Gore*, reported on Lincoln's eyes: "Mr. Lincoln's were slow, cold, clear and exact. Everything came to him in its precise shape and color. To some men the world of matter and of man comes ornamented with beauty, life and action, and hence more or less false and inexact. No lurking illusion or other error, false in itself, and clad for the moment in robes of splendor, ever passed undetected or unchallenged over the threshold of his mind—that point that divides vision from the realm and home of thought... Neither his perception nor intellectual visions were perverted, distorted or diseased. He saw all things through a perfect mental lens. There was no diffraction or refraction there. He was not impulsive, fanciful, or imaginative, but calm and precise." Herndon was himself not so calm and precise. What he meant was, "He saw all things through a perfect mental lens." He didn't let his vision get in the way of his perception. Lincoln would have been a good philosophical phenomenologist.

A Frenchman, the Marquis de Chambrun, writing to his mother back in France wrote, also about trees, of an experience with Lincoln that illustrated the precise and detailed, clear vision and mind of Lincoln,

> Mr. Lincoln stopped to admire an exceptionally tall and beautiful tree growing by the roadside and applied himself to defining its particular beauties: powerful trunk, vigorous and harmoniously proportioned branches, which reminded him of great oaks and beeches under whose shade his youth had been passed. Each different type he compared, in technical detail, to

the one before us. His dissertation certainly showed no poetic desire to idealize nature; but if not that of an artist, it denoted extraordinary observation, mastery of descriptive language and absolute precision of mind…I have heard him give opinions on statesmen and argue political problems with astounding precision. I have heard him describe a beautiful woman and discuss the particular aspects of her appearance, differentiating what is lovely from what might be open to criticism, with the sagacity of an artist. In discussing literature, his judgment showed a delicacy and sureness of taste which would do credit to a celebrated critic.

Abraham Lincoln was a backwoodsman. He was, without being a figure in a novel, the embodiment of much that we value and even romanticize about such frontier people. He was in fact related to Daniel Boone and his father's folks had come south on Boone's Wilderness Road. When we read James Fennimore Cooper, barring the deserved ridicule of Mark Twain, we have the character with the poetic name Hawkeye. Lincoln fits the role and the name. (The actor Daniel Day Lewis has played both Hawkeye and Lincoln in recent movies.) The name tells us of a natural phenomenon, the hawk that can soar and see great and yonder distances, and yet notes by eye the movement of a twig and then feeds upon its minute and violent calculation.

Lincoln was a master of many details, even battlefield strategy. He studied books on war after he became President. Sandburg quotes Lincoln, after the Battle of Second Bull Run, as the battlefield master, saying, "[McClellan] had he thrown Porter's corps of fresh men and other available troops upon Lee's army, he would inevitably have driven it to the river and captured most of it by sunset."

Lincoln read the telegrams at the War Office. He studied the maps. He knew the material world and how it works. He is the only President to hold a patent from the Patent Office, for a method of changing the ballast in rafts and boats to get them over sand bars, a trick he performed himself as a young man in New Salem, Illinois, to the amazement of onlookers on shore.

The eyesight of Lincoln is, however, even more remarkable than his ability to see aspects both close and visionary. Lincoln also had the kind of mental vision that can hold two things in his mind at the same time, two conflicting things. That is of course what he did with the country, seeing the South for what it was, and seeing the North for what it was, but also in his mind holding them together for what they were, the Union. That is what he dreamed and knew them historically to be.

Another 19th century agonized Calvinist with melancholy moods like Lincoln has some words about this kind of vision, eyes that hold two things in mind with insight. Herman Melville tells us early in *Moby Dick* of the wonder of the whale that has an eye on each side of its head. Yet still, he says, with one brain the whale knows what to do with its binocular vision. This natural phenomenon would deeply move Melville.

Binocular vision was a tragic aspect in Melville's life. He was a person who was looking, as a critic has said, with great lust for the ultimate and yet had seen too much of the world to trust a faith in the God of the 19th century Victorian parlor or church. Cynical ambiguity then haunts him. He wrote a book, *Pierre, or The Ambiguities*, as a kind of crazed sarcasm and satire. He had yet to find a way to bring his views of the world together. He is unable to do what he imagines the whale can do. As we see in the discussion of Negative Capability, holding ambiguities in mind is a leadership and spiritual skill that Lincoln mastered. Melville struggles endlessly to reconcile the ambiguities he sees.

He does present a one-eyed, full-faced, view of truth near the end of *Moby Dick*. He has his dark Captain Ahab encounter his first mate

Starbuck on the deck. He, Ahab, has just shed a tear into the ocean, and the ocean amplifies his tear, and he is redeemed, Melville suggests, by that amplification. He asks Starbuck then to look at him. He wants the experience of one human eye, just the look of a human eye. This is Ahab's moment of redeemed humanity before he plunges on.

Melville later places a Yonder vision before us. He sees this in the natural forces of a spouting whale. Like Lincoln, Melville shows us something up close and specific, and yet visionary and even distant. He paints a beautiful picture of an aspect of Yonder. The scene unfolds after two views of an unsolved ambiguity are accepted: Our view of Ahab redeemed by his tear, and our view of Ahab as evil. Melville's Yonder sight is the essence of a secular religious view. With one equal eye we see our doubts, but we also see, in some intuition of Yonder, a heavenly view of something we believe.

Melville explores and explains his vision, "And for this I thank God; for all have doubts; many deny; but doubts or denials, few along with them, have intuitions. Doubts of all things earthly, and intuitions of some things heavenly; this combination makes neither believer nor infidel, but makes a man who regards them with equal eye." He could be describing Lincoln, neither a believer nor an infidel, but one who can regard life with an equal eye.

The intuition, the Yonder vision, Melville cites is this:

> The rainbows that are made in the vapor of the spitting whale.
>
> And how nobly it raises our conceit of the mighty, misty monster, to behold him solemnly sailing through a calm tropical sea....
>
> ....[H]is vast mild head overhung by a canopy of vapor, engendered by his incommunicable contemplations, and that vapor—as you will sometimes see it—gloried by a rainbow, as if Heaven itself had put its seal upon his thoughts. For d'ye see,

rainbows do not visit the clear air; they only irradiate vapor. And so, through all the thick mists of the dim doubts in my mind, divine intuitions now and then shoot, enkindling my fog with a heavenly ray. And for this I thank God...

Rainbows are not made in the clear air, but air shot through with the mists of doubt.[4]

---

[4]　Herman Melville, *Moby Dick*, Chapter 85.

CHAPTER TWELVE

Lincoln's Clear-Eyed Words

L incoln had at least one real event of double vision, of actually seeing double. It was near the time of his tragic death. The atmosphere in the White House in those mysterious days seems to us now to be taken over by Shakespearean tragedy. His double vision event fueled the emotions and fears of his wife Mary. Lincoln's interpretation was that he would have a second term in office but might not complete it. However séance-like this and other such events seem, it is also likely that Lincoln came by his double vision physically, not metaphysically. As a teenager he had been completely knocked out by the back kick of a horse he was trying to hurry around the grinding stone at a mill. He was in mid-sentence when he was knocked in his eye socket. He completed the sentence upon coming to. But he was out and he referred to it as his being dead. Some medical opinion now is that the injury and trauma to his head would be a future cause for episodes of double vision. Regardless of his physical condition, the clarity of Lincoln's ideas and words belies any potential for confusion that might overcome lesser minds. Neither blurry sorrow nor wild-eyed hopes would make him lose his way, and what he saw became his words.

The historian William Lee Miller tells of a train ride in Connecticut that Lincoln had following his Cooper Union Address of 1860. A minister from Norwich named Gulliver encountered Lincoln on the train and remarked at how the speech he had heard the day before was the most remarkable speech he had ever heard. In response

Lincoln shared that he had been told of a Yale Professor of rhetoric who had heard him in New Haven and followed him to Meriden to hear him again and then lectured on him to his class. He then asked, as he engaged the Rev. Gulliver, what he found so remarkable. The minister replied, "The clearness of your statements, the unanswerable style of your reasoning, and especially, your illustrations, which were romance and pathos and fun and logic all welded together." Ambiguities were not ambiguous in Lincoln's mind, sorrow and humor were equally held in view and word. Clarity was the holding, welded result. While the far side on Yonder is bound to and bounded by the ideals and universal hopes that Lincoln embodied in his words, the near side, as we have indicated, would note trees, foliage, vines and other natural details, all clear illustrations. The good Reverend on the train was particular in his pairings that Lincoln's illustrations were "romance and humor" as well as "pathos and logic."

There are some rare finds on Lincoln's language, the specific and up close quality of his mind and word choice. They are again from Professor Dodge, the professor who founded the English Department at the University of Illinois the 1890s and wrote two small books on Lincoln's language. The first, *Abraham Lincoln: The Evolution of His Literary Style*, was published in 1890. The second, *Abraham Lincoln, Master of Words*, was published in 1924. Professor Daniel Kilham Dodge is another example of a student of Lincoln who shows a devotion that is extraordinary. His quest into the language of Lincoln, over a hundred years ago, is the same quest we are following here. In a close study of Lincoln's figures of speech Dodge finds the concrete homeliness of Lincoln's metaphors and similes are taken from the everyday, what we are calling the near side of Yonder. Yet they are figurative to ideas that were important, the far side of Yonder. In one chapter he notes three main tropes: card playing, ship of state, and eggs. Quoting Lincoln, "You must not expect me to give up this government without playing my last card." "You stand on middle ground and hold the ship level and steady." And "Broken eggs can never be mended...." "I should merely furnish a nest full of eggs for hatching new disputes." All these words are from the near view, real things.

In a special message to Congress, and against the advice of the government printer, Lincoln used another common figure of speech to refer to the South with the words "Sugar coated." "With rebellion thus sugar-coated, they have been drugging the public mind of their section for more than thirty years" He was told it was undignified. He replied, "The word expresses precisely my idea, and I am not going to change it. The time will never come in this country when the people won't know exactly what sugar-coated means!"

Professor Dodge concludes, "Lincoln's figures almost always serve a useful purpose in making an obscure thought clear and a clear thought still clearer." For example, in a telegram, "You must know that major-generalships in the regular army are not as plenty as blackberries." One thinks of the poet William Carlos Williams' rule, "No ideas without things." Lincoln had a consciousness, and a language, that the country would only come to in fits and starts, in poetry and rhetoric, a century later.

.

CHAPTER THIRTEEN

Sorrow

Tears seemed to release Lincoln. Sorrow and grief were engaged in his thinking on the issues that shaped his consciousness. The biggest change in Abraham Lincoln came in the early years of his marriage, and then again in 1850.

There were other changes, of course. Prior to the changes in his life in early marriage there were huge changes in moving to and then from New Salem, Illinois, where he was a near folk hero of both mental and physical abilities. There was the change in moving to Springfield as he tried to make a new life in the new capital city as a lawyer. During those first years of professional life Lincoln, while decent, thoughtful, sincere, and often energetic, was also erratic in his moods, sarcastic and satirical with his political opponents, and sometimes merely calculating in his political maneuvers.

Lincoln, as we most remember him, emerges when his sorrows and tears begin to be about others. Prior to this time his great reservoir of sorrow over his lost mother, his sister, his early love, were understandably also self-focused in some way: My mother, my sister, my love. Much of his grief over his older sister's death, when he himself was under twenty, was expressed in revengeful cruel humor against her husband whom he blamed for her death in childbirth. Then as a younger professional he was armored by the traditional masculine focus on the goals of fame and some success. But both fame and success eluded him when he compared himself to the men he competed with, notably Stephen Douglas and his friend Edward Baker, both of whom bested him in many ways.

Then, in 1850, just a month shy of his fortieth birthday, Abraham and Mary lost their son Edward Baker Lincoln. The next year Lincoln's father died, and Lincoln did the most uncharacteristic thing in his life. He not only refused to attend to his father as he was dying, he refused to attend his funeral. Prior, he had written a cryptic note to his relatives that it would be better for both them and him if he did not respond to his father's incessant calls to see his only surviving child.

This kind of cruelty and even moments of potential violence marked Lincoln during the years from 1831 to 1850, when he went from an extraordinary village youth to a moderately successful town politician. His love life was all but crazy during this time, with false proposals, broken hearts and, perhaps, suicidal despondencies. There was even, nearly, a duel.

But the next fourteen years, after 1850, Lincoln is a profoundly changed and changing man. All of his early strengths are there but the way they become composed within him change and become quite remarkable. In 1854 the issue of the extension of slavery lit a fire under Lincoln and he was never the same. From then on, he was on a mission. Prior to this time his speeches in Congress in 1848 had a 19th century verbose hoop-la that simply falls away from him after 1854. His sense of self-importance in his one term in Congress is embarrassing. Only as he begins to feel his failures, to see his sorry career as not culminating in anything like the greatness he felt called to, only then does he begin to become what we would call a great but also a sorrowful person.

Lincoln did not suffer from what psychologists would now call chronic or bipolar depression. He did not have manic episodes, and his events of extreme lassitude were short-lived and are not necessarily to be defined as depression. Despondency over love and the loss of love is not depression. Lincoln's early self-esteem was rooted in his beliefs in loyalty and reason. As young lover he was not able to hold to his values, mainly because women were wild cards for him. He was very interested in them but very clueless.

He also had a 19th century Calvinist religious sense of the abandonment of God from his life, a sense Allen Guelzo defines in his book *Redeemer President*. Lincoln did not feel himself to be among the elect and saved. While he was dismissive early on of evangelical ideas of God, he nonetheless had the moral burden of a Christian conscience whether he liked it or not. Rather than call him depressed, Lincoln was, in the now famous words from *Fanfare for the Common Man*, a melancholy man. "He was a quiet and a melancholy man." (For a fascinating study of 19th century and modern views of melancholy, see Joshua Wolf Shenk's *Lincoln's Melancholy*.)

The quality of silence in him was also enormous. But silences, sorrows, and guilt are not depression. His ability to sustain, endure, even to seek silence and solitude, was huge. Seeking silence is itself a spiritual calling valued in religious traditions. We could call this part of Lincoln his introverted and even his religious nature. But the paradoxes of his life continue. He was also greatly energized by extraverted activities. Sitting up late into the night in a tavern full of storytellers, being the sought-after center of attention for his stories and his humor, all this was a hallmark of his young lawyer life. He would shake hands for hours as President. He took what he called then his daily "baths" in the energy of the people. While he seemed not to lose his dreamy gazing eyes, he would often focus them deeply upon a visitor.

The words then that fit him best are despair and sorrow. These are not psychological diagnoses, and as his sorrow and his despair increase he becomes a changed person. Silences were creative for him. These are aspects of loss that are most deeply addressed by the categories of religion, not psychology. Their opposites are hope and joy. Those become the energies that balance his deepening life and move his life forward. He did not heal, therapeutically, from his old wounds. They were always there, unhealable, as they usually are. He did not ever "get over" a depression. He did not need cognitive reframing as a cure. He could hold dark and light in his brain better than anyone he knew. Instead, he had Yonder vision, close and far, but what changed him were relationships.

His primary relationship was with his wife. He was nearly bereft of the feminine aspects of the psyche within himself, except for the archetypal aspect of passivity that comes out in his leadership style. The feminine, as it presented itself in individual women, just floored him. Then in marriage, on a day-to-day basis, Mary was all he really knew. He had the memories of his mothers, and he had sought, prior to his marriage, the guidance and comforting care and attention of older matronly women. They responded with adoration and good sense, and some Quaker-Ladies deeply moved him as President. They prayed with him.

He mysteriously married just the kind of feminine energy that he most needed: high, ambitious, calculating, sentimental, literary, cultured, and selfishly devoted. But she would not be the kind of feminine energy he would most know how to relate to. He needed her but they did as much balancing as they did relating. There was real love between them. Mary Todd carried those ambitious aspects, and freed him for his more saintly ones. "Mother," as he called her, became the balance and also the lightening in his life. His relationship storms were with Mary and especially in the loss of their two children. Those were the losses that deepened his relationship with Mary and with the issues of his time. Grief bound him to his wife and to his country.

When Lincoln cried tears for someone other than himself he became the man who became the President we remember. He had always wanted the esteem of others. It was his deepest need. Not only fame, but also esteem—that was what he most desired. Esteem is something you earn from others but it is for one's self. Lincoln's biggest argument with his intellectual partner Herndon was over Lincoln's belief that all motivation is self-serving. The esteem he wanted was historical remembrance, and that he got. But the capability to sustain love, to show kindness, to contain the multitudes of issues and people, and his capacity to find a language that spoke directly to people, for all of that it took love for others not for self. That was what made him who he was, great. He had early on been unusually thoughtful of others, but then in his career that was more eclipsed by his ambitious if humbly expressed political manipulations. Grief and sorrow were not just motivations about the self, but about the other, and those feelings changed him.

After his son died, after he saw the American hope being lost to the slave powers, after he left Springfield for Washington, from then on—in those broken and breaking relationships—Lincoln carried his grief and sorrows on and near the surface of his face and readily flowing from his heart. One day, as President, he heard the recitation of a poem by Longfellow with the lines, "Our hearts, our hopes, our prayers, our tears/Our faith triumphant o'er our fears." His eyes filled with tears, his cheeks became wet. After several moments of silence he said, "It is a wonderful gift to be able to stir men like that…" That soulful moment was illustrative of his spiritual accomplishment, of how he had changed.

Later, after his second son had died, he read with great feeling some lines from Shakespeare's play *King John*, including, "That we shall see and know our friends in heaven"[5] and he said to a soldier on duty whom he had called into share his reading, "Colonel, did you ever dream of a lost friend and feel that you were holding sweet com-

---

[5]   Shakespeare, *King John*, Act III, sc. iv.

munion with that friend, and yet have a sad consciousness that it was not reality?—Just so, I dream of my boy Willie." And then, overcome with emotion, he dropped his head on the table and sobbed aloud. Willie was his second son to die, this time in the White House.

Tears are an uncertain teacher. But they can change and blur vision into a sense of heaven, a sense of a place beyond. Lincoln became intense, a quiet fire, burned in his vision of America's place in world history as an experiment in self-government and in the idea of equality. That vision became a mission. In the early 1850s sorrows stirred his inner fire. He seems unshackled. Losses of his sons, even his father, his brilliant career, seemed to free his stride. Hope in America's Yonder was a source of life energy for his plodding, his ploughman's foot, one in front of the other. Lincoln actually walked as though he was still behind the plow, lifting his legs from his knees. In the coming decade he was to plant huge legal and political fields, increasing freedom in America and a stronger bond of democratic union.

As a young man Lincoln said he felt like a slave. His indenture to his father was a bond not of union but of slavery for him. The new world of earning your own way through mental energy, rewarded with payment, was a far better world to him than subsistence farming and patriarchal loyalties. Lincoln, then, loved his sons with as much freedom and abandon as he had received in bondage and restriction from his father. He was to love his boys just the way his father had not loved him. These relationships were freeing to him, father and son. Neighborhood boys in Springfield flocked to Lincoln like a Hans Christian Andersen figure. He carried them on his shoulders, told them stories, and let his own sons play havoc in his law office. He delighted in giving father love. With the first death, his second born son, this precious and intimate passion turns more and more toward the national bondage he saw poisoning history's last best hope. That poison, slavery, he said he had felt personally. By the end of his life Union soldiers were singing to him as "Father Abraham," and that they are coming, 300,000 strong. In his re-election Lincoln won 55% of the popular votes, but 80% of the soldier's vote. That vote was over General McClellan who had been supremely popular with his men, taking care of them and looking good on his horse. Lincoln, who, although a good horseman, often looked like Ichabod Crane on a horse, called up something deeper in young men, and they responded. It is poignant to note that at Lincoln's assassination it was reported that a boy was asked to place his small finger in the hole of the pistol shot to Lincoln's head, to staunch the bleeding.

A year after Edward died, in 1851, Lincoln's father died. The nature of the father-son bond had changed for Lincoln. Although distant with own father, he was closer with his own sons. There is no psychological reason to assume that Lincoln did not have great anger, even hatred, for his father and his father's role in his life. Other sons might have loved working for their dad and handing over their earnings and supporting the family as the next little man in the family. Lincoln had a bigger view of himself. His intelligence and personal value rebelled against that role as the yeoman-like Thomas.

Thomas's own relationship with his father ended, as we have said, when he was six and his father was shot dead in front of him by local Kentucky Indians. Thomas sat next to the slain body of his father and was almost himself killed by the Indian, but for the saving rifle shot from his brother Mordecai. Thomas lost his father and his economic security in that one moment. He surely had limited psychological energies for his son. Actually, as President, Lincoln ended up having limited availability to his first son Robert, who still grew up to be a solid man. But in the matrix of Thomas and Abraham it is easy to see how free and safe Abraham Lincoln would have felt once his father was gone—free to love as he had been loved by his stepmother, free to love as he would have wanted to be loved, and free to be as powerful as he felt he really was, no longer with the legacy of his servitude to his father ruling his inner life. Most men compare their mark in the world with their father's and either fear or desire to do better. As a boy when Lincoln spoke to a visitor before his father had spoken, his father slapped him down. Lincoln had never feared challenging big men, but now he was also free.

The most important relationship in Lincoln's life, prior to his wife Mary, was with his stepmother Sarah Bush Lincoln. She rescued him from physical and material oblivion, and she rescued him from intellectual and emotional bondage by protecting him from his father. With such a great foundation of mother-love to balance his legacy of father-hatred, Lincoln had two psychological paths before him. With the kind of father-rage that Martin Luther carried into the Roman Catholic Church and the Reformation, Lincoln could have exuded the energy of righteous truth and the power to make a divisive stand. Lincoln could have become a firebrand abolitionist. Or he could hold a fragile and diverse community tighter as his stepmother had, and invest himself in the irenic energies of mind and spirit that she so valued in him.

His love for and from his mothers was behind Lincoln's use of the common term "Mother" for his wife Mary. A mother's love was the foundation for his respect, love, and tolerance of her, and it was the basis of the holding love, not the dividing truth, that so marked his leadership of the breaking apart nation. Holding together with his tormenting and tormented wife Mary must have been as hard a personal challenge as holding together the country, his public challenge. He had a core of strength for both of these. By the time his first son died in 1850, he was already in the orbit of a powerful relationship with Mary. Grief was a deep bond for them, for better and for worse. Lincoln speaks a great deal about the truths of the founding fathers, but we can see, better than he could, the power also of these three founding mothers.

CHAPTER FOURTEEN

Tears Are the Passion of Faith

T he mystery of how Lincoln came to be is comparable to the inexplicable rise of another unlikely person, Joan of Arc. But the mysterious feel to his death resembles the aura of his mysterious becoming. While it is possible to see him as an American Caesar, it has been, ever since his death, necessary to compare him to an American Christ. The vortex of the Hebrew calendar, Passover, the freedom from Egyptian slavery, setting the date for Christian's Good Friday, is a fate that shapes the ends of his life. He was, unmistakably a man of sorrows and acquainted with grief, as Isaiah said the Messiah would be. His policy of Reconstruction emerges as if from the parables of Jesus, especially the loving father greeting the return of the prodigal, lost son. In visiting the wounded in hospitals Lincoln always made a point to search out Confederate wounded. They were his sons too. His call for malice toward none and charity for all echoes the beatitudes of Jesus's Sermon on the Mount. As much as he never asserted himself as a professing Christian, as much as he sticks largely to Hebrew Bible, Old Testament, references, his love of enemies is, as Tolstoy acclaimed, Christ-like.

Lincoln took a carriage ride with Mary on the afternoon of Good Friday, the day of his death. They talked of world travel when this was all over. She favored Europe, he, the Holy Land, as well. Those were places of kings greater than he, David and Solomon, and the site of the Temple. We need not juxtapose these dates—Passover and Good Friday—to proof-text anything. What we do know is that Lincoln knew the world the way Jesus knew the world, through sorrow and grief born of love and passion for justice. The theme of Passover coincides with the life of Lincoln. Freedom from slavery is justice. Sorrow conforms to Jesus's Passion. Sorrow is the way love knows the world most deeply. Lincoln, like Jesus, was a man of passion for justice and tears for life's consequent sorrows.

Sorrow and tears in spiritual consciousness are explicated in the writings of the French philosopher Jacques Derrida. In a book about him John Caputo says that Derrida "was a man of tears, of faith and tears, for faith is driven by passion and tears are the passion of faith." Grief and sorrow shape awareness in the same way, near side and far side, that Yonder shapes awareness. There is a near side and a far side to grief. In the tight constriction of grief our eyes squeeze shut and if they focus on anything they focus on something small and immediately present, a picture, a memento, something that loss makes into a palpable relic, the near side. But then in the thunderclap of the broken heart the chest expands in cries, the eyes lift upward and the empty skies of unbounded time and space loom around us. These polarities of grief were with Lincoln from childhood. As he and his cat would walk the near mile down to the creek to get water passing his mother's grave he would have seen the particularity of his loss. Later as he mourned the death of Ann Rutledge and feared the night's constant rain upon her grave he knew the near endlessness of his losses. Though historians have raised questions over the facts in these stories, David Herbert Donald's authoritative biography gives the Ann Rutledge story credence, as does Fred Kaplan's biography of Lincoln. Lincoln's near tears and long passions is our point, and stories abound of his life accumulating the near and far sides of sorrow.

Sorrow then shapes his nature, his soul. His is a life grounded in these twin dynamics, both of grief and of Yonder. There was near and blinding grief that opens the soul. See the boy Lincoln staring at his mother's casket. He knew that sightless sorrow. There were far horizons, not seen but felt, that led him on. Lincoln during the 1850s would walk the streets of Springfield with his hands clasped behind his back staring down or up and far away and not knowing where he was.

There is an agnostic quality to Lincoln when it comes to philosophical and theological matters. There is a kind of blindness, not a kind of knowing, that forms his kind of faith. Caputo says of this phenomenon that there is about it a "quasi-transcendental" quality or condition. Quasi-transcendental is neither here nor there. What the heart knows when the eyes are shut with tears or lifted in blurry vision is that life is not lived by knowledge but by the giving up of knowledge. This is the tone of Lincoln when he talks of God and faith, of being driven to his knees. His is not a tone of affirmation but of resignation. Caputo quotes Kant saying, "I have found it necessary to deny knowledge in order to make room for faith." Similarly Derrida contrasts knowing with seeing. His heart can know what he cannot see. "Believing depends upon blindness and has to do with the desire for what is out of sight." Yonder is the ground of being for this not-knowing place. In Lincoln's favored source, William Shakespeare, the poet John Keats saw this quality of standing in the dark without grasping for any particular fact or beam of light, what he called Negative Capability.

CHAPTER FIFTEEN

Lincoln and Books

Without books Lincoln would have disappeared into the prairie or been lost from view down some river. Not that his native genius and eventual good heart would not have made a difference, somehow. As the only President who holds a patent, Lincoln still might have invented his ballast shifting gizmo for getting rafts off of sand bars. As a dark lover of something missing in life he might have been a local legend. If Johnny Appleseed needed a pal, or John Jacob Audubon an assistant, Lincoln would have been perfect. Huckleberry Finn and Jim could sorely have used his help in some of their fights and trials, or more realistically wouldn't he and Samuel Clemons have hit it off as friends? Twain might have immortalized that lonely Lincoln Man in a story or two. But it was books that loosened the bolt and let his door fly open, to borrow images from William James. Books let Lincoln loose in a wide world and so we did not lose him in the prairie or down a river.

The few books he saw in his scant months of formal school were spectacular. From our view they are unique in their ability to capture the grammar of good English, and the rhetoric of good speech and thought. They portray the heroic sweep of political history, and the moral heights and depths of both Enlightenment and Biblical systems of morality and virtue. We saw how those sources and values worked in his encounter with his friends who were stealing the family melons.

Historiography has moved in a Lincolnesque direction towards the stories of the common person and their alternative narratives. But it was the grand narratives that were available to this common farm boy. His books referenced the ancient classics, heroes in history, fables, the allegory of *Pilgrim's Progress*, and the archetypal story of Robinson Crusoe. Lincoln then had an appetite for the big world that had happened and was happening around him. For him and his meager society it was the grand movements that were at stake. In his book, *Abraham Lincoln: The Theologian of American Anguish* (1973) Elton Trueblood names Alfred North Whitehead's concept of "the habitual vision of greatness." Lincoln, says Trueblood, had this habit. His own inner capacities found a match in greatness and it became the habit of his vision.

It is not just that he would have heard of Moses, read of Washington, dreamt of Robinson Crusoe, but that even his speech and vocabulary were forged in those early books. One of his Readers emphasizes the initial learning of words of only one syllable. The Twenty-third Psalm was an example of a text with many simple words and it was to be memorized. The prayer of "Now I lay me down to sleep," derived from another psalm, was simple monosyllabic speech. In Lincoln's *Gettysburg Address*, 73 percent of his 265 words are monosyllabic. The Twenty-third Psalm is 78 percent monosyllabic. Turns of phrase like "of the people and by the people" originated in phrases from his early readers. The sweep and the clarity of his mind were grand, history and the Bible were grand, and the language that carried such great themes was bold. It was also simple and clear, like much of the King James Bible and the Shakespeare he read.Shakespeare is where Lincoln's imagination found its hearth, home and society. The Bible and the Enlightenment were like his real parents. His passion for justice, his compassion and mercy, are Biblical. Justice, compassion, and mercy are not only Biblical and Enlightenment values. They are clearly evidenced all throughout Shakespeare, and without ideological mandate.

Shakespeare engendered Lincoln's sense for human character and his own roles in life. He was alert to the drama around him. He had been schooled by the many plays he knew. From intrigue among his cabinet members, to the high drama of his marriage, to the tragedies and the comedies all around him, Lincoln could see the cast of characters that he had read. Shakespeare made him wise. The Bible made him good. The Enlightenment gave him the tool of reason. Shakespeare is the link between Lincoln's secular Enlightenment persona and his religious Biblical spirit. From books, all these books, Lincoln developed the art and imagination to grasp the history unfolding around him and through him.

It is fun to imagine how Lincoln handled Secretary of Treasury Salmon Chase's overwhelming ambition, a foolish Malvolio indeed, or balanced the power struggles between Chase and Seward, all with his grasp of the kind of intrigue that comes from Shakespeare. These secular plays offered a subtle and psychological language for human drama without the moral lessons found in the Biblical stories. Lincoln never quoted Shakespeare in his speeches, however. He never left his frontier roots to put on literary airs. After he had he pocketed both Seward's and Chase's tendered resignations—off-setting their power plays—he gloated to John Hay, his secretary, that now he had "a pumpkin in each bag."

Books were his religion. Recall, also, that Lincoln went to the theater on the Good Friday of his death, not to Church. *Hamlet* was his first theologian, and *Macbeth*, not the Gospel Passion, (as much as Americans put him into the crucifixion place after his death) was his source of self-understanding in his last week of life. While steaming up the Potomac, Sunday April 9th, 1865, Lincoln delighted his companions by reading Shakespeare. This was at the time of the fall of Richmond, the end of the war, and his preparations for Reconstruction. In his tour of the fallen Richmond he made sure it did not turn into a Hosanna Palm Sunday parade, despite what some of the local, newly-freed, black population desired.

A unique source for this Potomac shipboard story comes from the founding professor of the English department at the University of Illinois. When Daniel Kilham Dodge had taken the job in 1873, he moved from New York to Champaign-Urbana and to the four buildings "huddled on a bleak prairie," 714 students, 48 faculty.

Dodge quotes Lincoln's fellow voyager, the Marquis de Chambrun, telling this story and adding his conclusion concerning Lincoln's capacity to grasp Shakespeare: "His judgment evinced that sort of delicacy and soundness of taste that would honor a great literary critic." He had just witnessed Lincoln reading from *Macbeth* while on this historically timed journey. One wonders how and why Lincoln had *Macbeth* with him. "That day the conversation dwelt upon literary subjects. Mr. Lincoln read for us for several hours passages taken from Shakespeare. Most of these were from *Macbeth* and in particular, the verses which follow Duncan's assassination. I cannot recall this reading without being awed at the remembrance, when Macbeth becomes king after the murder of Duncan, he falls prey to the more horrible torments of mind. Either because he was struck by the weird beauty of these verses, or from a vague presentiment coming over him, Mr. Lincoln paused here while reading and began to explain how true a description of the murderer that one was…and he read over again the same scene."

Dodge's remarkable early research had already led him to write of a poignant moment when Lincoln called on a randomly stationed Colonel to share some lonely moments in conversation.

Dodge quotes Noah Brooks,[6] "In the spring of 1862 the President spent several days at Fortress Monroe… He bore with him constantly the burden of his public affairs. His favorite diversion was reading Shakespeare. One day as he sat reading alone, he called to his aide in the adjoining room. 'You have been writing long enough, Colonel. Come in here; I want to read you a passage in 'Hamlet'." He read this discussion on ambition between Hamlet and his courtiers, and the soliloquy, in which conscience debates of a future state. This was followed by a passage from 'Macbeth'."

It was then that Lincoln made reference to the Shakespeare passage we have referred to before, that may have helped him form a sense of eternity. Opening to *King John*, he read from the third act the passage in which Constance bewails her imprisoned lost boy: Closing the book, and recalling the words:

> 'And, father cardinal, I have heard you say/That we shall see
> and know our friends in heaven;/If that be true, I shall see my
> boy again.'

This inspiration from Shakespeare and the hope of seeing his boy again in heaven came in the spring of 1862. Elton Trueblood tells a questionable story from the late winter of that same year where the source for such hope and affirmation comes from Dr. Francis Vinton, rector of Trinity Church, New York. In their conversation the clergyman reportedly said that it was rational to conclude that God himself is continuing and would continue his interests in and concern for persons even after the death of their body. This would not be a new theological idea for Lincoln.

---

[6]   Noah Brooks (1830-1903) was a journalist and a friend of Lincoln's who wrote two books about him after his death, *Washington in Lincoln's Time* and *Lincoln and the Downfall of American Slavery*. This story is cited by Dodge.

Dr. Vinton, Trueblood reports, drew attention to Christ's teaching in Luke 20:38, "For he is not a God of the dead, but of the living: for all live unto him." Lincoln was stuck with Dr. Vinton's then confident words, "Your son is alive." Others who report this scene quote Lincoln as saying that he is being mocked and that his grief is being mocked by this assertion. The jury is not in on this story.

But these words of "seeing your boy alive" are parallel to his gripping recitation of the words of Shakespeare. Lincoln may be drawing on two traditions to find a faith to live his sorrow and despair. Whether the event with Rev. Vinton is historical, and depending on how it is interpreted, it is consistent with Lincoln's long theological conversations with both Rev. Smith and Rev. Gurley, his two Presbyterian minsters, pursuing with them a rational claim and then reaching for faith as a comfort.

Trueblood quotes the inspired biographer Ida Tarbell who cites this conversation with Dr. Vinton as the turning point in Lincoln's own courage to assume that God would not be defeated by the Civil War any more than Lincoln and his love for his son need to be defeated. These are strong interpretations. This may be a case of too much Christian interpretation of Lincoln's spiritual journey. But it is consistent with the outcome of his personal and public courage by the time of his Second Inaugural Address to envision a positive future and appeal, in terms that were new to Lincoln, to "a living God." What is clear is that as sources for the faith and the courage to live his life Lincoln had two sources, one secular and one religious.

Lincoln was just as deeply involved with Shakespeare and Shakespeare's wide, wide world as he was with the Bible, its grand narrative of God in history and God's love in mercy to the enemy. Professor Dodge tells us of times when Lincoln challenged and queried famous Shakespearean actors for the why and the how of different interpretations and deliveries. Lincoln had his own opinions.

He thought that "Oh, my offense is rank" was a greater soliloquy than "To be or not to be." He thought that the king's passage was often slurred over, and he was himself capable of giving moving and dramatic, even spellbinding recitations of it. Because he grasped the political context of intrigue and the plotting of destruction he was critical of how the opening lines of Richard III, "Now is the winter of our discontent" were delivered. He saw the bitterness and satire, the hate and jealousy, in Richard, and knew also how to recite that with a force and power that simply be-stilled his listeners.

Having seen Edwin Booth as Shylock he reportedly said, "It was a good performance, but I had a thousand times rather read it at home…tragedy is best read at home." Lincoln loved the plays as he could see and feel them in his own imagination better, often, than going to the theater, as much as he loved the hour or two of diversion the theater offered him. Diversion reminds us that Lincoln would have greatly loved the comedy in Shakespeare, not found in either the Bible or the church. Lincoln was of course very funny himself and as in love with humor as any fool or disguised character in Shakespeare. Professor Dodge, in quoting the Marquis de Chambrun, may have overstated Lincoln's powers as a Shakespeare critic, but that does not diminish the importance that Shakespeare played in Lincoln's own mind and spirit. Dodge, by the way, did well at Illinois. When he retired in 1928 the English Department at the University had twenty-two faculty members and sixty-four instructors and assistants.

Daniel Kilham Dodge is another persuasive example of a scholarly person writing about Lincoln who, like the religious and spiritual writers we have cited, clearly has a personal affinity for Lincoln, and a personally shaped professional perspective as to what is important about Lincoln. In Dr. Dodge's case it is not Lincoln's spiritual and religious life but his literary life and his love of Shakespeare.

A photograph of Dodge in the centennial re-issue of his essay reveals a very handsome young man of dark intensity. His own arrow-winged collar, wired spectacles, perfect pocket-handkerchief reminds one of another figure of that era, out of the mid-west, who wrote deeply on Lincoln, Albert Beveridge. These were handsome accomplished meticulous intense, even proper men, devoted at times to the rustic pioneer giant.

Dodge was born in Brooklyn in 1863, the son of a doctor and his Danish wife Astrid. Dodge also married a Danish woman, having grown up fluent in Danish and English. His degrees were from Columbia and he was new to the mid-west when he made his career, and he and Astrid made a family of four girls and a boy. His focus in curriculum development was on a common education for cultural elevation, not vocational specialty. His democratic approach to education was part of the values that also lead him to be, for a year, the Champaign Fire and Police Commissioner.

Lincoln began to haunt this dark-eyed man as he has so many others. At one point Dodge confesses, "During the past twenty years and more I have been so deeply interested in the study of Abraham Lincoln as a man and as a writer that some of my friends have charged me with showing that same tendency to revert to the subject, whatever my original intention, that is noted in Mr. Dick in connection with the execution of Charles the First." This in *Abraham Lincoln, Master of Words*, a Centennial re-issue by the University of Illinois in 2000.

Dr. Dodge's easy reference is to what may be a less than well-known reference to Dickens' *David Copperfield*. Such a literary reference illustrates his 19th century rhetorical point of view: commonly cultured people would read works that are beautiful and true. In the essay introducing this Centennial volume, James Hurt, recently a professor of English at University of Illinois, asserts that literary criticism has changed since Dodge's day. Moral aesthetic criticism has changed to a post-modern textual analysis.

We look then, in terms of Lincoln's religious and spiritual importance, at the changes in context and point of view from earlier Lincoln devotees. Just as religious and theological formulations have changed, so too views of rhetoric and textual criticism have changed. It is not only that Lincoln changed but that our view of him changes, age to age. How Lincoln used Shakespeare, how Lincoln used the Bible, how Lincoln loved literature, how Lincoln loved things spiritual, all are redefined for us now because of how we look at both literature and religion. We have, in our time, redefined from Dr. Dodge's day, what it means to be immersed in literary texts. We have also redefined what it means to be infused with spiritual and religious awareness. Lincoln's view of literature is not the view we have today. We see literary texts having multiple lives as cultural documents with silences as well as implications. In Lincoln's early Romantic time texts were a matter of truth and beauty, and that was all we knew and all we needed to know. To understand Lincoln's spiritual life or his literary life is to also see how his views of these issues are different from our own. In Dr. Dodge's case Lincoln's view of literature was also not his own, professorial, view.

As a gentleman teaching literature, then, Dodge is troubled that Lincoln did not quote the Bible and Shakespeare more in his speeches. This is a fact that concerned him and one he could not explain. In his essay he says, "The number of quotations from Shakespeare is even smaller than that from the Bible." But his evidence is also that it was in his personal conversations that Lincoln would often quote Shakespeare. This bothers the Eastern teacher. Had Lincoln been in his English class Dodge would have encouraged him to show how Shakespeare could be quoted in his public speeches. After all, that is what higher education was for, was it not?

We know from many sources, including the dated essay by Elton Trueblood, that it was in conversation, more than in speeches, that Lincoln would either quote the Bible or, more often, make reference to Biblical themes and concepts. In his 1970s volume on Lincoln as America's "theologian of anguish," Dr. Trueblood, also a midwestern scholar and a Quaker, takes an awkward pride in the Biblical references in Lincoln's Second Inaugural Address. In the present context this can be a kind of "our team wins" mentality. This comes from the same kind of outdated definitions of what religious and spiritual truths are all about. It parallels Dr. Dodge's moral-aesthetic view of Shakespeare. Higher education and Christianity, among the elites, were the fancy clothes you wore. Rustic Lincoln seems not to know how to dress up.

Lincoln was a man of many silences, and what he held dear and unspoken, especially from public speeches, is something we can make educated reflections about. We can ask, first, what might be the political gain or loss of Biblical or Shakespearean quotations in speeches. Since Lincoln was, as William Lee Miller so well reminds us in his biography, *Lincoln's Virtues*, a politician first and always if not last, we can assume that he saw no rhetorical gain in such quotes. But, more importantly, since both Shakespeare and the Bible did come up mostly in personal conversations we can assume Lincoln would then be speaking more personally, less publically, and from his heart and mind. This would be a place where his moral core and his soul would be very alive, in talking directly with people. Lincoln had a strong boundary between his personal life and his public life. We know he drew a big line between his personal views on slavery and his public role as President. We can assume he had a line, too, personally and publically in speaking. He would be open, in personal conversation, to his heartfelt life with both the Bible and with Shakespeare in ways that he would think improper publically, and he certainly never liked putting on airs. This line makes his Bible quoting in his Second Inaugural all the more powerful, because he brought in the Bible not as political filler as some biographers think, but as his deepest personal convictions. He was talking but the Bible and God personally to the American people.

Lincoln, in a speech, would need only one allusion to a New Testament passage, such as a house divided against itself cannot stand, to tell us of the Biblical worldview that held his ethical views. We also know that he had read the very same metaphor of a house divided not standing in his secular Blab school readers. Those secular books were infused with Biblical as well as Enlightenment values. The few Biblical references in his Second Inaugural about the judgment of God tell us the high value he put on that concept. Likewise, it was only one line, *Hamlet's* fatalism about the divinity that shapes our ends, that Lincoln often spoke to show how deeply defined he was by Shakespeare from that one play. Thus with only a few powerful Biblical references, and no Shakespearean references in public speeches, it would be in personal conversations that we see those sources in Lincoln's mind.

It was in personal self-reflection that Lincoln would spend long hours reading Shakespeare's plays, as well as his favorite poets, Burns and Byron. These would be hours of deep self-definition. The time he spent with himself with literature meant he could quickly go the shelf, pick out a book of Shakespeare, turn to his companion and find the passage he wanted. Then he both would read it and recite it. Hearers reported how dramatically and persuasively he would recite. He must have done this alone many times, as the pages were well worn, the passages immediate to find. This would be personal time spent with those voices and stories. A kind of theatrical therapy would be a way for us to understand what Lincoln was doing with Shakespeare, even with the Bible. This was inner work. What he was doing, for and with himself, with Shakespeare or the Bible, and then in his personal talking, was of a different order of magnitude than the texts of public speeches. These books made him himself.

The theologian and literary scholar John Philip Newell names this psychological use of Shakespeare in his book, *Shakespeare and The Human Mystery*. In his personal Preface Newell says, "Year after year in my life, like century after century for countless others, I have chosen to place myself before his (Shakespeare's) characters to watch in them something that also is in me. The experience is sometimes laughter, sometimes tears, sometimes shame. Always it is the experience of looking into a mystery that I am a part of."

Is this what Lincoln was doing sailing up the Potomac from defeated Richmond, reading *Macbeth* to his friends? Was he looking into a mystery that he was a part of, including—could he feel—the coming assassination of himself as the king?

Lincoln took the dramatis personae of Shakespeare as his human family and a source of self-reflection. Lincoln also grounded himself in a spiritual value distilled from Shakespeare. John Keats, as we have said, identifies it as Negative Capability. This is an intriguing defined psychological characteristic. Traditional religious pieties will not define Abraham Lincoln's spiritual poise, his leadership and his presence in the eye of the worst storm in American history. It was, of course, a storm of Biblical proportions, and Lincoln's role on the national stage was nothing less than Shakespearean. Scholars of Lincoln, David Herbert Donald, in his keystone biography of Lincoln, and John Burt, in his literary criticism and philosophical exploration of the Lincoln-Douglas Debates, *Lincoln's Tragic Pragmatism*, both name Negative Capability, this unusual passive ability. With it Lincoln can stand in the midst of turmoil and not reach for certainties that are simply not available. We find then, from how Shakespeare was read by the poet John Keats, the essence of Lincoln's psychology, this essentially spiritual trait, that Keats called Negative Capability.

CHAPTER SIXTEEN

Negative Capability

N egative Capability is a concept with psychological and spiritual implications. John Keats' term defines a practical and spiritual stance in the world that might have remained undefined except in some religious traditions but for the inspiration Keats drew from Shakespeare. Keats uses the term to argue that the brilliant Coleridge was trying to find a place of certainty in life that just was not there. In Shakespeare's totality Keats saw a man with a creative consciousness, one who could live fully in the world without a point of view, an ideology. Charlotte Herbold, a teacher of Shakespeare, says simply that Shakespeare loved all of his characters so much that he saw something human in all of them. He made that his point, rather than having some point of view be the point.

This wide compassion flows unceasingly into and out of Lincoln as his life progresses to his Presidency, culminating in his "we must not be enemies…better angels of our nature" First Inaugural and his, "malice toward none and charity for all" conclusion to his Second Inaugural. Lincoln, like Shakespeare, sees humanity in all its forms.

As much as Lincoln individually wished to rise within the American System from subsistence farmer to capital-earning public professional he did not ultimately believe in free will. Like that other determinist, the 18th Century American theologian Jonathan Edwards, Lincoln paradoxically urges the exercise of freedom within a context of the absence of free will. By the end, Lincoln's view of Providence has the same absolute judgment and love that the Calvinist Edwards saw in the Divine Will. But it came to Lincoln through a pitiless eye that saw cause and effect first in nature, then in social determinism, and then as expressed in the plays of Shakespeare—all the world was a stage and we all have assigned lines given to us.

Many people thought Lincoln was the most unlikely of candidates to become President. He must have had reason to think so too. Unlike a believer, he felt he did not know if he was doing God's Will. He did not have the resolve of solid faith. In his Farewell Speech you hear longing, hope, and a prayerful desire for God's blessing but not an onward Christian soldier's confidence. For Lincoln, it was just the opposite. He didn't know God's will for a long time. Much of life was a mystery to him, the "accident" of his being elected President, the unexpected length of the war. He wanted, fiercely, to know. He had always wanted to know why and how mechanical things worked, like implements and barges and bridges, but now also people, then war and life and death. Why and how does all this, most especially the Civil War, happen as it does? His meditation on the Divine Will, a secret paper of his own during his first term, variously dated, became the origin of the Second Inaugural, and his answer.

In Lincoln's life he works his way up the ladder—just as Jacob's angels do—to the Providence of God. He begins on the low rungs of reason and observation, not from some cloud of revelation or some emotional inspiration.

How to remain able to keep a course of action, to sustain one's self in ups and downs, in the midst of uncertainty, that is the strength of this concept, Negative Capability. It is not a term Lincoln would have known. The English poet was born fourteen years before Lincoln and died when Lincoln was only twelve.

There is a painting of Lincoln that once hung in a restaurant in Cape May, New Jersey, a town once visited by Lincoln on vacation, and now is often frequented by several famous Lincoln scholars. In the foreground of this contemporary picture is a darkened almost silhouetted image of Lincoln. More dominant behind him is a large perfect red circle, perhaps an iconic sunrise or sunset on a near horizon. It presents the artist's intent of images of East and West, as if the red circle were an image in a Buddhist temple, and in the foreground the American President framed now by a spiritual symbol from beyond the world as he knew it. The painting works as an image, a way to begin to understand the concept of Negative Capability. The large red ball is the force of a determining and holding reality, the presence of gravity, a force field that both backs up and holds, sustains, the lone man in the foreground. But it is not something that he looks at, knows fully, or believes in as a truth or ideology. Living within that unseen field is how Lincoln's sense of Yonder became for him a sustaining, not fully known, presence.

We know from the story of the melon thieves that Lincoln had a strong sense of how to relate to human behavior from a point of view larger than just right and wrong. He clearly had energy for the right and against the wrong, but he didn't identify himself as the arresting officer, the judge and jury, over his neighborhood friends and thieves. Some greater sense of value backs him up and defines the drama of that telling event. Similarly, in terms of the law, he could in fact as an adult lawyer argue cases for and against the freedom of individual Black slaves in different legal circumstances. The law was his containing temple of reason, and not his own flag-before-his-eyes view of justice. Lincoln never became an Abolitionist. Negative Capability is a way to suspend judgments more than to make them. By the time of the Second Inaugural, the end of the war, Lincoln still refers to the Jesus' injunction against judging lest we be judged.

The story of Lincoln and the Blue Umbrella, well-told by Edmond O. Wilson in his book *Patriotic Gore*, is a stunning story of how Lincoln lived sustained by more than his individual ego and ambition, much less by his point of view.

Lincoln, as this true but nearly parable-like story opens, is a medium big fish in the Illinois legal profession. He was picked by a very big East coast law firm to be the local guy in a hugely significant trial on the patent of the McCormick reaper. The trial was set for Chicago and the East coast guys thought that a local man might help with the judge. But the trial was shifted to Cincinnati, Ohio. Lincoln had already gotten a large retainer, and he was interested in the case. In fact he had gone to a great deal of trouble to investigate the actual design and production of the farm equipment. He took his extensive research and his blue umbrella and went off to Ohio. Meeting the two big-deal lawyers he greeted them warmly with, "Why don't we fellows go off here together to eat." They just left him behind, standing there, with his too short pants, his blue umbrella, and his research. Throughout the trial he was never mentioned, consulted or acknowledged. Nor was he asked to dine with the other lawyers on this team. We know one of these men. We know that his future Secretary of War, Edwin Stanton, who at his death cried and said, "Now he belongs to the ages." was the most arrogant and offensive of these men.

What did Lincoln do? He stayed to watch the trial. He knew that these Eastern lawyers were the top of the line and he wanted to see and learn from them. He wanted to be able to compete with them and he knew he had a big learning curve. In the most humiliating of circumstances he found a way to hold his balance, to stay on task and to simply keep his emotions from taking over. We could assume that he focused only on his ego-goal of becoming an important lawyer and person, but that would hardly explain how he both stayed with this terrible situation and maintained good humor and balance. Ambition alone would not explain this kind of personal balance and focus.

We don't know from any personal notations how Lincoln sustained his ego, or his mind and heart, through this. We only know that he reported to his fellow Springfield lawyers that those Eastern lawyers really knew their stuff and that the next time they were out his way he would be ready for them, ready by his own self-improvement in terms of speaking, law, and knowledge. He didn't mention his too short pants, if he even knew. It is, however, easy to see in the scene Lincoln playing the role of the Fool in a Shakespeare play—oddly dressed, clearly not one of the elite, yet having a place in the play. The Fool in Shakespeare is most often a character of superior wisdom with a point of view outside the ego-driven limitations of the king or princes. Immersed in Shakespeare, Lincoln, consciously or unconsciously, found a healthy-minded way to appreciate all life's roles, including the seeming fool.

There was, however, in contrast, a man of great ambition who used his point of view to keep himself going. We could call this the characteristic of Positive Capability. That was General McClellan. We know from his letters to his wife during the war that he had a supreme view of his own greatness. The single-minded focus on himself sustained him through many difficult tasks in building the army and through several ups and down in command. The famous story of McClellan shunning the waiting President shows us once again Lincoln's continuing ability to either dis-identify with his role, or re-identify with a greater role, but clearly not only identify with himself as the role.

Lincoln, in this story, waited and waited at McClellan's home one evening, having decided to call personally on urgent war business. When the General returned home he went up the backstairs and took himself to bed. When the President was informed that the General was now asleep, he and John Hay, his young secretary, left. Hay asked him how he could stand such an unseemly rebuff. Lincoln replied that he would hold the General's horse if the General would but do his job.

Lincoln in these true events was egoless, as Jesus preached, but he does not identify himself as a Christian trying to live in the way of the Master, nor the Sermon on the Mount. A more practical, secular, explanation is that Lincoln's ego was shaped by the self–reflection that began when he was sixteen and continued in his long devotion to the broad and balanced worldview of the Bard. While what Lincoln did in these two stories was practical; his ability to act with egoless poise was cultivated. He had been reflecting on ambition and his own ego through long readings of Shakespeare from 1825 on. Fred Kaplan tells us about his sustaining reading of Shakespeare, in his biography of Lincoln as a writer, suggesting that Lincoln may even have considered himself as a person of Shakespearean magnitude. Lincoln's egoless poise is then to manage his own sense of greatness, not his own sense of smallness. His disappointments in his career are because he had a high inner sense of worth and value, as strange as that must also have been for him to imagine. Shakespeare was a way to learn how to be. As Harvard professor Stephen Greenblatt says in a New Yorker article on his book on Shakespeare, "Will in the World," his "...literature was not a self-enclosed system of signs, but rather it was a way of being in the world, a form of agency, a human act." Shakespeare would help Lincoln find a way to be in the world.

What appeals to Keats about Shakespeare is that it is a literature of "life on the pulse" not a literature of signals for ideas or beliefs. Lincoln reads and re-reads Shakespeare in these terms. There were times when Lincoln actually was ego-driven, foolishly and cruelly so, as in his early satirical barbs at others, his shameful near duel, and his early inflated speeches on the floor of Congress. He was wrestling with greatness. What Lincoln learned from Shakespeare was a way to understand his own ambiguity about ambition and to feel the humanity of all human roles.

CHAPTER SEVENTEEN

Lincoln and Ambition

L incoln had long legs, as we all know. One day, the old story
goes, while consulting with a woman client in his law office he
lifted one leg to rest on the corner of the table next to them. Lincoln
often elevated his legs or just reclined on a long sofa. The woman
exclaimed something like, "Why, Mr. Lincoln, that is a terribly long
leg you have, there!" Swinging up the other to join it he remarked,
"Yes, and I have another just like it."

For our purposes in this story we have a metaphor, at least a
suggestive image of the fact that not only was Lincoln a bit of a giant,
he was twinned in many ways. About any one thing he might think
he'd have another long thought just like it, only opposite. There was
enough in half of Lincoln for any one man.

He embodied many paradoxes: melancholy and comic, strategic and idealistic, well read and rustic, talkative and silent, and
of course secular and religious. One can wonder how he contained
such separate universes. In his adolescence, a normal time for unin-
tegrated and conflicting sides, Lincoln began to form two of his most
fundamental polarities, ones that form the basis of his secular and
his spiritual natures. Lincoln, on the one hand, had ambition. Lincoln had great driving throbbing energies for self-advancement, self-
improvement. We could call it self-realization. He also, on the other
hand, had a nearly equal and consuming awareness of the vanity, the
gloom and doom of fame, which he saw as the fate of ambition. Between humor and gloom, as well as poetry and reason, he managed

to balance his many paired opposites. He did not overtly use religion as way to moderate ambition. His gloomy view of ambition had a Calvinistic hyper-conscientiousness about it that practically cried for a redemption that eluded Lincoln as it did so many 19th century intellectually formed Calvinist writers, thinkers, leaders.

As a youngster he was a talented show-off. It revealed a basic belief in himself and his potential. He had no trouble mimicking an authority figure, the local preacher, who was one of the leaders in his small southern Indiana community. He was cheerfully cooperative with his stepmother, but there was an almost sullen obedience to his father reflecting his own sense of the high difference between who he thought he was and who his father assumed he was or should be. He was required to turn over his earned money, to do major work for others including thousands of split rails. He even helped move his family to Illinois when he is about to be twenty-one and free.

Later his ambition showed a dark and sinister side. In a speech, The Lyceum Speech of 1838, as a young professional in Springfield he warned of the dictatorial power of a politician who assumes too ambitious a role in settling national disputes. That speech is also studied in the chapters on the Warrior and the King archetypes. A psychologist can easily see his projected shadow self-image in that speech. He warns people about the ambitions that he himself could succumb to or would have to overcome.

However, Lincoln as a young man put his lamp under a cover with his melancholy. His poetic imagination, his residual sadness, perhaps from his mother's death, but perhaps just from his Yonder spiritual nature, saw life both as a great expanse and great nothingness. The frontier and the prairie could inspire vision but also reveal an abyss. The land of southern Indiana he remembered as without poetic inspiration. He did a lot of plowing and tree felling in Indiana.

Lincoln was himself anything but "un-poetical" as Fred Kaplan reminds us in his *Lincoln: The Biography of a Writer.* Poetry is one place he yokes the many opposites he sees and feels and thinks about. Poetry, the writing and the reading of it, was in his temperament and he responded strongly to its emotional force. Often it was on the sad side. He would memorize poems on loss and bereavement. "Thomas Gray's Elegy Written in a Country Church-Yard" being salient. A hallmark line from that poem for him was, "The paths of glory lead but to the grave."

It was sadness and Shakespeare, not a sense of sin that moderated Lincoln's ambition and muted his taste for some kind of glory. While he was often emotionally down about his failure to achieve fame and success, such as his two-time failure to become Senator from Illinois, he never got very up about his achievements. "Uneasy lies the head that wears the crown" from "Henry IV Part 1" is Kaplan's notation on how, "Shakespeare assured him that overweening ambition leads to an inevitable fall." Lincoln takes his lesson here from *Hamlet*, "All that lives must die, passing through nature to eternity," not from Jesus. He tries in his life to "o'erstep not the modesty of nature." Lincoln, for example, holds his public speaking up to the mirror of nature, not unlike how a Taoist or a Buddhist might, and keeps himself bound to what he thinks of as reasonable. Even when, as President, he often quotes Claudius's soliloquy, thinking of his own "offence" (a word he got from his childhood readers not the Bible and uses in his Second Inaugural) it is not his nature that is offensive, not sin, but only deeds caught in moral ambiguities, entailments and consequences. From his Scott Reader he learned to quote Alexander Pope's twin principles of human nature, self-love and reason, with reason restraining the urge to self-love. This kind of thinking governed Lincoln all his life. He agreed with *Hamlet*, "How noble in reason" is humanity.

We know that Lincoln read Shakespeare even as a young boy. One of the two Readers his stepmother Sarah brought with her from

Kentucky was Scott's. By 1821, at the age of 12, Lincoln was, as Fred Kaplan says, an avid reader of poetry, including William Scott's "Lessons in Elocution" which contained thirty pages of Shakespeare's histories and tragedies. The passages from these plays, which he read out loud, brought him a whole new world. It was a world, thereafter, he never neglected. Of course reason didn't persuade the hot heads of the North and the South when emotions and partisan passions overtook the middle ground and tore the country apart. But reason never tore Lincoln apart.

Lincoln's self-restraint, emotional and verbal, in word and deed, has a saintly quality to it. He is strangely egoless, or ego-restrained. It is not a religious renunciation of power that saves him. In the temptations of Jesus, the role of ruling the world and feeding the people is adjured because Jesus will not swear loyalty to the Devil. Neither would Lincoln submit to the devil of personal glory. But he did assume power. He has been accused of being America's Caesar. The record of his restraint, his lack of revenge, his respect for the law, and his belief in the will of the people, all restrain him and his ambition. His glory was in his idea of the country and his earned esteem, and that gave him a path away from the oblivion of melancholy or the mania for power.

His tragic sense, his sadness, was in his nature and his spirit. Some of it is from Shakespeare, and later Burns and Byron, and some of the Bible. It did not come from the history he read or believed in. The great men that inspired Lincoln as a boy, particularly Washington, were not tragic heroes. Jefferson did not appear tragic, nor did Jackson or Henry Clay as Lincoln grew up to know them. It was not American history, nor the Biblical stories of Moses, David, or Solomon that damped the flame of Lincoln's ambition. The passion of Christ seems just to have not registered in his vocabulary. Oddly he avoids or represses one story line, Jesus's Beatitudes and Passion that most of his countrymen come to identify him with. Rather Lincoln had a gallery of mirrors in the Kings of Shakespeare to study, to learn from, and to avoid. Often the King's ambitions are reflected and corrected by the Fool. John Philip Newell in his *Shakespeare and The Human Mystery* catalogues the role of the Fool as the one who sees all things as passing, and that for whom tight boundaries are inadequate. Fools also reveal the falseness in others, observe what others fail to see. They have a freedom that comes from a lack of ambition or station in life. Fools offer wisdom, especially about the pitfalls of Kingly ambitions. More than in any one play or role, Lincoln had the all-encompassing, non-partisan, compassion of the author, William Shakespeare. Shakespeare was the one in whom John Keats saw such notable balance and neutrality.

Lincoln's reasonable modesty, his perspective on ambition, is captured in the last line of a memorized and often quoted poem. He so often quoted it that people thought he had written it, William Knox's, "Mortality." The last line is, "Oh why should the spirit of mortal be proud!" The poem starts with "So the multitude goes, like the flower or weed, /That withers away to let others succeed;"

Lincoln held to these poetic words, this stoic reasoned wisdom. His was not a bitter pinched reasonableness, but a living restraint upon himself and a sympathetic guidance in his dealings with the folly and the ambitions of all who surrounded him, often as President.

CHAPTER EIGHTEEN

The River of History

The dogmas of the quiet past are inadequate to the stormy present. The occasion is piled high with difficulty, and we must rise with the occasion. As our case is new, so we must think anew and act anew. We must disenthrall ourselves, and then we shall save our country.

Fellow-citizens, we cannot escape history. We of this Congress and this Administration will be remembered in spite of ourselves. No personal significance or insignificance can spare one or another of us. The fiery trial through which we pass will light us down in honor or dishonor to the latest generation. We say we are for the Union. The world will not forget that we say this. We know how to save the Union. The world knows we do know how to save it. We, even we here, hold the power and bear the responsibility. In giving freedom to the slave we assure freedom to the free—honorable alike in what we give and what we preserve. We shall nobly save or meanly lose the last best hope of earth. Other means may succeed; this could not fail. The way is plain, peaceful, generous, just—a way which if followed the world will forever applaud and God must forever bless.

- Abraham Lincoln (To Congress. December 3, 1861)

It was the tradition that such a Presidential message to Congress was not read in person, but by a clerk. With language like this it is a great loss that Lincoln didn't give these words in his personal voice before the members of Congress. Lincoln is defining how he and the Congress and the people can respond to the tide of history they all are in. We can see the way Lincoln thinks here, his unique blend of passivity and action, his own call to personal and national transformation. The metaphor of the river is a key way to understand how Lincoln sees and feels history. He shares with Emerson the desire to join in the flow of nature. "Life is a search after power," Emerson had written, and "All power is of one kind, a sharing of the nature of the world." Emerson is echoing the ancient sages of India of which Tagore writes. "The challenge for Lincoln," Fred Kaplan states in his biography, "was to find a way to increase his share in and to live that power expressively." Emerson had stated, "The mind that is parallel with the laws of nature will be in the current of events, and strong with their strength." Lincoln read these thoughts and might have heard Emerson in 1853 in Springfield. Emerson asserted that self-reliance and original action would, in leaders, make things happen, and things had to happen because events happened by laws of cause and effect not by luck.

Such a law of cause and effect would fit nicely into Lincoln's one true article of faith, his belief in a doctrine of necessity, a cosmic principle called fate. This was a principle that would work for Lincoln until the on-going Civil War became for him and the nation an overwhelming whirlwind, a mystery, needing a further explanation.

Lincoln then is Emersonian in his appeal to Congress to be leaders, to make things happen. Implied in his appeal is that they, like he and all, will have to change in order to make happen what needs to happen. Lincoln's doctrine of necessity was inclusive of a larger fate than mere cause and effect. But like Emerson he also makes his paradoxical appeal to the apparent freedom to change so that what has to happen will happen. The metaphor of the river helps sort out the process of this paradox. Our apparent free choice is to find the right river and to enter the river. Once in the river, following cause and effect, one navigates from point to point, but not with control over the river. Lincoln, after all, as we have seen, like Mark Twain later, had mastered the charts of the ever-changing Mississippi and had navigated downriver on actual voyages.

Lincoln's life experience renders the metaphor of the river journey as appropriate. With this metaphor in mind then, after such a detailed, point-by-point address, Lincoln says that when the occasion is piled high with difficulty, we must rise not to, but with, the occasion. As boats rise and fall with the flowing water so we meet the ebb and flow, swells and currents, of the river. The river we rise with is history. Rising with the river of history is the way to understand what some prominent Lincoln scholars refer to as Lincoln's passivity. It is at first hard to see or understand the idea that an ambitious and then engaged and active President could be passive. We can, however, see that poetry and metaphoric language is better able to explain this reality of Lincoln than political science or objective history written without images. Lincoln calls on Congress—using one of his simple favorite images—to save the ship, to hold the power and to take up the responsibility. Lincoln had chosen, and had desired to choose, the river of history, and a certain moral current in that river. There he would test his greatness and fulfill his ambition to be worthy of the esteem of his fellow citizens. He had a deeply held moral belief that America was in the most worthy river ever navigated. But the river was the river, and it was the boat that was in a struggle with the river, and the captain was in a struggle to guide the boat. The captain never tried to control the river. He would control the crew as much as possible (and even the captain's wife, but, of course, never his younger children!). This is an example of Lincoln's accommodation with nature, mentioned in the Foreword, and how it directed his vision of political action. Some could call it a kind of passivity. From a spiritual point of view it is rather simply wisdom. This so-called passivity of Lincoln is a crucial quality of his psychology and his spirit and much of his complexity is explained by taking it into account. The great Harvard historian and biographer, David Herbert Donald, states directly in the preface to his gold-standard biography of Lincoln, "More important, this biography highlights a basic trait of character evident throughout Lincoln's life: the essential passivity of his nature."

In other words, his own self-understanding, his self-image, comes from what is acting upon him, the river. He saw himself, he often said, as drift wood, and he used that image and the verb "to drift" at crucial times to explain himself to himself and to others. This image also explains his willingness to change courses in terms of policies and even pledges. He credits not his own "sagacity" but this: "I claim not to have controlled events, but confess plainly that events have controlled me."

Another historian, James B. McPherson at Princeton, when he reviewed Donald's book, seemed not to see this quality and failed to see how it worked even within the biography Donald wrote. Donald had gone outside of the methods of professional history to include an epistemology not definable by historiography. Passivity is not an empirical category of meaning or knowledge. Yet Lincoln found his touchstone in Shakespeare's *Hamlet* saying, "There's a divinity that shapes our ends, /Rough-hew them how we will."

The doctrine of necessity was Lincoln's sense that a higher power, a larger force, but not an evangelical Christian God, was impelling the actions, the powers, and the minds of humanity. Donald goes on to point out that Lincoln's lovable compassion, his willingness to overlook mistakes, comes from his sense of fate and his passive stance in regard to it. This is his pragmatic approach to problems. "My policy is to have no policy" is the compass that directs his approach to problems.

This passivity infuriated and confused the doctrinaire people on his right and on his left. Yet, in the end, he achieved the ideological goals of the doctrinaire Abolitionists, and he defeated the ideological goals of the Nullifiers and Fire-eaters of the South. It is valuable to explore again just what the strange power of this passivity might be. The term "expectations" is a helpful way to understand this principle by which Lincoln conducted himself. If he has no policy and river navigation was to just get from point to point, then he has clear and simple expectations of himself. Perhaps "self-expectation" is the best term to define how his passivity worked. Clearly in one sense he had a policy goal—the preservation of the union—and he had an end point in mind for the journey—the hope for self-government and freedom of opportunity and equality before the law. So it is on the level of self-expectation, even in the spirit of that self, that we see Lincoln's passivity open up into a deeper and more complex characteristic. The long-established name of this characteristic, including a version of passivity, comes, as we have said, from a poet, not a psychologist nor an historian, "Negative Capability."

Donald, in his preface, cites this by saying "...Lincoln in his own distinctively American way had the quality John Keats defined as forming 'a Man of Achievement', that quality 'which Shakespeare possessed so enormous...' Negative capability,' that is when a man is capable of being in uncertainties, Mysteries, doubts, without any irritable reaching after fact and reason." Donald closes his biography's Preface with his notation of Keats' concept.

John Burt, in his literary criticism and historical interpretation of the Lincoln-Douglas Debates, opens his Introduction with the subtitle "Negative Capability." It is through this de-centered self that one is able to disenchant oneself of ideologies, and the conflicts necessary to them, without abandoning principles. Eventually this attitude of the spirit opens and allows tragedy and fate to become meaningful. Tragedy then is more than an end-game defeat. When the self is open to the tragedy implicit in values-conflicts, one can understand Lincoln's spiritual life, including his apparent passivity.

Lincoln calls on Congress to "disenthrall' themselves. He is beginning to invite the transformation of self that the historical fires require. The ability to act together in a new mind to save the country will be the result of changes wrought in those responsible for guiding the inflamed nation.

Ambiguity about ambition was an early knot in Lincoln's psychology, one of his paradoxes. He unties this knot, releasing a tremendous amount of energy, in the four years of willing sacrifice that marked his leadership of the destroying country. That he had ambition like a constantly stoked little engine is a truth named by William Herndon, his last law partner in Springfield. Even as a youth in Indiana some of his friends reported, if we can believe them, that he had told them he would become President! He may even have thought he could be as great as Shakespeare if he turned to language not to history. While his Shakespeare-fed notions of reason and nature, his knowledge of kings and fools humanized and moderated his ambitions, they did not cripple him nor turn him into a wandering saint or fool from Dostoyevsky. Shakespeare, like a good parent or therapist, tamed him but did not break his spirit and drive.

He allowed some of his ambition to be carried by his high-spirited and openly ambitious wife, Mary. She had said herself she intended to marry a President. One early candidate for her was Stephen A. Douglas, but it was to be Lincoln. Shakespeare, not Biblical ethics, was his, but not Mary's handbook for knowing how ambition worked and didn't work. His real nod to Christianity in this regard was his wholesale compatibility with the Whig Party's formulation of the moderate modern man. Whigs had a different wardrobe. A Whig man dressed differently than the Jacksonian ruffians or elites. They drank less, swore less, spent less on ostentation, if not on national expansion. They cultivated learning and education, not the manners of a Sir Walter Scott hero, nor the lack of them in a Davey Crockett. Lincoln was a Whig more than he was a Christian in terms of personal ethics, although many in the North wished to merge the two codes.

It was rather something more personal than Whig ethics, something more heartfelt, that re-emerged in Lincoln as the vitality empowering his ambitions. It was his love of people and his love of being loved by people that reignited the firebox of his ambitious engine. In the sorrows of his heart, in his deep relationships, his thinking became more heartfelt. He began, as we see significantly in his Farewell Speech, to be a man with a thinking heart.

There is luminosity about Lincoln, a word that an English professor and Protestant minister, Eileen Sypher, came up with. The word shows him to be more than a reasonable Whig, or a chastened Shakespearean king, or a re-frocked fool. There is a truth about Lincoln to be seen by seeing him with a feeling heart, as in seeing his image by moonlight at the Memorial in Washington, D.C. There is more to be learned about Lincoln in those shadows, including his poetic passivity, his dreaming Yonder sense, and his heavy heart. His truth is not fully seen in the glory that one might wish to see in his American rise and his inspiring legacy. The deeper light here comes in the words: his heavy heart. It is his heart that makes him want to love and be loved. It was his thinking heart that drove him back into politics when the expansion of slavery looked more than plausible. He saw things, in Shakespeare's coined term, feelingly, and that brought him close to the spirit of that religion he had never fully embraced.

One of the most endearing documents from the hand of Lincoln is his early petition to run for state office in Illinois. The subtext, as we shall see in the next chapter, is simply this: Love me as I love you, and that will be enough, no matter what happens. He ran for office like one of the lilies of the field in the Sermon on the Mount. If his flight be like the sparrow that falls, rather than like the young eagle that soars, that will be just fine. He told William Herndon, his partner, when he left Springfield, that when the Presidency is over "I shall return and we will put out our shingle and practice law just as before, as if nothing had ever happened." This sentiment is more than Negative Capability, this is a love of life, a love that is self-emptying and yet truly fulfilling, to both the lover and the loved, to himself and those he served. He opened up that heart for loving life and then also became a wounded, angry lion roaring back in his Cooper Union Address that right must validate might and we must do the right! He had thought this through and now his heart gave him the drive that political glory never did. He rose with the occasion. One reluctant attendee at his Cooper Union Speech, once won over to Lincoln's words, called him simply a "wonderful man."

Thinking heart is a term widely used now to describe the life and written testimony of a victim of the Holocaust, Etty Hellesum. This young Dutch Jewish woman volunteered to go with her people to the camps because she wanted to serve, to be their thinking heart and conscience as they endured, or did not endure, the enslaving power of Nazism. Her testimony is largely one of a religious mystic and yet without conventional religious loyalties of membership. Like Lincoln, her thinking heart crosses traditional boundaries and gives witness to and care for the victims of war, the widow and the orphan, those that so haunted the war-making, heart-broken, President. The ambitious melancholy boy had become the tragic leader, finding his greatest power in the thoughts of his heart, his most spiritual place. Like Etty Hellesum he followed his people into their, into our, fiery furnace.

The kings and fools in Shakespeare were a realistic peer group for what Lincoln called the theater in his mind. Almost everyone he met as President was convinced that he knew better what to do and how to do it. His vaunted cabinet of presidential rivals, the newspaper editors, the power people in the Senate and the House, and almost all of the clergy, approached Lincoln with a degree of contempt that could have undone anyone who did not have a secret sense of their own enormous mental, spiritual and even physical power. Lincoln had that sense, it was what made ambition so dangerous for him.

He had been in deep dialogue with the Shakespearean giants for years. Those giants were his peers along with his other peer group, the figures he met in the Bible. The Biblical figures and all the scripture that surrounded them made for yet another world for Abraham Lincoln. Along with his Shakespearean theater, and his poets' retreat, he was an active and constant reader in the sanctuary of the Bible. He knew hundreds of Bible passages by heart and had surely taken the measure of the Patriarchs, the Prophets, even the Devil. Jesus as the Christ was to him largely a mystery, but his was not a smug rejection.

On the last afternoon of his life he was with Mary. While on their famed Good Friday carriage ride, they talked of world travel after "all this" was over. While she favored the European capitals he is said to have mentioned Jerusalem. Where else was he to meet the memorials to other true greatness, the ambitious King David and the wise King Solomon? These would be the men he would have wanted, even needed, to meet, if only in imagination. While it was Good Friday, he was on his way to the secular theatre, not to a Christian worship event. He was about to become forever a figure understood by the willing sacrifice of Jesus. He was truly in one way, despite himself, the most Christian of men. Leo Tolstoy proclaimed him to be a Christ-like leader because of his love for the enemy. Whitman called him our first Martyr Chief.

CHAPTER NINETEEN

Christ and Lincoln

Those who want to make Lincoln a Christian, or even Christ-like, as Tolstoy said, had better to look again. Jesus did not begin his ministry modestly like Lincoln began his career. Jesus boldly announced in the synagogue the Isaiah prophecy of release to the captives, sight to the blind, all being fulfilled before them that day in him. He began active ministry working a miracle of water into wine, with a rebuke to his mother. Jesus was not seeking an office but had a voice and teaching role within a prophetic tradition. Jesus had settled the ambiguity over ambition with his rebuff of the Devil in his Temptations. None of this applies to humble Lincoln.

What does invite comparison is that in the end both had egoless obedience to the will of God, as each one knew it to be. Both evoked love and even worship from their followers, and suffered a death by willing sacrifice to evil.

The spiritual path has a secular direction for Lincoln, with all the ethical contradictions and half-measures, political compromises and even mistakes that humans are involved in. The humanity of the divine-human Christ, to those who believe, is not marked by any of that. Nor was Jesus responsible for involving a nation in over 600,000 deaths by war.

Yet if the messages of Jesus, and the example of his de-centered, God-centered humanity are to live in other lives, then Lincoln's life truly echoes Jesus' love of humanity. Lincoln sometimes embodied Jesus' gentleness of spirit, sometimes his fiery passion for freedom and truth, and sometimes the fear of the Lord in judgment. There is also in Lincoln the radical message of expansive love, across tribal boundaries, of mercy and compassion for the lowly as well as a rebuke to the high and mighty.

We could say that Jesus didn't need an ego but that for a while, Lincoln did. Jesus was not ambivalent about his ambitious role, but Lincoln was. Unlike Jesus' bold synagogue announcement of his identity and mission, Lincoln breaks forth into the public world by posting a truly humble notice that he is available for election to the State House but that it is O.K. if he is rejected.

"But Fellow-Citizens, I shall conclude. Considering the great degree of modesty which should always attend youth, it is probable I have already been more presuming than becomes me...Every man is said to have his particular ambition. Whether it be true or not, I can say for one that I have no other so great as that of being truly esteemed of my fellow men, by rendering myself worthy of their esteem...But if the good people in their wisdom shall see fit to keep me in the background, I have been too familiar with disappointment to be very much chagrined."

This he posted in New Salem, Illinois, in his twenties. Lincoln shows none of the Isaiah-enhanced self-assurance that Jesus shows in his synagogue debut.

CHAPTER TWENTY

Prophets and Lincoln

P rophets are thought to predict, but in fact they reflect. The Biblical prophets whom Lincoln read were, as was he, both secular and religious figures. The prophets were deeply "involved with his people" as Abraham Joshua Heschel tells us in his classic study, "The Prophets", and they reflect on God-past and on God-future because they know God-present.

Prophets, intimately aware of the people, are also achingly aware of the moral arc of the universe. They identify with the forward vision as well as the back-looking wisdom of that high arc. They look to where God is going and who God has been. Increasingly as President, Lincoln steered America into the history that was sweeping him and the nation along in an unknown future current. He also looked deeply to the past for guidance.

Lincoln's most dominant personality trait, even more than his deep desire to be worthy of the esteem of his fellow citizens, was his fierce need to know. As a boy he would be truly angry, and would pace the floor of the cabin at night thinking, if he had heard someone talk of something that he did not understand. He needed knowledge, as well as their esteem that he knew something. As a young man he studied and surveyed and waded out into the Sangamon River so he could figure out how to navigate a steamboat down it, and also to be able to propose state legislation for its improvement. With practical and thorough knowledge he figured out how to dislodge a stuck raft by shifting its cargo and drilling a hole in its bottom to allow incoming water to angle the boat off a sand bar, all this to the amazement of town folk watching along the New Salem shore. Lincoln needed knowledge and he found it again and again.

Deep in the Civil War and at the highest moments of his life he also passionately needed to know—looking back—what all this horrid war meant, and—looking forward—where his country could be going. He wanted to know the perspective of the moral arc of the universe, and nothing less.

This knowledge was the underlying theme of many of his conversations, especially with visiting clergymen, but also even intimately with several Quaker women. This was also what he wrote about in a secret document he kept in his desk, his reflections upon the Divine Will.

Lincoln sat down at dinner with his wife, with whom he shared the recent loss of their dearest son Willie. Also at the table was his sister-in-law who had just lost her husband, fighting on the Southern side. Why, he asked, was all this the way it was? Everywhere he turned, his mind and heart were filled with tragic suffering. He would then go deeply into his mind and heart, suffering his added punishing prod, to try to understand and to know. He lived in what Heschel calls the three dimensions of the prophet: himself, the people, and God. What is most theological about Lincoln at the end is that he was passionately seeking knowledge of God: What was God doing in history, personally with him as an instrument, and nationally with God's almost chosen people?

Prophets are not born atop the arc of the universe; they struggle like Sisyphus to climb its heights. Lincoln didn't say he was carrying a rock, he would rather say something quaint about the disasters and defeats like, "the bottom is out of the tub." Prophets begin in silence, in bottomless pits, like Moses, a fugitive in exile, speechless before the burning bush. John Burt describes in rhetorical detail in his essay "Collective Guilt in Lincoln's Second Inaugural Address"[7] how reticent to speak, how reverential, nearly speechless his syntax is in that Address. As if, says Burt, he knows the deeper spiritual response to this whole war and its cause is reverence and silence. When Prophets do speak they speak from their secular and religious identification, their sense of self, and their sense of the people. It is within the prophetic tradition then that Lincoln is speaking in that final speech. When they speak they bring into the world the third dimension of their existence, God.

The reason that the language of the prophet is convincing, Heschel tells us, is because it is authentic language, true to itself, true to the people, and true to the claims of what is understood to be God. The ultimate tool of the prophet is language. It is in words from a holy silence that the prophet binds self, people, and God together.

There were two tools in Lincoln's life, the axe and the pen. We think of him as an iconic young man with an axe. He was, however, more than just handy. He became a master of this heavy tool in the way a Samurai warrior masters a sword. Apprenticeship on the Indiana frontier began when a boy was nine. That was also when his mother died, 1818. Lincoln probably had used an axe since he was seven. It was from then on that his daily tool was the axe. Virgin forests with gigantic trees were on their eighty, then one hundred, then one hundred and sixty acre farm. Reports vary, and it grew over time. Soon he was making hundreds and hundreds of split rails, eventually also making a huge raft to go down the Mississippi River. When he was on his deathbed, stripped of his evening theater clothes, men who stood by were said to be shocked and amazed at the sheer size and strength of his arms, his axe-handling muscle. Once when tour-

---

[7]   "Collective Guilt in Lincoln's Second Inaugural Address," John Burt, *American Political Thought* 2015 4:3, 467-488.

ing out among the troops he was known to have held an axe out at shoulder height and arm's length to please the crowd of soldiers. You can hear them whoop with delight, for they would have known what strength it took to do that. The story goes that after he left several soldiers tried but could not do it themselves.

Yet, as biographer Fred Kaplan says in his book on Lincoln, it was the pen that was mightier for Lincoln than both the sword and the axe. It was with the pen that he wrote the words that gave him prophetic speech. He almost always wrote before he spoke and he was loath to speak without first writing down his words.

The speech of the prophet, says Heschel, is emotional. It is "authentic utterance" in that it comes from a total identification between the person and the words the person speaks. There is urgency and magnitude. There is also poetic imagination, diction, rhythm, and artistic form. A prophet is not just inspired, a prophet is eloquent, and it is a secular rhetorical skill that is being used. The secret of the prophetic style is, "his life and his soul are at stake in what he says and in what is going to happen to what he says." It is appropriate to think of Lincoln in these terms. It is necessary to remember that Abraham Joshua Heschel himself is the man with the long grey beard and dark glasses in the photograph standing arm and arm with Martin Luther King, Jr. on their way to Selma, Alabama. Rabbi Heschel had just published his study on the Prophets a few years earlier. Heschel had the authenticity of the prophet himself.

The prophet identifies with the people, and from within that secular identification comes his prophetic speech. In that enduring identity come words for the moment, and beyond the moment. Heschel says, and we can think of Lincoln, the prophet's words have not dignity but grandeur. His words are, "luminous and explosive, firm and contingent, harsh and compassionate, a fusion of contradictions." Lincoln was a man abundant with contradictions, yet he spoke from his ultimate identification with the people, all the people, of the country. Contradictions gave him a wide view of many views. His was a secular democratic identity. Between himself and the people he looked to know what in our past made this war last so long. What about our future could make this war be meaningful? He needed to know.

It is not that a prophet sees into the future as a seer, a prophet sees where the moral arc of the universe is going because he or she sees where it has been. The prophet has suffered to know by reaching feelingly back and longingly forward to find the words to say what is to be known. This knowing speech, Heschel says, begins with an extreme sensitivity to evil and ends in an epiphany of the highest good. It is grounded in the practical knowing of the human heart when, as theologian H. Richard Niebuhr says of revelation, the human story we are all living is revealed to be also God's story living through us. The prophet speaks a reflective revelation. It is a knowing that says, looking back, that what has happened is in some sense what should have happened. The past, our past, makes moral sense, even with the evil in it. The past tells us, the prophet says from knowledge of this arc, what should happen now and in the future. It is a call to human agency in life. Complete secular identification, like Lincoln's, one's self with the people, is the stepping stone to this kind of prophetic revelation.

Lincoln was, as we can so easily see now, becoming his deepest truest self in this ordeal of knowing. His last pictures show us the face he was always being drawn toward, a face of ultimate kindness, of the sweetest compassion, the face his stepmother and mother must have seen in him as a boy. But his face, no longer awkward or callow, now a pure face, exquisite by suffering, fragile and spent, a face that all humanity aims at when emptied in greater love. Secretary of the Navy Wells said his aspect in death was never more beautiful.

This self with its pure real face is what Niebuhr says it means to have a God. To have a God is to have a history, because your story connects you to your past and to your future. When the story of your face, your history, become joined in the community of others, then, in that union, the face of God, says Niebuhr, is revealed. It is a matter of all stories becoming one history. This union with history and the future is how Lincoln spoke a prophecy, a revelation, about our past and future, our world, now. We hear it in the *Gettysburg Address*.

The last photographs of Lincoln, just days before his death, reveal images of what the poet David Whyte portrays in his poem "The Faces at Braga." There he pictures the wooden hand-carved faces he saw in an ancient monastery. He asks us, in the poem, to let life be the carver of our faces such that our deep grain of love is brought to the surface, letting even our flaws lead our life's searching chisel to our very core. Then we are no longer in a fight with our failings, hooding our eyes with grief, our mouths drying with pain. Rather we have given ourselves over to the blows of our life. Then the lines of our faces become like rivers feeding the sea and meeting the land and sky. This is where our faces fall away and we grow "younger toward death". Our flaws are now gathered in celebration of our essential self, we having merged perfectly and silently, and are wedded to our life-carved face. One can see Lincoln's ancient face. This poem's truth would be one way to explain the otherwise inexplicable truth that Lincoln's really strange face, by the end, and sometimes earlier, became totally beautiful. Lincoln let life carve his face. He famously had told his secretary, John Hay, that after the age of forty a man is responsible for his own face.

Part II

The Warrior Archetype

The Idea of the Warrior

Like the planet Mars the warrior archetype is one sphere in the solar system of each self. Most scriptures tell of the warrior, a core figure in the spiritual journey. Whether it is Arjuna in the Bhagavad-Gita, or Peter and the sword at Gethsemane with Jesus, or Joshua taking up the battle of Jericho, the image of the warrior emerges and, like Mars, orbits the light of the central Sun, the greater light.

Lincoln engaged the warrior archetype as a boy, in early manhood, and as an elder, President. As a young man he was a Captain in the Black Hawk War. The Warrior for him was a traditional initiation into the glory of leadership and the self-esteem that came from a cohort. This proved to be a crucial networking experience for his future. He proved himself and showed something of his magnetism. But it also fueled his quest for greatness and gave him a narrative for that common male desire, glory. The quest then led him into rigid and ego-haunted roles of traditional ambition. His idealism became ideological and absolutist and his generous spirit was overtaken by flaming desires—the kind that can lead a warrior astray. His eventual enlargement of the warrior spirit included an accommodation with the feminine, in a home setting, and a deep experience of grief that led his heart to a larger spirit that transcends the warrior self.

Men, the Jungian psychologists Moore and Gillette point out, become aggressive before they have the social context of established relationships and cultural controls. In other words, men become warriors when they are still just boys. Herman Melville called war a boy's game.

Women, they point out, access aggression within their social, biological and psychological selves at mid-life when some home and temple have already been built and need protection and defense.

Ancient myths and religious texts contain the story of the Warrior archetype. A study of most holy texts will show the dynamics of the self that arise in the context of conflict, fights and wars. The secular and the sacred often meet at the boundary when the self meets the other, a flash point of conflict and the beginning of warriors at war. The issue at stake is the survival of the self or the group. Jungian studies also define these dynamics of the self in the context of a culture.

Jung's concept is that the archetype is a psychological instinct in the development of the personal self, and then in the expression of the transpersonal Self. This concept can show us Lincoln emerging from his boyhood first as a warrior, then seeking and finding a larger way to be. The idea of the warrior can take us through the confusions of his life into the grips of what Jung would call the Shadow Warrior. Lincoln, we shall see, struggled to define himself as someone other than the Shadow King. His eventual spiritual achievement is to become part of the redeeming concept of the Grail King. The Grail King is the one who serves the other, and becomes redeeming and glorious by doing so.

Lincoln and the Warrior Archetype

Archetypes come to us in history, our own, and larger social history. There are two Captain Abraham Lincolns in American history. One was a Revolutionary War soldier, who later, as a civilian while tending his corn field, was shot dead by a party of Indian warriors resisting white settlements in Kentucky in the 1780s. The other, of course, was his grandson, a militia-elected leader of a party of white men formed to fight off the attack of desperate Black Hawk Indians in northern Illinois fifty years later. That fight never happened.

The Warrior is a member of a caste that destroys or defends a social enclave. They are the vanguard. If they win, their enclave—usually after the destruction of a pre-existing one—can then become a nation or an empire. They do this at the cost of thousands of lives. In the paradoxes of Lincoln's life none is more extreme than his nearly pacifist personal nature and his determined leadership in a warrior fight that spilled out into total war.

Lincoln loved his young-man membership in the warrior caste. He was elected Captain Abraham Lincoln in the militia in the Black Hawk War in Illinois in 1832. Once he had his legal freedom from his father, at the age of 21, Lincoln held a wide number of jobs: postal clerk, store clerk, surveyor, raft maker, temporary steam boat pilot. None however was a calling. Being a warrior is a calling. It has transpersonal value. Lincoln had taken various and sundry jobs, but he became, for a short while, a warrior. Afterwards Lincoln chose his life-long calling, to be a politician, and being a lawyer was his means. But being a warrior was his first step.

The brief time Lincoln spent as a warrior is crucial to understanding his later life. Those months were the stepping stones from subsistence work, to work for pay, to work that both paid and had a higher definition. To be a warrior was both real and ideal, it protected the enclave, but it also assumed the higher value of the enclave. In that sense it was Lincoln's first spiritual identity. In the American Revolution, and its blood, Lincoln first read and felt his own covenant with society. But when he became Captain Abraham Lincoln, elected by his ruffian pioneer fellows, he took his place alongside Captain Lincoln, his grandfather, a warrior from that American Revolution. He acted on the covenant he had only read about.

While his forefather had been shot, really murdered, by Indians, Lincoln showed no blood-thirsty revenge when he and the other enthusiastic volunteers went after the seriously threatened yet threatening Black Hawks. In the midst of their wild-goose chase one day a lone Indian wandered into their camp. Lincoln, with the threat of physical force, defended this hapless man. He stood down his blood-hot militia who wanted nothing more than to kill the Indian. It could have been easy for Lincoln to want to repay a debt by killing this Indian.

Black Hawk and his people had been exiled and tricked and were in desperate straits. They were trying, for what was to be the last time, the warrior solution to their threatened enclave, their tribe and society. Their fate was like that of Chief Tecumseh who, two decades earlier, at the very time of Lincoln's birth, lost the entire Illinois and Indiana land of his ancestors to General William Henry Harrison from Fort Wayne. It was then a wild west and the warrior caste presaged the real rule of law and the political chiefs to come, the greatest of whom would be Lincoln.

Lincoln did not seek revenge for his grandfather's murder. Revenge did not flow in his veins. From the boyhood event with his melon-stealing friends, to the many occasions of ambitious and contemptuous cabinet members and generals, Lincoln never took revenge. And yet to become a warrior, to become his father's father's namesake and rank, appealed to Lincoln's desire to be worthy of the esteem of others, and to amount to something outside of his father's limited orbit of subsistence farming, carpentry, and hunting. In that way he avenged his life with his father.

As a warrior, Lincoln, showed a natural mastery of the first spiritual step in the warrior archetype—mastery over hatred. In the warrior traditions a sacred warrior, as opposed to the shadow warrior, has control over his violence because he has control over his emotions. The honorable warrior does not kill in hatred or from hatred, but only from skill for more objective purposes than revenge. What the spiritual warrior does is to remove his ego from the incident he is enacting. Lincoln completely mastered this. That very ability later enabled him to master the warriors, mainly a whole slew of generals, he had on hand as the Civil War began.

In the warrior code the virtues that have meaning are more than physical abilities, they include courage, and a reliable concern for the well-being of fellow soldiers. Men bond in such groups by way of initiation events. Lincoln had already gained respect and membership in the informal group called the Clary's Grove Boys. He had met the challenges of their big leader, Jack Armstrong. Stories differ as to who won those wrestling matches. But win or tie, but not lose, Lincoln showed his willingness to mix it up physically in a fair fight with other young men. His size and strength would have spoken for themselves. Even when he was an older adult, his political friends or opponents, simply as men, would never have been far from feeling just how strong Lincoln was. As we have noted, when he was on his death bed, as his clothes were removed, men remarked on just how massive and strong his long-concealed arms were. The warrior archetype lurks under the surface of most power relationships for men, and the warrior is first and foremost a strong man. Lincoln's warrior abilities, physical and spiritual, were foundational—if not often historically noted—to his beginning achievement in life.

We cannot grasp Lincoln as a spiritual person without under-standing his relation to the archetype of the Warrior. Warriors are a psychological and cultural form for masculine identity, used to cross the threshold from hunter-gatherer tribes to agricultural settlers and then to city culture and society. The warrior is the initiate into what we call history, ever since The Iliad. The warrior has roots in myths such as Gilgamesh, Beowulf, and the Bhagavad-Gita. Lincoln is a prototype of such mythic figures and then, in real time, crosses the boundaries from near-tribal life to agricultural life, to city life. He makes his per-sonal transition out of the nearly primitive west to national power. He crosses the threshold into history. Many presidents had been warrior generals. Lincoln's identity comes from classical archetypal traditions. The pre-history in the West, such as the myths of the sacred feminine, were, of course, completely unknown to Lincoln. The archetypes of the feminine, however, do figure in his spiritual life.

The Warrior exists in culture and consciousness as a symbol but shows up in individuals in history and stories in books. We know from Lincoln's speech to the New Jersey State Assembly, on his way to Washington, D.C. and the Presidency, that one of his significant childhood thrills was the story of Washington crossing the Delaware and the Battle of Trenton. It was etched deeply in his mind and heart. He shared this memory with the Assemblymen and reminded them that they had all been boys.

In the 12th and 13th century myths of Parsifal and The Fisher King, the rustic youth in the far country is thrilled to see The Red Knight come riding by. It changes his life. He is called by that warrior image to leave his widowed mother and go off, like his unknown father, to be a knight. The allure of the Red Knight is strong in boys. Young Lincoln reading about Washington crossing the Delaware would be such a story. There is another story, told by a contemporary of Lincoln, that while the family was still living in Hardin County, Kentucky, veterans from the War of 1812 came by their cabin. The witness says the boy Lincoln himself fed and cared for them. In Fred Kaplan's biography we read that the Lincolns may have heard about the victory of General Andrew Jackson in New Orleans in 1815 before it reached the nation's Capitol, and that would have been just before Lincoln's sixth birthday. Would he remember feeding and attending to those uniformed giants?

There would be more Red Knight stories, but stories with rhetoric added. When he is fifteen, in Indiana, he read Lindley Murray's *The English Reader* and there he read Demosthenes' speech to the Athenians, as Kaplan points out, exhorting them to perform heroically like the men of the previous generation. He would also have read Publius Scipio's speech to the Roman army as well as Hannibal's speech to the Carthaginian army as they do battle, each one appealing to God to be on their side. To fulfill the glory of the previous generation, to fight with God on your side, these were twin deep concerns to Lincoln and his generation. These were to become real problems for him to solve one way or another.

Psychologists such as the Jungian Robert A. Johnson tell us that each boy on his way to fulfill his notion of masculinity has to come to terms with his inner Red Knight, his aggression and his ambitious desire to be the top man. In the Parsifal Fisher King myth the boy kills the Red Knight. This means he gains power over aggression. The spiritual issue is: does he have to become the Red Knight in order to master the Red Knight? Lincoln, eventually, becomes a master of this spiritual issue. But a knight gains his status by defeating another knight. It is a zero-sum game in the mythology. For a boy to become a man, Johnson says, he must master his own aggression as well. To be a man he must have his aggression but it must not have him. Unless he masters his fighting spirit he will be mastered by it and become a bully, a tyrant, the shadow side of the Red Knight only. Lincoln would meet plenty of men who had failed this inner ordeal.

The Red Knight is the mythic figure we see in the movie *The Fisher King*. There we see the raging horse-mounted figure who will destroy both the wounded man, played by Robin Williams, and the angry man, played by Jeff Bridges, until they join forces. The angry man is redeemed in the service of the wounded one. We see Lincoln finding spiritually inspired ways to solve these issues: his friendly solution to the melon thieves in his youth in Gentryville, for example. Eventually he solves the problem of living up to the past warriors; and he finds generous solutions to aggression and hatred in the Civil War.

Along with his "Readers" and their Classical references and their American history, Lincoln was a deep reader, a memorizer, of the

Bible. The Bible would another source for understanding the warrior. The Bible was the currency of society. Moses and the Exodus story is an alternative to earlier, pagan or traditional scriptures. It tells of a non-violent, if miraculous, revolution: Freedom without war. However, Moses does lead to the warrior, Joshua, and then to battle of Jericho. In the Exodus story itself the Red Sea does the killing of the Egyptian warriors, and the escaping slaves are not themselves ever warriors. In the Biblical stories that Lincoln read less is made of the warrior as a sacred figure than other mythologies. Not until King David does the Warrior King emerge in the Hebrew story, and George Washington was the Warrior King model to Lincoln. Lincoln became a Warrior King. This is as unlikely as the story of Joan of Arc, the woman warrior saint, whom, like Lincoln, we cannot fully explain.

As Lincoln went from young boy to young adult to President he became an old soul. Always his life was defined by wars. It was the defeat of Chief Tecumseh that opened up the Indiana territory that his father moved them to when Lincoln was seven. The Black Hawk War initiated Lincoln into a sense of his own glory and into his covenant with American history. He was Captain Lincoln, his most thrilling achievement. He then opposed the U.S.-Mexican War (1846-1848) as a one-term Congressman, with nearly disastrous results for his career, but also finding principles for his later stands against slavery. Then there was the Civil War. It defined America, and Lincoln defined the Civil War. And warrior glory took on a serpent's eye.

Lincoln was little more than a homeless man, a day laborer living in the homes of those he worked for, when he went off to fight in the brief Black Hawk Indian War. Like the young Parsifal in the Fisher King myth, he left home and followed the glory of the Red Knights of his time, some of whom were also to become the educated leading men of New Salem and then Springfield. These very warrior men would be the core politicians and leaders of the frontier civilization being built in Illinois in the early 1800's.

Did he make the right choice in following the hot blood of the men called up as a volunteer militia? Did he know what he was doing to protect the white community? Did it need to be done, to make war on the desperate, tricked, displaced Indians who were starving and looking for something back from their former lands? It was the right choice for the development of a self, without which no one has a spiritual journey. But it was also a choice deeply involved in moral ambiguities. Lincoln would fight his way through moral ambiguities for the rest of his life. As we shall also see, once he is back in his community and more established, he struggles to find a way to channel the warrior energies in a time of peace. His Lyceum speech of 1838 shows us a man mightily fierce and yet looking for a worthy fight, a fight not like the first one he volunteered for, the Black Hawk War, but a fight like the one his Grandfather got into, the American Revolution.

In his early post-warrior life Lincoln is often an awkward man. Not only did wars involve Lincoln, as all Americans, in deep moral ambiguities, but the choice of the warrior archetype itself presented him, as it does all young men, with ambiguities. The warrior archetype has an arch if not awkward relation to the feminine. Warriors get close to women by putting scarves in their armor, and bowing and serving at great sacrifice. But they do not, as warriors, know much about how to have relationships with women or the feminine itself. Knights may worship the feminine, but they hardly share life. Thus they are often awkward. Lincoln had two wonderful and powerful mothers and a significant sister and probably a significant first love. But it would take more than the fighting honor and male camaraderie of a warrior for Lincoln to come to spiritual and psychological terms with the feminine. More important than any one influence in his life Lincoln had splendid mothers. The Mother archetype, the image of the protecting, guiding, nurturing, good feminine or Anima, spirit was huge in Lincoln's soul. It became his way to go beyond the warrior.

He did not, like Parsifal in the Fisher King myth, leave home in order to follow the Red Knight. He left home to be free of his father and subsistence farming. It was only then that he got a glimpse of the Red Knight, the man with a horse who goes to battle. To be a warrior was a transition, not a goal, for Lincoln. To be a warrior was not a way to separate himself from his mothers and their world. He achieved initiation without rejecting his mothers. This is an important distinction. He mourned his blood mother, he revered his stepmother, he angrily grieved his sister's death in child-birth, and he lost his heart in love early on to Anne Rutledge. Once he returned from his short adventure into the warrior world he then needed to find a way to negotiate the women who surrounded the new life in the frontier capital of Springfield.

It was not till he had sons, and lost one of them, and learned to call his wife "Mother," that Lincoln found a way to be both aggressive in a worthy fight and spiritually mature, self-less, in his ambitions to achieve power. While over half his eventual work life is spent away from home, he becomes king of his family and he values them greatly. By mid-life he found the social, cultural and personal context into which to plunge his fiery self. It is then that he can, as a mature Arthur, truly pull his sword out of the rock and show himself not only a good warrior but a potential king.

But that was Springfield. The warrior archetype would not be all he needed in order to come to terms with his great self. He was awkward early on in Springfield and we will look at that and the Shadow Warrior difficulties he had. But the Warrior archetype was a very good way to leave New Salem, his first home way from his family. The fire was lit as he mounted his horse and rode north to the Black Hawk War. Some say his real sword at the time, if he even had one, was really just made out of wood. He, like most of the militia men, had no arms of his own. He himself later claimed, comically, that his bloodshed in the war was from mosquitos. Lincoln re-enlisted twice more, but as a private. Some say his election as Captain was because he was so ridiculous looking and hardly one to impose order. Yet he won the confidence of several future political leaders in the state. After his fewer than one hundred days of trekking through the woods, burying Indian-killed fellow militia, Lincoln walked and canoed home, his horse had been stolen the night before his discharge. He never engaged in combat, although his company came upon the disastrous carnage of a troop like their own, killed and scalped by the Indians. There is always a little Don Quixote, if not Ichabod Crane, about Lincoln as a warrior.

Why did he, years later, refer to his time in the militia and his being elected Captain as the thing that had given him the most pleasure of all his achievements? Lincoln's deep and acclaimed satisfaction with his short war adventure makes sense when we understand the building blocks of masculine psychology and the role that the language, if not the reality, of war plays in spiritual life. As a man, and as an always growing spiritual person, being a warrior then was crucial to Lincoln.

More than Lincoln's psychological identity and aggression is at stake in the story of the Black Hawk War. The warrior archetype is important to the journey of Lincoln. But war itself is an event with symbolic and rhetorical power. It is the intensity of war as life's story and the language of sacrifice and decisive turning points, even victory and defeat, that define war. War, as we have seen, surrounds Lincoln's life and defines it, and he defines war. More than aggression and the self are at stake in the greater story of the Civil War, which became his war, as it became the war that reformed America. Identity through story is as stake, history for individuals and for the nation. War is one of several major story lines in history. War is a narrative. The psychologist Karl Scheibe in his book *Self Studies* says... "adventure has a central role to play in the construction and development of life stories...life stories, in turn, are the major supports for human identities." Adventure, of some sort, is the stuff of history. Scheibe is taking his cue from Erving Goffman's dramaturgical theories of human development, life as story.

In William James' famous essay on the moral equivalent of war, James says such an equivalent is hard to find. But he knows that we humans thrive on a story, a strong story. He says that appealing to the horrors of war as a way of stopping war will have no effect. "The horrors make the fascination. War is the strong life (italics); it is life in extremis; war-taxes are the only ones men never hesitate to pay.... Through man lives by habit, what he lives for is thrills and excitement. The only relief from habit's tediousness is periodic excitement."

Recall that Lincoln is still living, in 1832, in the little "two-rut" town of New Salem when word came that the "British Band" of Indians was moving south from Wisconsin back into Illinois. Lincoln had just announced his candidacy for the state legislature. We see him proclaiming himself a politician, desiring more than anything the esteem of his fellow man, as he would say. Then he also signs up for war. A sorry war it was from the view of the present, a war full of the usurpation and trickery of American policy and President Jackson's "Indian Removal" plan. Yet the potential of an alliance of many Indian tribes, with possible British or Canadian assistance, was real to the boundaries of the emerging United States. Half of Black Hawk's thousand-person troops were women and children. That tells us, like all war, that the ambiguities are high. This is a war story fraught with histories.

Some years later, caught up in his post-warrior moral rigidities, Lincoln took up words against the Mexican War. He mounts an intense and specific analysis of the demagogic circumstances around that war, including his famous speech asking President Polk to name the actual "spot" (his word) of land where the Mexicans invaded Texas. Lincoln knew that the spot was ambiguous at best. Were he to apply a similar moral and factual inventory of the Black Hawk War of 1832 he would find much to trouble his soul. But not when he was twenty-three and really at complete loose ends trying to build a free life of his own, not when his grandfather was "Captain Abraham Lincoln" in the American Revolution, and not when he never got a man's respect from his brow-beating father. No, the war and being a warrior gave this gangly giant everything the masculine self needs to establish an ego—the status of a horse to ride, the title of leadership, the esteem and camaraderie of other men, some cash, and something exciting to do. Especially it was something exciting to do that would make this idea of America more of a reality. That was a vision that fueled Lincoln like no other. It was his secular religion, even as it would lead him to become spiritual about what was first for him only secular.

Young Warrior and Beyond the Warrior

More than his psychology and his social and economic situation were at play in his brief emergence into lasting membership in the warrior caste. His mind was at work. Lincoln's boyhood history of reading shaped his choices and actions here. The rhetoric of war was shaping his vision of history.

Allen Guelzo points out in his biography *Abraham Lincoln: Redeemer President* that in his early education, his remarkable subscription school curriculum, came the images of revolutionary war. There were the soldiers from Parson Weems' book on George Washington, the archery bowman under Henry V at Agincourt from William Scott's "Elocution." These were the images that "fixed themselves in my memory," said Lincoln.

It is one thing to be nine and thrill at the courage of the American Revolutionary fighters and the noble George Washington. This was pure inspiration to the young Lincoln. He was thrilled again to have a small taste of this glory in the Black Hawk War when he was 23.

But one day shy of his fifty-second birthday Lincoln refers to Washington in a less thrilling tone. He is boarding the colorfully-painted train bound to Washington, D.C., to become President. His personal eloquence is unsurpassed in his brief impromptu remarks. This "Farewell" speech stands in stark contrast to all his early speeches, especially the Lyceum Speech that so much reflected his struggles with the warrior archetype and its direct road to the king archetype. We can ask what has transpired for him with his inner warrior and its early glory. He sounds no notes of fight and glory even as he has won the presidency and is about to enter the biggest fight Americans have ever known. The context of this speech begs for a warrior speech. He has won his fight. He is clearly going to have to lead the nation in some kind of fight. There is a field for him to win.

But he says nothing of that sort. He was always loath to speak without prepared notes. This speech was written down on the train after its delivery, by hand, first by himself and then by his secretary, as the fast train was bouncing too much. This speech is about his soul. It is about memory. He reminisces over the heart-warming details of his friendships and family life. It is about place and about gratitude. He mourns leaving them and wonders if he will return. When he does not return the nation mourns him with the same full heart. He shares the national story. He compares his situation with George Washington's. This was every boy's dream, at least every boy of the depth and breadth of Lincoln. But he is not glorious. He is humble. He asks for help, help from them and help from God. This former skeptic defines the mystical presence of God, who stays with them and goes with him. With their help and God's, he has faith that he will not fail. And he doesn't fail. But it is also about not knowing— and he doesn't know. This speech is almost a prayer. He traces his life story, and it is one of birth and death, the births of all his sons, and the death of one. He will be in this stance again at Gettysburg. This has been the turning point of his life. As he gravitated to the national struggle over the extension of slavery he moved personally, in the bosom of his family, from a young warrior to what he calls an old man. He has now passed into being an elder. It was a passive passage, his rhetoric says. He is about to enter the king archetype and with all the wisdom that a true warrior can bring to that new role. Grief over the death of his son is an event the historian who looks only at the Kansas Nebraska Act and the Dred Scott case misses. If we listen to his words we see where his heart is first and foremost; it is with people, the national hope, his family, and with the hope of the aide and presence of God. That is what he says.

The heart is an eloquent organ. Lincoln expresses himself in this short impromptu speech with the beauty that comes easily when a well-read person speaks from a pure heart.

This is what he said, and he doesn't sound like a warrior. We will need to come back again to what went on in him, as well as in the country, to produce this king's prose, his Farewell Address in Springfield, February 11, 1861.

My Friends:

No one, not in my situation, can appreciate my feeling of sadness at this parting. To this place, and the kindness of these people, I owe everything. Here I have lived a quarter of a century, and have passed from a young to an old man. Here my children have been born, and one is buried. I now leave, not knowing when or whether ever I may return, with a task before me greater than that which rested upon Washington. Without the assistance of the Divine Being who ever attended him, I cannot succeed. With that assistance, I cannot fail. Trusting in Him who can go with me, and remain with you, and be everywhere for good, let us confidently hope that all will yet be well. To His care commending you, and I hope in your prayers you will commend me, I bid you an affectionate farewell.

Something is happening here within the powers he had won as the warrior. How could he comprehend himself carrying a burden greater than his childhood hero? How is it that he appeals to God and prayer so readily, now? What happened to Lincoln was not easy, it was not pretty, but it was profound.

To answer the mystery of his transformation we go back to the status of the young warrior Lincoln at age twenty-five. In a certain kind of religious language we could say that the Devil doesn't take a real interest in a young man until he has some power of his own. Innocence is left untouched by the Evil One because, after all, what can a boy do? But a man, a man with ego power! That's a Devil's catch. Turning thirty is a good time for the Devil to take notice of a rich young ruler type. Jesus is thirty, the Buddha is a young man leaving home to be a pilgrim, and Lincoln, at twenty-nine—all three have their mighty battles with the temptations of ego power, or Self Power, as Tolkien calls it in "The Lord of the Rings."

However, the challenge to Lincoln is perhaps greater because of his secular mind. When Jesus is tempted by the Devil he has scripture and his knowledge of God to fight back with. When the Buddha is faced with a similar temptation to kingly power, he has the awareness of the beckoning Holy Man he has seen on the road. But when Lincoln achieves early status, becoming a rich young ruler, a lawyer in the Capital city, with a family and a house, he has only his wits and his Whig Party ethics to gather about him. It is his wits that become his path. He is, he knows, smarter than almost everyone he meets, and so it is the mind, it is reason itself, that becomes the way to insure the new kingdom, the American Republic. Reason has produced Law and reason and law become Lincoln's religion. He even calls it a political religion. But it does not protect him from power, ambition, and the potential betrayals of himself that he encounters. He mournfully, maybe fearfully, recites poetry about the empty vapor of ambition.

Jesus is offered by the Devil, among other things, all the kingdoms of the earth, but the Savior in the name of God turns him down. The Buddha is told he can be the ruler of the united kingdoms, and he chooses rather to be a redeemer of humanity. Lincoln dreams of being... well, let's read on about that in his Lyceum Speech of 1838 when he is twenty-nine. But for now the point is that in his vision he struggles with his temptations without a real sense of religion as a guide or God as his companion. The touch of glory that he felt as a warrior could, and he seems to know this, take him the way of Alexander the Great, Genghis Khan, and the other mighty men of history. He, ironically, is later accused of doing just that, as if he fulfills in his opponents eyes his own worst fears.

The danger for him is that in his secular idea of America there is no King in the way there had been a Divine Right of Kings for centuries. He is more than thrilled by the American Revolution. He believes in its vision, the fulfillment of the English Civil War vision, the Puritan Revolution, the stripping away of the Bishops and the Church from the King, leaving the King as a secular figure. But, as we shall see, this leaves anyone who would be king vulnerable to ruthless power because the check, the balance, of the Bishops and the Church, and even perhaps God, have been removed. Wouldn't the Devil have a field day with a Godless King? Walt Whitman bemoaned this demise of virtue and character in the political men who took up the democratic and secular power of America before Lincoln's election.

Lincoln's grandfather's war and then Lincoln's own Civil War come out of the religious and political history of England. The motto with which the Puritan Revolution fought in 17th century England was: "No Bishops. No King." The Puritans wanted to get rid of the Bishops. To do so meant the King no long ruled by Divine Right. Defenders of the church thought that by showing their connection to the status of the King they would stop the Puritans. But the legacy of the Puritan Revolt meant that in the Colonies between 1760 and 1770, suddenly, the Divine Right of Kings had lost its hold on the mind of the people. The bulwark idea of the Divine Right of Kings went out of fashion as quickly as did men wearing wigs. All this was crucial to Lincoln's view of America as the alternative to despotic monarchies.

However, even before the Bishop-King connection, there was the warrior. The sacred role of the warrior preceded the spiritual status of both the Bishop and the King. The prior, less-spoken, truth was, "No Warriors. No King." In the myths that Lincoln knew, the story was that without the Knights of the Round Table there was no King Arthur. Not Moses and Joshua but George Washington and the English king drew Lincoln into the secular version of warrior and then president. Lincoln was thrilled to know that without Washington, the warrior, there would be no America.

Lincoln loved the American Revolution for its freedom from the king. He had a personal as well as national, indeed, a worldwide vision for this good news to the common peoples of the earth, to be rid of the despotism of the old European monarchies. We see, however, that his existential and spiritual situation is exposed to the free-reign of the naked human ego. In this sense he is more vulnerable than that other spiritual leader that he so remarkably calls to mind, Joan of Arc. That rustic girl is like Lincoln in the extreme unlikelihood of her becoming who she becomes. In Mark Twain's twelve-year project of writing her biography, he acclaims that it is a mystery how she became who she became. She too is a warrior, one who is said to have never actually killed anyone, just as Lincoln did not. A saintly warrior, she still leads men into battle, as did the executive actions of Lincoln. But she, above all, had God as her shield and protector. What would moderate her ego was her iron-clad belief in the divine right of kings. That was her defense of God's rule on earth. Not the man who was the king, but his office was everything to her, it was the incarnation. Lincoln's situation was quite the opposite. Indeed he ends up running for his second term entirely dependent on the generals in the field. Were it not for Sherman in Georgia and Grant in Vicksburg, Lincoln would not have been re-elected. No Generals, No President.

It is interesting to note that the American Civil War repeats and plays out the consequences of the English Civil War. That is the thesis of a book by David Hackett Fischer, *Albion's Seed*. The anti-bishop and anti-king Puritans who fueled that revolution were centered in eastern England. The supporters of the church and the king were located more in the south and west of England. The cultural migration from England to America places those eastern English Puritans in New England and Pennsylvania and those who were on the church and king side, the south-western English, migrate to the American south. Hence the more hierarchical, aristocratic Cavalier Southerners end up once again fighting the descendants of their old enemies, the Puritans, now the Whigs, of the American north.

Lincoln's family, unknown to him, goes back in America six generations. His first forefathers in North America settled in Hingham, Massachusetts, in the early 1600s wishing to be free of the English crown and church. They were from Hingham, England, in the heart of eastern England. That was the Puritan stronghold. Lincoln becomes, in legacy, an American ruler believing in a land without a king, and a government without bishops.

What then, without the King's God, or God and Bishops, or even just the church, would govern his warrior ego and his ambition?

What would lead him to his prayerful, humble farewell speech in 1861? What would govern his ambition was something more than classical republican virtue. No version of Rome, classical or ecclesiastical, fully translated into Lincoln's spirit. But what does lead to the soulfulness of his farewell speech as well as its trust in the national story and the providence of God?

In 1838, in 1845, he was not so humble and he was often a foolish warrior-politician with harsh words and rigid ideas. His face in his first known photograph, a daguerreotype by N. H. Sheppard in Springfield, Illinois in 1846 has an icy emptiness, a slicked-up pose, with only the beautiful intelligence of his eyes redeeming the image. He was congressman-elect Lincoln. His right hand is huge and strong like the axe handler he was. His left hand has his index and forefingers aligned in a pointing gesture that could not have been natural to him. He had become as one who could strike poses and figures. He is about to do just that in speeches against the Mexican War and President Polk. Nobody paid any attention to that grandiose maneuver on his part in Washington, and back home in his congressional district he was widely criticized for being against a popular war. We will learn that he had his reasons. He felt it was done unconstitutionally, and he is beginning to see the connection between the Mexican War, annexing Texas, and the extension of slavery. The northern abolitionists and folks like Henry David Thoreau saw that connection, too.

The man at mid-life is leaving behind the glory of war. This is when he sees the eye of glory as the serpent's eye and the rainbow of glory as raining blood. He is just not caught up in it like almost everyone in his district, and he is forming ideas about deeply moral issues based on his Yonder vision of what American can be. He is striving to be an ethically moderate and reasonable Whig Party disciple, which is not unlike being a secular Puritan. That is his spiritual life at this point. He is a sober man in all regards, and it shows in his dead-pan face. He is not fully a humble man and he has been following his ego-driven "little engine of ambition" insistently. Given the size of his self-image he was not being very successful either. He is more smoldering than on fire. He is posing as a Congress Man. It is hard to see where the spiritual undercurrents of his love of the poetry, of Burns and Byron, would be in this photographed man.

In the Warrior archetype the good warrior has an arch and strained relation with the feminine. He is not the rape and pillage Shadow Warrior, he is the virtuous knight who has a damsel's scarf in his armor and worships her on a pedestal, but hardly relates to her. The book that Lincoln could never finish, *Ivanhoe,* shows the wounded knight having a passionate relationship with the Jewish healer, Rebecca, but a failed one, as he goes off in the end with his ivory Saxon bride. Lincoln would not have known what to do with Rebecca from *Ivanhoe,* unless that had been his feeling for Anne Rutledge, and it may well have been, and it gets buried then with her.

He just had no idea, and he said so, how to handle himself around city women. So when he gets thrilled with Mary's intelligence, wit, charm and plump body, he also lets her ego ambition drive his own. In sharp and foolish newspaper political correspondences he lets her and her women friends write or edit a letter that he is responsible for. It attacks the Democratic politician James Shields. The letters are, interestingly, signed "Rebecca." Being called a liar, Shields challenges the newspaper to produce the author. To protect his lady, Lincoln claims ownership and he is challenged to a duel.

Here is the one time a real sword comes in handy to Lincoln. As the respondent he gets to pick the weapons. As they cross the state border to have this illegal and lethal event Lincoln has, counting on his extra-long strong arms picked the broad sword. The shorter Shields sees his mistake. Lincoln in a comical and shrewd move lops off a tree limb as they are walking to the dueling grounds. That convinces Shields to drop his challenge. Lincoln never gets over his shame at this event. It was illegal, irrational, violent and foolish, and he knows it. His ego and his ambition, and his relationship with the women he is trying to please, have all gotten the best of him. Only his rustic humor with the lopped off limb, playing to his strength, saves his life. Shields himself goes on to become a U.S. Senator in three different states.

The Shadow Warrior and the Lyceum Speech

How did Lincoln get to be this arid way? We see the seeds of his rigid political religion being preached in his Lyceum Speech of 1838. Lincoln did retain his marvelous compassion and mercy in his speeches about temperance. He identified with the unfortunate drinkers with his heartfelt wisdom as to how to respond—not the way the Presbyterians who sponsored his temperance spoke. They would respond not with sympathy but rather with judgment. Lincoln never got judgmental. But when America was threatened, Lincoln grew rigid and reactive. The violence that was along the borders of the expanding country was a serious threat. But more than the Black Hawk Indian threat, it was the extensive lynching and newspaper editor killings and mob violence in Missouri and Mississippi that were serious threats to law and order and to the future of a democratic republic. Lincoln's spirit became one of religious rigidity, in the secular language of law and reason. In his reaction his shadow warrior and the shadow king ego got full play, unconsciously to him but not to us.

The spiritual temptation of the warrior is to let the ego attach to personal power. As a future leader, lawyer and then politician, Lincoln did let his ego get involved. Some early political speeches are sarcastic and his humor is flamboyant and not very funny. As a young boy his humor was fun and sociable as when he held his siblings upside down to walk their muddy foot prints across the cabin ceiling—and then cleaning it all up. When he was older, as President, his humor was often joyous, as when telling young War Department officers a story of just how a picture of George Washington worked successfully in outhouses in the British Army during the Revolution.

But his rhetoric and wit, in mid-life, could be ego-centered in a way it was not in his youth or in his maturity. Early in his adult career, as in his Young Men's Lyceum Address in Springfield in 1838, he has fustian and absolutist language proclaiming shrilly that everyone should "swear by the blood of the Revolution" and never violate in the least particular the laws of the country and never tolerate their violation by others. Using the warrior history, Lincoln falls under the sway of the ego warrior who is arrogant, almost a brow-beater if not a bully. Lincoln was not a Holy Warrior in the Black Hawk War nor by the time of the Civil War was he a crusader, and he boldly opposed the Mexican War. But in mid-life he fell under the young man's temptation of the Shadow Warrior. In his early speeches, especially about the US-Mexican War, as we saw, in his one term in Congress, he is just full of himself as he takes on President Polk, to the notice of no one, in an anti-war speech.

Yet to his great credit Lincoln avoided the passions of war and its license for hate and revenge. He was aware of such dark forces in human nature. In the late 1830s lawless mobs and lynching were taking place along the western frontier, and even the borders of Illinois. Lincoln at this time also struggled to navigate his own passions, his own ambitions, and the urges and the threats they posed. He was never a John Brown, but he understood what made up John Brown and even grander historical figures. Remember, he is a young man standing up with his warrior-engendered ego without any invisible means of support, and without sanctioned visible ones like the local Presbyterian church, which he avoids. In his 1838 Lyceum speech he quite unconsciously reveals his own relationship with the shadow warrior, as well as his own answer to its temptations: absolute allegiance to the law and to nothing less than a religious respect for George Washington and church-like loyalty to the country. As troubled as he is by the lawlessness in the west he thinks, in this speech, that he understands why.

The reason for lawlessness in his generation, he argues, is that they have no glorious revolution to fight for. The glory days are over. All that is left is pedestrian ambition, aspiring to "nothing beyond a seat in congress, a gubernatorial or a presidential chair." But he also reveals an inner sense of himself with a series of exclamations about how unsatisfying these public offices would be to men who have a different sense of themselves. His shadow self becomes evident in his oratorical fantasies about the rule of law and the emergent potential of a dictator. These mere elected political offices would not satisfy a man from "...the family of the lion, or the tribe of the eagle. What! Think you these places would satisfy an Alexander, a Caesar, or a Napoleon?—Never! Towering genius disdains a beaten path. It seeks regions hitherto unexplored. It thirsts and burns for distinction; and, if possible, will have it, whether at the expense of emancipating slaves, or enslaving free men....!"

It is stunning that he could picture the ambitious man as a man going one way or another on this central issue, as if he is speaking with foreknowledge of the Lincoln-Douglas debates where that is exactly what happened: two men with presidential ambitions each willing to do the opposite with the slave question. By the time of those debates, however, Lincoln is almost twenty years older and has found his moral compass and has reformed his unmapped if still mighty ambitions.

What will protect us, he asked stridently in the Lyceum talk of 1838, from men and warriors with this Caesar-like ambition? You can sense the internal argument that is being posed to himself and his own ambitions, not unlike Jesus's encounter with the Devil and the temptations to rule the Earth from the height of mighty towers. Lincoln, understandably, seems a little shaky in his dismissal of ambition compared with the account of Jesus. He asks about the men with the "loftiest genius coupled with ambition," who will save us from them? Only the people, "....it will require the people to be united with each other, attached to the government and laws, and generally intelligent, to successfully frustrate this future dictator's designs." You can see how his faith in democracy also fills in a real check and a real balance to all men—even himself—who have the towering ambition to disdain the beaten path of earlier generations.

Who then, he asks, will sustain the people, what will keep them from the passion of revenge and hate? It was, he argues, not some superior spiritual or religious virtue that may have worked in the past. Lincoln was in many ways a social determinist. The Revolution itself had turned these base human instincts, hate and revenge, against the British rather than against each other, in order to establish and to maintain this noble form of government and religious liberty. The warriors were saved from hate and revenge by a belief in this new form of government. That was the salvation of that generation. But the "silent artillery of Time" has killed that history and there is no way to live in direct continuity with that history now, now in 1838. So what must we do? We must substitute Reason for Passion. "Reason, cold, calculating, unimpassioned reason, must furnish all the materials for our future support and defense." Then with "general intelligence, sound morality...and reverence for the constitution and laws" and a taboo against any desecration of Washington's grave and a faith in this free government that rivals faith in the church, we will... what? We will let the proud fabric of freedom rest.

This is hardly spiritual fulfillment. It was, however, his secular spiritual practice and his secular theology in order to avoid dictatorship on the one hand and lawless mobs on the other. This was a time of spiritual crisis for him, his own passion and ambition, and so he thought also for the country. Eventually neither the abolitionists of the North nor the fire-brands of the South would be so devoted to reason, to Washington, and to law-loving. Lincoln ended up preaching to a smaller and smaller choir and he underestimated the feelings in both the North and the South, until some moral passions and compassions of his own caught up with him and he made war without hate and took up political authority without revenge.

Yet he used sharp wit and ridicule as verbal sword play early in his career, egged on by the one thing he was never at ease with, young passionate women. These are the women he is attracted to, but as we have noted, they nearly end his career in an illegal duel based on some newspaper writing that they did in his name. Eventually he mastered his absolute devotion to the law by an even stronger sense of value rooted in the idea of equality and the humanistic, progressive world defined by the Declaration of Independence. By the time he is married in the fall of 1842, and the woman in his life is called "Mother," he begins to return to his more easy-going self. His Temperance speech of that year shows his perceptive compassion toward alcoholism. Once he has young sons he moves further from the ego voice, if not yet the rhetorical flourish, of his Lyceum talk. He plays with his boys like he played with his fellow militiamen. He was always more at ease with men than with women and eventually he shared a broad range of emotions with a broad spectrum of men.

Lincoln was a young lawyer on the move in Springfield when he gave his Lyceum speech. Four years later when he is about to become a married man, his Washington Temperance speech is different. It is built with the compassionate reason, if not the soulful rhetoric, that we have come to remember him for. In fact, his Temperance speech out-Christians the Christian clergy with his Gospel-based call to compassion, friendly persuasion, solidarity and healing for both the ill and the community. In the progression of his life we see that there is something about domestic life, as troubled as his marriage was, and family loyalty and love that sustains and opens Lincoln in a way that the warrior archetype did not. His Temperance speech, four years after the Lyceum speech, begins to show the pragmatic love in his deepest spirit even while it is still expressed in the bloated language of traditional 19th century public rhetoric. That would change as he gets closer to the bone of life, mainly by way of tragedy personally and his latent passion for the American vision of freedom and equality. The context of his Farewell Speech in 1860 is that he has to leave his domestic life, including the grave of his son, and that opens his heart, and he has to carry the burden of the national trauma, and that opens his spirit. Hence the prayerful prose of those remarks.

Camaraderie: Youthful Fun and Ageless Grief

Now he had enjoyed being a warrior, not really fighting, because he loved comrades. One day while drilling his Black Hawk company, without weapons, he marched them, by mistake, to a standstill in front of a fence and didn't know the close-order drill maneuver to call out to solve this dead end. His solution? He called for his men to halt and he dismissed them for two minutes with the order to reassemble on the other side of the fence! This became his leadership style. It recalls his fun-loving, thinking out of the box, non-hierarchical way to run things. He was an administrator in the same haphazard way. He would find a way out of an impasse through a mix of creative chaos, practical wit, and teamwork: Be at ease, disassemble, and re-assemble, on the other side of the fence! He let common sense and chaos pragmatically solve his oddities as a warrior leader. That good humor and freedom of mind became a hallmark trait as he became, eventually, the masterful

Commander-in-Chief over multiple ego-centric warriors who often could not solve the problem in front of them. It often was Lee's Army that was in front of them.

It is, then, playing with boys, first comrades, then soon with his own sons and youths in the neighborhood, that restores Lincoln's spirit, returns him to his heart. Herman Melville once wrote "Never forsake the dreams of thy youth." In some ways Melville did. Lincoln as a family man begins to make those dreams his keepsake. He lets his boys go wild in his office, unreasonably so. It is his unconscious compensation against the caustic spirit of his highly temperamental wife. In the spiritual life of Lincoln his fellowship with men, especially young men, is restorative and nurturing. Lincoln's spiritual journey is essentially the masculine spiritual journey. His secular spirit is always enlivened by male company. Neighbor boys, his own boys in Springfield, young army officers, and his own two secretaries, Hay and Nicolay, in Washington, all become favorites of his for rough house play and jocular conversation and, eventually, deep shared grief. Men on the legal circuits were a great source of brotherhood and human community.

It is then the deaths of his sons, 1850 and 1862, and the deaths of young men in the war that drives Lincoln to his deepest spirit. His Farewell speech from Springfield is remarkable in its very mention of his buried son, along with his own foreshadowed death. His *Gettysburg Address*, with all its latent imagery of birth from death, follows closely upon the death of his son Willie. All through his adult life, Lincoln's wife Mary was an emotional, intellectual and professional partner for him. Her sorrows and her thoughts must have moved him. He binds himself closer to her as the years go on, in his own fatherly and husbandly way.

It is the death of his son Edward in Springfield that begins the spiritual turn in Lincoln. The change in Lincoln begins not just with the passage of the Kansas Nebraska Act nor his reading of the Dred Scott case and his fears for the country. It begins when his boys are born and one dies. It was at the death of Eddie in 1850 that he started seriously reading theology with books that were shared with him and authored by his Presbyterian minister. They engaged in deep conversations on religious themes. Indeed, Reverend James Smith, and his 650-page book "The Christian's Defense," became favorites of Lincoln. The Presbyterian minister was noted for his appeals to reason not emotion, and he was one who had been a doubter first, like Lincoln. He was to baptize the Lincolns' fourth son, Tad, the only one to be baptized. It was at this time that Lincoln was driven to share the fate of grief with Mary, who was deeply undone by the death of her son. She had lost her father, her only stable if distant parental figure, just five months before.

In 1862 with the death of his son Willie, Lincoln again turns to a highly educated and powerful Presbyterian minister for conversation, consolation, spiritual and theological thought. Dr. Phineas Gurley, his minister at the New York Avenue Presbyterian Church in Washington, tells Lincoln outright that God is a living God and that his dead son is with the living God. In most of Lincoln's speeches when he refers to God it is in terms of "the Almighty" but in his Second Inaugural he uses Gurley's term, "a Living God." On these occasions Lincoln was greatly shaken. He turned to these powerful and intellectual ministers. He opened to a sense of a living God who not only ruled all life but who was eternal. Lincoln's sense of the eternal life of his son Willie, who was himself a religious boy, is twice given him, once by his conversation with the Rev. Dr. Phineas Densmore Gurley. But at the same period of time Lincoln read Shakespeare's *King John* and is struck by a mother's reflection on her dead son, known in a dream. He shares this passage and this hopeful secular idea with some young officers at the War Telegraph Office, and he bursts into tears of grief over his own deep sense of longing and also communion with his dead son, even in a dream. There are always sacred and secular sources to Lincoln's spiritual life.

The death of a child, to the parents, is transformative in any event. For Lincoln, loving his sons was the singularly most transformative event in his middle years, between his law practice and his Presidency. The lover of absolute homage to the law celebrates his boys as little law-breakers. He is extraordinary in his latitude with their wild, playful, and even disruptive behavior. Spilled ink-wells at the office were common as he let them do whatever they pleased, and he would just laugh. These boys would not have their spirit broken as his father had come close to breaking his, or as his punishing and violent wife might do. Neighborhood boys in Springfield would follow him home in little flocks, and ride on his shoulders as if all in a Hans Christian Andersen story. He, like Jesus, was a "let the little children come onto me" kind of a man. We see then, in terms of archetypes, the warrior as a believer in the absolute codes of the law becoming a gentle, wise, playful and extremely flexible man personally, spiritually.

The transformative potential of his grief not only changed Lincoln it became his deep spiritual language for the nation. John Burt reminds us that Lincoln wore a black band on his hat at Gettysburg for the recent death of his son Willie. Burt centers his rhetorical analysis, in *Lincoln's Tragic Pragmatism*, of the *Gettysburg Address* on the transforming new birth of freedom that comes, can come, to the parents of a lost child. "The citizens' watch over their imperiled Republic was analogous to the parents' watch over their dangerously ill child, a touchstone of nineteenth-century fiction....In all these novels of the death of children...the dying children become a source of transformative wisdom to their grieving families." The aggrieved parents can become, as Lincoln calls the nation to become, rededicated to the new wisdom brought about by their terrible grief. In our case the wisdom is that human equality and its maturation was at the root of the Civil War, more than just the restoration of the old Union, or the rule of law, or democratic majority rule. It is then the promise of a living thing, a form of real life, like a child, a re-born nation.

Grief is not compatible with the absolutism of Lincoln's 1838 nearly hysterical advocacy of reason and law, the revering of Washington and the Revolutionary Fathers. Grief and sorrow return him to his mother and his sister and his early love, all gone, make him gentler, restore his silence, and renew that sweetness his step-mother had seen in him. Fatalism, as well, always made Lincoln more compassionate not more bitter. That is one of his unique, certainly signature, contributions to the spiritual life.

More Than a Warrior Among Warriors

The other turn in Lincoln's spiritual life was his rising passion about limiting the extension of slavery. The 1857 Dred Scott decision, and all that it meant in terms of the status of Black people in the country and the future of slavery, blew fire into the embers of Lincoln's deepening heart.

As Lincoln began to see how a house divided against itself over slavery could not stand, his own inner house unified. His ambition and his sense of justice annealed into a terrible swift sword, his pen and his voice. He wrote and spoke with a new light, a spiritual passion that drove the darkness of his early images of dictatorial ambitions away. When someone identifies with what Reinhold Niebuhr called one of the Children of Light, then the Children of Darkness can become the Other. Here is where Lincoln's spiritual life offers another of his unique and signature gifts: he was able to see the darkness that had been in his own psyche in others without hating them as an enemy. Truly he judged not, as he eventually warned the nation to not do.

Particularly the shadow figures for Lincoln's newly enflamed passions would be, first, Judge Stephen A. Douglas from the famous Lincoln-Douglas Debates and then General George McClellan in the Civil War. Douglas embodies all of the cynical expediency and rationalizing that Lincoln had envisioned in his Lyceum speech, and McClellan all of the ruthless ambition that Lincoln no longer had as his pole star. Both Douglas and McClellan were shorter, dark haired, stoutish men. Douglas has been an "opposite" for Lincoln from their early years as opposing political figures in the Illinois legislature. Douglas has been a potential suitor for Mary Todd, Lincoln's eventual wife, and a more expected choice by her family. Lincoln's long and significant battles with Douglas involved a war of intellectual and ethical ideas. The definitive rendition of those enormously significant debates is explicated in John Burt's massive book *Lincoln's Tragic Pragmatism*. Lincoln's battle with McClellan is one between two warriors, one who gravitated to the Shadow Warrior, McClellan, and the other, Lincoln, toward the King.

The Warrior archetype is rooted in physical power, a power we might say, on the ground. Because of his moral and intellectual power we can overlook that Lincoln also must have had a very strong sense of himself as a physical being, starting with an axe in his hands at age seven. He was not afraid to use physical gestures to establish points of view. In a seldom reported scene, some days after the Battle of Antietam, being disgusted with General McClellan's inability to pursue Lee's army, Lincoln turned abruptly as they were walking the fields and left the short, shocked, General in a field alone. Lincoln was tired of hearing excuses. He acted not out of uncontrolled pique but out of controlled purpose. It was an unmistakably symbolic and embodied slap in the face to this tiresome and treacherous general. Upon returning to Washington after this dramatic interview and silent confrontation, Lincoln reported to his aides, "I am now stronger

with the Army of the Potomac than McClellan." There are historians
who think that McClellan might have been willing to use the army
to pull off a military coup and take over the government. Lincoln
had an instinct for such things and he knew how to fight and to win.
That is what warriors are supposed to do.

McClellan, too, was a master of the warrior archetype, not
the least by appearance, and yet with a fatal, Shadow Warrior flaw.
He was greatly loved by his soldiers because he took such good care
of them. Such good care that they were kept out of fight after fight,
but were well-supplied, well-fed, well dressed, and well-protected.
McClellan looked good as a soldier. He was called Little Napoleon
and he had the bearing that was assumed to be that of an elite military leader. One of Lincoln's unintended achievements as a warrior
was his eventual transformation of the image and the reality of the
warrior from West Point and society gentleman to Western warriors,
the plebian, low in his class at West Point, straightforward, Ulysses
S. Grant, and the fierce, harsh, William Tecumseh Sherman. Grant
and Sherman would have fit in with the Clary's Grove Boys in a way
that McClellan never could. Lincoln, simply by being who he was,
brought a new type of warrior, a westerner, into the top leadership
the Union Army. His area of Illinois never had to use the draft and
it oversubscribed its volunteer quotas, even while also being heavily
Democratic, not Whig like Lincoln. In many ways Lincoln was a
western man's man, and the Illinois boys knew it.

McClellan early on was thought of as the ideal military man.
He was handsome, and he took himself seriously, very seriously. He
was proud and that was looked on as a virtue. Were Lincoln to have
taken his own ego seriously he would have been more universally
laughed at. Many soldiers, especially at first, did think Lincoln was
a laughable sight with his dangling legs off a horse and his sad, odd,
face. But his twinkle, his heart-felt good humor and deep respect

for the common soldier eventually made the army a strong base of support. It was crucial for his re-election in 1864. While McClellan received 45% of the popular vote as a Presidential candidate opposed to Lincoln, Lincoln received 55% and the bulk of the Electoral College. Warriors had become a big part of his base.

To care for the fellow soldier is the common warrior's unspoken covenant. Lincoln simply loved other men. He had a good heart for them. The young officers in the Civil War became some of his favorite companions. Soldiers felt this from him. They would record positive observations or snippets of conversation with him in their journals or letters. Perhaps even more than care for each other, comfort with each other is the trait that bonds warriors. The ability to get along, of course, is crucial to a cohort of soldiers. Close-order drilling is a good example. Humor is the oil and the salve for the friction and discomfort warriors feel when forced to be close with each other. Lincoln's phenomenal ability to tell jokes, to crack jokes, to poke fun at himself most often, are traits popular with soldiers and Lincoln exceled at such humor. So not only would he would laugh and joke, he would care and comfort and be comfortable. As Commander in Chief Lincoln was forever bailing out deserters from their just punishment. He wanted these boys to live and have a life and he found numerous ways to help them.

This all started—the jokes, the physical prowess, the fun, the care, with the boys he served with in the Black Hawk War. Those fighters really became his first cadre of voters and supporters upon his return to Sangamon County. At an early election as he began to run for state office, those "boys" would accompany him. You can picture them almost as a gang of body guards. One day one of his supporters was being severely heckled in the crowd. Lincoln stepped down from the platform and took the man, it is said, by the back of the neck and the seat of his pants and threw him twelve feet away.

That may stretch the truth but it is a snappy story of just what Lincoln accomplished for friends as a warrior. And he had Clary's Grove friends there with him, to back him up.

Military people refer to the arena of battles as the war's theater, and it is in the theater of this Black Hawk Indian war that Lincoln met also the professional men he would be able to assume connections with especially later in Springfield. Here future leaders had heard of him, and he them, men who were the leading lawyers and politicians in Springfield where Lincoln was to make his professional stand. Several of his eventual law partners were also leaders in the Black Hawk war and so Lincoln became a member of a circle, a network, that proved essential to his success in establishing himself as a man among men. The warrior cohort, not unlike a religious or monastic brotherhood, functions as a calling place for men to some higher purposes, and it also becomes a network. While Lincoln would jokingly refer to the blood he shed in the war—those terrible mosquitoes!—he earned secular professional status from joining the warrior brotherhood.

Roots of a Deeper Identity

There are, as we have seen, many distinctive traits to Lincoln's spiritual identity. He is an original.

Those traits begin to show as he navigates the role of warrior. He was basically a southerner but never identified with the southern warrior cast. Lincoln was born a southerner who moved to the southerner's enclave in central Illinois. He was never aware of the six-generation deep roots he had back to New England in the 1630s, those ancestors who had come from the Puritan strongholds of eastern England then migrated to New Jersey and Pennsylvania generations before Virginia and Kentucky. But, uniquely, he also never identified himself as a southerner nor certainly with the southern military cult. He failed the Sir Walter Scott test! He could not, as noted, finish reading *Ivanhoe*. Sir Walter Scott was the source of much of the southern mythology of the warrior caste.

Lincoln's father was a yeoman, a carpenter, a subsistence farmer, a hunter and gatherer. He might have been the kind of man Thomas Jefferson envisioned in his pastoral small-farmer Republic, but he didn't think of himself that way as nearly as we can tell. Lincoln's mothers, while both southern women, were home folk devoted to the life of the family, not the manners of Southern society.

Lincoln was a lower-class person compared to the men who were in the class of southern warriors. He became a rising middle class lawyer for the wealthy railroad companies as they built their tracks and made their fortunes across the former Indian west. But before he pursued employment in the cash-economy and worked as a politician and then a lawyer Lincoln was really just a country guy, in the frontier mid-west. His friends were both the Clary's Grove boys, real ruffians who played sadistic bloody games, as well as the debating society men who were doctors and shop keepers with real intellectual interests.

Lincoln walks to us out of the imagination of Mark Twain, flatboats down the Mississippi, steam boat pilots, and a knowledge of and horror at slavery. Like Lincoln, Twain had southern origins and a northern future. Both men worked out their spiritual life moving through the dark forests of evangelical Calvinism, with its melancholy thoughts about God's rule in man's life, to a clearing of skepticism and rationality, and a real longing for faith. Lincoln like Twain had unique and early rustic identifications with merry bands of men that put them more in the Robin Hood camp, not the Sheriff of Nottingham, and certainly not with bad King John. Friar Tuck would have been Lincoln's and Twain's idea of a good clergyman.

In the midst of the paradoxes, roles in life, complexities and near self-contradictions, did Lincoln know who he was? Is there a spiritual thread that he could follow out in the labyrinth of his nature? He is a three-month volunteer warrior who becomes the hands-on Warrior-in-Chief of the Civil War. He is the failed store keeper, a one-event river boat pilot, who becomes the head of the ship of state, not just as a president but as a nearly kingly one, and a liberator with his Emancipation Proclamation. He is a non-believing, rational skeptic, who becomes America's emotional pastoral care-giver in his abundant kindnesses and tender mercies. He then becomes a poetic preacher at Gettysburg and a theological prophet, in his Second Inaugural. What is the thread if there is one and how strong was it?

What was the spirit in the heart of this warrior? As a child Lincoln had shot one wild turkey. He did it from inside his cabin, much like his uncle had shot the Indian that killed Captain Lincoln and was on the verge of killing Thomas, Lincoln's eventual father. When young Abe went out to see his kill he was astounded by the purple beauty of the turkey's feathers and was ashamed of his action. He never killed anything again. Did he have a warrior's heart?

There is a parable told in the Samurai Warrior tradition. A lone Samurai comes rapidly riding into a village lopping off the tops of fence posts with his sharp sword as he gallops by. He calls for all the villagers to come to the public square and show him proper respect. He notes a trail of smoke coming from the chimney of the Temple and realizes the priest has not come out. Banging into the meditation hall, he finds the monk sitting before his Buddha and incense in meditation. The warrior clangs his sword against the door pillar says, "You do not know who I am! I could kill you in the blink of an eye!" The monk turns his head and says, "You do not know who I am. I could die in the blink of an eye." The two men bow to each other recognizing a common spiritual way of life.

Lincoln would have understood this parable—egoless willing sacrifice is the true spiritual code, for both warriors and for holy men. It lies at the heart of the warrior and is its continuing thread. This was the willingness Lincoln grew into as a leader of warriors and as a person. From his griefs, from his defeats, from his marriage, from his theological struggles, from his battles with Stephen Douglas and George McClellan, from all this, Lincoln became one who is willing to die in a blink of an eye, an egoless warrior, a king, and a lover of the world. We shall see it soon in his face.

The Emerging Face of "Father Abraham"

When Lincoln was elected minority President, without a vote or a state from the entire South, he was, even among the northerners, considered a most unlikely of presidents. Lincoln brought something of the American West into the center of national life. He was carried on a demographic shift that was new to the vocabulary of New England, the Mid-Atlantic, and Washington culture. But he also brought a spirit within his person that was unique. As the Young Eagle, as his long-time friend Joshua Speed called him, he soared on new western winds. But he also had large and strange wings of his own.

He was by any account a strange man. It is his own powerful spirit that most accounts for his prevailing. While he was elected Captain of his militia group he was not re-elected. He re-enlisted twice more. He didn't care that he was no longer Captain. He just always loved that he had been Captain. He had no ego-based shame, ever. While never seeing any fighting at all he loved the camaraderie and the occupation. His prospects in clerking and in politics back in New Salem were daunting. He arrived back home from the Black Hawk War on foot. Was he egoless or lost? He said of himself he was like driftwood.

But what of the warrior spirit in him? He had not shot and killed another animal since his boyhood and the wild turkey. He was in no sense a dashing young officer. Yet the gang of tough men, the

Clary's Grove boys, had come to admire him. He was a superior wrestler and a funny and reliable comrade. These are the virtues of the warrior. Something sincere would have been seen in him, and something strong. This would be, then, what the hundreds of thousands of American warriors in the Civil War eventually would see in him.

On a horse reviewing troops he was an oddity for sure. We hardly ever hear of his horse's name; one was "Old Bob." We often hear that Lee had "Traveler," Chamberlain had "Charlemagne," and Grant had "Cincinnati." In the middle ages a knight was not a man unless he was on his horse. Hence a knight unhorsed was unmanned. George B. McClellan had "Kentuck." As we have seen, Lincoln, born in Kentucky, had said he would hold the McClellan's horse if the General would but fight. Lincoln, especially when you add on the stove pipe hat, looked like Ichabod Crane on a donkey not a horse, even at Gettysburg. He was often unable to get his ankles well-covered with pants. On a horse the cuffs would ride up and expose his boots and shins. Many commentators, especially his opponents, described his face and features as almost grotesque. We have only to contrast him with the handsome, compact, well-built, and soldierly General McClellan to wonder what the thousands of men would have seen in Lincoln. Yet even McClellan's men cheered him as he rode by reviewing troops. Soldiers wrote letters about "Father Abraham." Eventually a song was sung, "Here we come Father Abraham, 300,000 strong." While there were serious draft riots such as in New York City even after the Battle at Gettysburg, and serious disenchantment with his leadership and the military direction of the war, including thousands of desertions, he continued to build and gain respect among soldiers and among generals.

This is because at the core of the warrior is heart. Love, egoless willing sacrifice for some cause, and even more for each other, is what holds the warrior and holds warriors together. Warriors would have seen into Lincoln's heart. His many, many clemencies for deserting soldiers testified to his absolute respect for the individual. It was as if he could see himself as one of them, always.

That was not how military leaders were usually seen. Except for Robert E. Lee, perhaps the most loved military leader in American history, the West Point warrior class was lofty. Lincoln was a common man's man. He could see through the ego of his early slew of generals. Many were either full of bluster and over-confidence, intrigue and self-advancement, or chronic hesitation and just plain fear. No one had seen war like this before and no president had been so involved in being the active Commander in Chief. Washington and Jackson had their wars before they were President. Polk didn't involve himself in the Mexican War the way Lincoln did in the Civil War. This war, and a warrior President, was all new to these men. Most of the early generals Lincoln had to work with were either over-confident or strangely paralyzed. There were some remarkable men on both sides, such as former West Point Superintendent John Reynolds, another former Point Superintendent, Robert E. Lee, and Joshua Lawrence Chamberlain, a Congregational minister and professor of rhetoric and classics at Bowdoin College in Maine, in the North. (The noble Lee, the devout Jackson, and the solid Longstreet were in the South.) But there was also real decadence among the northern military leadership, and the common soldier would have seen it, and he would have seen how this odd man Lincoln was not a part of all of that. His originality, his difference, his heart and lack of ego, all became why he was the leader, instead of why he was not. McClellan was the poster boy leader who led by organizing and looking the part. Lincoln led by caring beyond himself and looking very different.

Lincoln had a ready and often a winning smile on his face. We know that the esteem of his fellow men was the supreme need of his youth. You can imagine then his smiling at soldiers in a troop review in the Civil War. There would be, for both to see, the mutual need and recognition between the man at the top and the men at the bottom, needing each other's recognition, approval, respect, and giving it. It was the seeing of "a human eye" that Captain Ahab in Melville's *Moby Dick* most longed for. He cries out to see a human face. Once the crazed and evil Captain lets a tear fall into the ocean. His heart awakens to the memory of the dent in the pillow he'd left in his bridal bed back in Nantucket. He becomes in that moment a human being. It is then he cries out for Starbuck, for what we know he will never see, a human eye. The human face is beyond him. This is exactly what Abraham Lincoln was capable of—to see and to be seen, with a human eye in a human face.

One trait in Keats' concept of Negative Capability is the ability to extend human sympathy to the particular and the concrete. In "Hyperion" he writes that the poet is not a dreamer. Instead, "They seek no wonder but the human face." This is the quality of recognition we find honestly reported by Walt Whitman. Standing like the common man he was, he would watch Lincoln pass by his street corner. There they would catch each other's eyes, see each other's spirit, at least as we read from Whitman and can imagine in Lincoln.

> —I SEE the President almost every day, as I happen to live where he passes to or from his lodgings out of town. He never sleeps at the White House during the hot season, but has quarters at a healthy location some three miles north of the city, the Soldiers' home, a United States military establishment. I saw him this morning about 8½ coming in to business, riding on Vermont avenue, near L street. He always has a company of twenty-five or thirty cavalry, with sabers drawn and held upright over their shoulders. They say this guard was against his personal wish, but he let his counselors have their way. The party makes no great show in uniform or horses. Mr. Lincoln on the saddle gener-

ally rides a good-sized, easy-going gray horse, is dress'd in plain black, somewhat rusty and dusty, wears a black stiff hat, and looks about as ordinary in attire, &c., as the commonest man. A lieutenant, with yellow straps, rides at his left, and following behind, two by two, come the cavalry men, in their yellow-striped jackets. They are generally going at a slow trot, as that is the pace set them by the one they wait upon. The sabres and accoutrements clank, and the entirely unornamental *cortège* as it trots towards Lafayette square arouses no sensation, only some curious stranger stops and gazes. I see very plainly Abraham Lincoln's dark brown face, with the deep-cut lines, the eyes, always to me with a deep latent sadness in the expression. We have got so that we exchange bows, and very cordial ones. Sometimes the President goes and comes in an open barouche. The cavalry always accompany him, with drawn sabres. Often I notice as he goes out evenings—and sometimes in the morning, when he returns early—he turns off and halts at the large and handsome residence of the Secretary of War, on K street, and holds conference there. If in his barouche, I can see from my window he does not alight, but sits in his vehicle, and Mr. Stanton comes out to attend him. Sometimes one of his sons, a boy of ten or twelve, accompanies him, riding at his right on a pony. Earlier in the summer I occasionally saw the President and his wife, toward the latter part of the afternoon, out in a barouche, on a pleasure ride through the city. Mrs. Lincoln was dress'd in complete black, with a long crape veil. The equipage is of the plainest kind, only two horses, and they nothing extra. They pass'd me once very close, and I saw the President in the face fully, as they were moving slowly, and his look, though abstracted, happen'd to be directed steadily in my eye. He bow'd and smiled, but far beneath his smile I noticed well the expression I have alluded to. None of the artists or pictures has caught the deep, though subtle and indirect expression of this man's face. There is something else there.

Walt Whitman's Lincoln is a most unusual man moving along in a clatter of soldiers. The face that Whitman saw, and the face that Lincoln saw, are the faces of men, equal but at opposite ends, involved in the war and the sufferings of their time—spending their hearts and words on the wounded and the grieved. Lincoln always looked for the Confederate wounded men as well in his hospital visits.

Lincoln never thought of himself as a warrior in any continuous way. He emerged as one when he began his adult life free from servitude to his father. He looked like a candidate for Goliath. He had visions of a unified kingdom like David. He loved his fellow men with a natural heart and humor. He had the brains to lead in practical and strategic situations. He had loyalty to ideals that moved masses of people. He began as a warrior and of course he died as a warrior.

His personal physical power was legendary. Once after visiting soldiers and wounded men for many long hours he was asked if he were not tired. This was near the end of the war. He said he felt fine, and took up an axe and lustily went after some chopping to show how fine he felt. He had been mastering this instrument since he was seven. Then he took the axe and held it out straight, at arm's length, without a waiver. After he left several of the other men tried it and no one else could do it.

Several times Lincoln used sheer physical power or physical movement to make his point. In the story we have told, while on the battlefield at Antietam and tiring of General McClellan's explanations for his hesitations, Lincoln dramatically, physically, turned suddenly and walked away leaving the General standing there. Who then was left holding McClellan's horse? There was physical stagecraft and power in his gesture, and just plain physical self-confidence. When Secretary of the Treasury Chase offered his resignation one too many times Lincoln snatched it out of his hands and just physically would not let it go. Often Lincoln bravely would stand in dangerous places to watch military action. There is a story of the young Oliver Wendell Holmes Jr., a tall man himself, knocking him down to get him out of danger. One night when the White House stables caught fire, maybe arson, he raced across the lawn, in his night shirt, and hurtled several bushes to get there in a courageous attempt to rescue the horses.

He had the traits essential to the warrior, physical power, control and a bond to other men. What made him even more trustworthy to the warriors in his life was his hatred of war. This is the real warrior's essential paradox, a hatred of killing despite a skill at it. Early volunteers and political generals have parade-ground emotion in their blood, but battle-seasoned warriors do not. What thoughtful men such as Oliver Wendell Holmes Jr., Robert E. Lee and Joshua Lawrence Chamberlain felt about this war is that there is magnificence to the movements and a rarity of intensity that has its own deep value and pull. Holmes called it the "action and the passion" of this times. But he was also dulled and made cynical about life by war. The twentieth century writer Walker Percy mused that men must love war in some way because they keep doing it. Melville, we know, called it a boy's game. Men do love something about boyhood and most boys "play" war as children. But to most warriors it is a horror in the end. Lee cautioned at Gettysburg, that we must not love it too much. Lincoln loved being a captain, but he did not love war.

Lincoln's early political career, as a one-term Congressman in Washington, took an almost permanently disastrous turn when he took it upon himself to object to the war with Mexico, and to Democratic President Polk's designs for instigating the annexation of Texas from Mexico. Lincoln was strongly anti-war, anti-military glory, the rain of blood, the serpent's eye. Lincoln was not fooled by these ploys nor was he excited by the military expansion of the west into Mexico—an expansion that would eventually raise the pressure to extend slavery and thus the potential for Civil War. If Polk and the

American expansionists had not wanted Mexico it could be argued there would have been no Civil War. From the floor of Congress Lincoln engaged extended legal and logical speeches with also wildly emotional, graphic attacks on the conscience, even the dream-life, of the war-tricking President Polk. Lincoln pictured Polk's brains as being fried in the guilty conscience of a hot skillet. Polk, said Lincoln, falsely accused the Mexicans of crossing the boundary line near Texas. That spot of land that Lincoln featured in his speech became a verbal taunt, "Spots," for him back home where the war was becoming very popular. Most of his fellow political men were in favor of the war and several went off and even died in it. Lincoln was troubled for years by his reputation of being a near-traitor for not supporting America's successful war with Mexico.

An unlikely looking warrior, if still a large man, with no war record, and a history of being truly anti-war, Lincoln made a very strange candidate for being president and commander in chief over a war that cost America 600,000 casualties, casualties he took as his responsibility. In other words, Southern losses were his too. To Lincoln, every Southern casualty was an American casualty. While he never recognized Jefferson Davis by his title, he always considered the Southerner his fellow American. When General Meade did not pursue Lee directly after the Battle of Gettysburg, he said that they had at least driven "them" off of "our" land. Lincoln was furious. He believed and felt the south was no less American land than the north. It is all our land, he fumed. These then are also our losses. That was how he viewed the Southern dead. Gettysburg was a national cemetery even if most Southerners did not feel so. He had moral and practical reasons to be intent on reconciliation and reconstruction of the South. He cared about the future life of the southern warrior, and he had a practical fear of what would happen in the South if the southern society were not re-built. They, the southerners, were his countrymen, and he, whether they liked it or not, was in his mind and in the Constitution, their President. The house was not divided, really. This is the mind and heart of a warrior who has become the king, the ruler of a kingdom.

The war was not just to preserve the one house, the Union. Lincoln added a provision in the final Emancipation Proclamation that had not been in the preliminary document, a provision for what he called "black warriors." That black men could fight for the union and for their freedom was a radical choice that Lincoln made. Two hundred thousand did, and forty thousand of them died. And it made a big, military difference. In an intimate warrior-eye view of the Civil War Lincoln wrote a letter to a friend in Springfield in 1863. He pictured a white southern warrior and a black warrior, "…there will be some black men who can remember that, with silent tongue, and clenched teeth, and steady eye, and well-poised bayonet, they have helped mankind on to this great consummation; while I fear, there will be some white ones, unable to forget that, with malignant heart, and deceitful speech, they strove to hinder it." He could see the war as a warrior would, and he could see the war as a ruler would.

The Archetype of the Grail King

"I am taken captive by so striking an utterance as this. I see in it the effect of sharp trial, when rightly borne, to raise man to a higher level of thought and action. It is by cruel suffering that nations are sometimes born to a better life. So it is with individual man. Lincoln's words show that upon him anxiety and sorrow have wrought their full effect."

— Lord Gladstone, on the *Gettysburg Address*

"Pain and conflict have a meaning: they are the working out of an ideal, and that which they produce is a similar working out. Their excellence consists in the soul which they fashion: and that of the soul, thus fashioned, in its ability to sympathize, understand, and aid."

— John Keats

The movement from warrior to king is deep in our culture, almost as if it were the natural order of things. In the election of 1848 Lincoln gave up supporting his long-time ideal statesman, Henry Clay, for the non-descript Zachary Taylor, a Louisiana slave owner, because he was a General from the Mexican War. The Democrats were running a General, and Generals were electable, and statesmen like Clay were not. Lincoln at that time was himself already deeply unpopular in his own home district for opposing the Mexican War. A warrior for President was in order.

The movement is from warrior to king and not usually from king to warrior. Few presidents are elected in order to take us into war, although some (Wilson, Johnson, the Bushes) do so after the election, but not by becoming warriors themselves. We may want the sword to lead to the crown but we do not openly want the crown to lead to the sword. This is because our expectation of a warrior turned king, a general being president, is that they will know how to make peace and create a safe new homeland. This was the promise of George Washington; it was part of President Eisenhower's World War II legacy to then end the Korean War. These are also promises for change that we enshrine in our religious and cultural myths. Biblically, David was a warrior before he was the king.

Symbolically we expect something about the warrior's sword to change when it is taken into the precincts of the king. As the sword changes so does the one who holds it. The transition from warrior to king is a psychological transformation. But the transformation from king to Grail King is an increase in spiritual magnitude, when the psyche becomes more truly the soul. Such comes with the tale of the sword that will not stop from its own bleeding in the myth of the Fisher King. The sword of constant bloodshed, whether it is imagined as Cain's sword that killed Able, or a weapon that pieced the side of Christ on the Cross, is a sword in need of healing. In the Fisher King myth the suffering of the wounded king is what redeems the sword. We can understand this in archetypal terms as the effect of Gandhi's hunger strikes in stemming civil violence. His suffering, at times, moved people to end Muslim-Hindu violence. The Fisher King myth also points to a confluence of the images of warrior and king. The warrior who turns king, such as Caesar, or the spiritual leader who becomes a certain kind of king, such as Christ, both come together in the Fisher King myth. A myth that would bring such divergent images together, Caesar and Christ, is a myth for our time, and it is one that sheds light on who Lincoln was. Certainly some see him as America's Caesar, others as a Christ-like American.

The story, or myth, of the Fisher King arose in several places in Europe in the 12th and 13th centuries. It is the source from which the King Arthur stories come. It is the story of Parsifal, which means "innocent fool," a country boy, who saves the Grail Castle and its land from the confusion, chaos, and destruction caused by the illness that has befallen the Fisher King. Unless the Fisher King is restored to health the kingdom will decline into devastation and the sword of constant bloodshed will not stop its bleeding. The king will only be restored when the question is asked, "Whom does the Grail serve?"

Innocent Parsifal eventually is the one who asks that question and the answer emerges. He has a long journey to the castle from the country and from his homespun life with his mother, named Heart Sorrow, who taught him not to ask questions. The Holy Grail of Jesus's Last Supper, the Chalice, as well as the sword of unending bloodshed, exist in the Grail Castle where the Fisher King lives. There is an answer to the question concerning who the Grail serves. Only at the time when the answer emerges—that the Grail serves the Grail King, not the people who want the Grail for themselves—will there be health and wellbeing in the land and balance between the sword and the grail.

Parsifal, however, has to be willing to ask the question. When he left home as a boy his mother told him never to ask questions. She also told him not to seduce or be seduced by women and to always know that if he needed food to go to the church. He is the model initiate into the ethics of the patriarchal world. He must leave his mother, avoid sex, go to church and seek worldly glory. Even while he has to leave his mother, his mother admonishes him to stay away from the feminine. He leaves home against his mother's pleading because has seen five knights riding by their country cottage. He is thunder-struck by their glory. Even though he breaks his mother's heart, he does leave. While not finding the five knights, he encounters the Red Knight, a man of ruthless violence, and he eventually kills him. He also meets Blanche Fleur and falls in love with her but forgets her in his ongoing adventures eventually ending at the Fisher King's Grail Castle.

The Fisher King's illness is caused by an event in his youth not unlike the event that caused Parsifal to leave home. He is struck by an overwhelming sense of life, of an experience too wonderful for his young ego to hold onto. As a boy he wandered into a knight's camp that was empty except for a fireplace with a spit on which was roasting a salmon. He grabbed it with his hand and burning his hand put his fingers in his mouth and tasted a magnificent pleasure that he cannot satisfy, comprehend, or cope with. He too is glory-stuck with an appetite that he cannot handle. Thus he becomes a king bereft, lost, and ill.

The answer to the question, "Whom does the Grail serve?" comes when it is revealed that in the center of the castle the Grail and the Grail King abide together. They are in a relationship of deep mutuality wherein the Grail itself serves the Grail King and the Grail King's purpose is to enjoy the Grail. This mutual pleasure is not unlike the original order of creation in the Garden of Eden, nor unlike, in church dogma, the relationship between Christ and God. It is the beauty and wisdom of that relationship, that communion, that brings health to the ruler and to the land.

In this important myth, as we hear from the Jungian therapist Robert A. Johnson, in his book *He: Understanding Masculine Psychology, Based on the Legend of Parsifal and His Search for the Grail, Using Jungian Psychological Concepts.*

> Parsifal is torn between his masculine, sword-wielding quality and his feminine Grail hunger. These two interplay constantly. In the Grail castle the sword that drips blood and the Grail

are held close together. They represent the unification of the man's aggressive quality with his soul, which searches for love and union. Unless they can be brought into balance these two things create warfare in any man. The sword is redeemed when it is drawn into the crucifixion and fulfilling a holy purpose. This is the case with a man's swords-wielding masculinity. It is redeemed only by suffering. Some people interpret the whole myth as a war between the masculine bloodshed and the redemptive feminine, but both are brought into balance at the end of the myth in the form of the Grail King.

The possibilities of the Grail King are the terms of fulfillment to the secular and spiritual story of Abraham Lincoln. To apply the myth of the Grail King, and its symbolic ideas, to the real life of Lincoln is almost impossible. The archetypal role of king is difficult to connect to a man as "un-royal" as Lincoln was personally. His legacy as a man for the common man comes from the deepest qualities of his nature. How do we get a king out of that? A Grail King seems even more impossible.

The ultimate and impossible paradox is the joining of the sword of Caesar and the crown of Christ. There exists a sword that never becomes a ploughshare. Does there also exist a crown of Christ is this world? Lincoln's personality and his mind incorporate numerous paradoxes, and the Caesar-Christ dichotomy is fundamentally impossible to resolve. Yet it is one whose tension is powerfully relevant to our time when America struggles to still show something of the original idea of America.

The Grail King, as an archetype, needs, in American history, to cope with the "un-royal" idea of democracy as well as with the reality of Caesar's sword versus the transcendence of the Christ ideal.

Lincoln would look blankly upon the notion that he and a king had anything to do with each other. Yet, we could remind him that a version of human sovereignty is basic to the origins of democracy in the Greek city state of Athens. The legitimacy of democracy is rooted in an inner value, the equality, of the enfranchised men. Citizens, then, are equal and sovereign. This is, fundamentally, an idea from a spiritual impulse. It is not materially evident. It is a value assumed, proffered, and then believed in. And Lincoln did. He also grew up in the Protestant context in which the priesthood of all believers was abundantly practiced in the frontier churches of his youth. The soul, too, was sovereign, in each person. The King Archetype then, paradoxically, points to the integrity and authority of the person and how that value becomes central to the formation of lives individually and in community. In our time we might express this archetypal idea in the psychological language of an "inner king" in the psyche of everyone.

Democracy could even be the secular fulfillment of the spiritual idea of blessing from an all-loving God in a universe of created abundance. In other words, not only does every person have an inner king or queen but the world is a gifted realm. This too would be a spiritual notion with obvious sources within the Christian vision and Jesus' teachings of the Kingdom of God. The idea of the Kingdom of God in America was a huge part of the frontier spirit deeply known to Lincoln even as he rejected church itself in favor of a more reasonable and enlightened version of these ideas.

Lincoln as a good king, if not a Grail King, might be acceptable to him—although we can certainly see him impatiently waving us off with his big hand or twinkling with bemusement at the ridiculous notion of him as kingly. But, we could argue, the Whig ideal that so moved him into the political world was also an idea derived from the concept of the good king. In the Fisher King and other ancient myths the kingdom prospered when the king was healthy. The whole integrity of the king was crucial to the welfare of the land. His inner orderliness and his creative and procreative powers were crucial to the idea that the land would benefit.

Lincoln would recognize these mythic concepts as classical Roman ideas of Republican citizenship and virtue. Personal and public morality became basic to Whig moral ideals. The spirituality of the Whigs had Puritan roots as well. These were rooted in evangelical Christian awakenings and branched in Abolitionism. Thus, for Whig Americans, in a land where, mythically, there was a sword that would not stop bleeding, slavery, it would be impossible for a good leader to also be a slave owner. The polity of the north and the south became different versions of different virtues. These became drawn and terrible swift swords.

While the idea, itself, of a good king creating a good land might appear superstitious to the rational Lincoln, the good man and good government were in fact guiding principles in his life. These principles he would fulfill. He was an honest man. He was integrity personified. Reason and the Law became the guiding authorities in Lincoln's life. He held these as basic virtues personally and nationally and they had political and spiritual consequences he had not thought of.

We can recognize aspects of Lincoln in the characteristics of the archetype of the king outlined by the Jungians Robert Moore and Douglas Gillette in their book on the masculine archetypes, *King, Warrior, Magician, Lover.* Here is a summary of these early kingly characteristics; they were marked qualities of Lincoln's life:

> The king archetype in its fullness possesses the qualities of order, of reasonable and rational patterning, of integration and integrity in the masculine psyche. It stabilizes chaotic emotion and out-of-control behaviors. It gives stability and centeredness. It brings calm. And in its 'fertilizing' and centeredness it

mediates vitality, life-force, and joy....It looks upon the world
with a firm but kindly eye. ...In its central incorporation and
expression of the Warrior, it represents aggressive might when
that is what is needed when order is threatened. It also has the
power of inner authority....

Lincoln could be this man in his early adoption of the law, and
then reason, as his life guides. His attraction to the Whig party was
not just its policy of national improvement, it was its emphasis, in
a secular way for sure, on the essential relationship between proper
personal behavior and a good government and a good nation. Gillette and Moore continue, "It is the mortal king's duty not only to
receive and take his people this right order of the universe and cast it
in societal form, but even more fundamentally, to embody it in his
own person, to live it in his own life." Whether this is simply called
Right Order, The Torah, the Law, the Dharma or the Tao, it is all the
archetype of good order. It is integrated into the person who leads
and then the people receive the blessing of that integration.

While we may not assume the cause and effect of this inner
and outer law, we may not be as far from these traditional concepts
of human organization as we think. Historians largely agree that cra-
ven leadership in the years before the Civil War contributed greatly
to its happening. We might see then what an ancient Egyptian saw
when he saw the ruler lose his connection to the good way. This is
what Lincoln saw when he looked upon the destructions of the Civil
War. The Egyptian ancient reference here is to the Middle Kingdoms
from Nefer-rohu, quoted by Gillette and Moore. It states that when
there has been a chain of illegitimate rulers who have not followed
right principles then "...the land is helter-skelter...Men will take up
weapons in warfare, the land lives in confusion. ...I will show thee
a son as a foe, the brother as an enemy, and a man killing his (own)
father." In other words, the American Civil War.

In Lincoln's mind the restoration of authority, right order, was his first goal as President. As the Thirteenth Amendment and the abolition of slavery, he was to say "a king's cure" for the evils of the land, so his first order of business was the king's job of restoring order. It was not to defeat the enemy. In fact he never considered the South the enemy, just the wayward brothers who had the wrong idea about how we are to live together, and who also did not have the legal right to destroy the union. Law and order then made up his kingly flesh and blood.

But that just makes him a king, not a Grail King, whatever that is. A leader who is in touch with the Grail King archetype is in touch with more than just the king. In Lincoln the Whig virtues did go deeper than law and order, they went to justice. As William E. Miller points out in his book, "Lincoln's Virtues, an Ethical Biography" Lincoln was a prudent man, and prudence had classical roots, but also spiritual reach. His orderly prudent mind starts with the quality of attention, as noted in Lincoln, even to his awareness of trees, trees he remembered and trees he would see while riding in his carriage around Washington. A prudent person, Miller states, is one who "pays a careful attention to the particular situation in which one acts. In calculating, for example, who to vote for it was pragmatic and more, to not just look at ones hopes dreams and fantasies, but to consequences intelligently understood, to the world out there, outside of oneself." Lincoln, prudently, would not miss the forest or the trees. For example, he was very upset with free-soilers who had cost the Whigs the election in '44. That had led to President Polk and the Mexican War and the potential expansion of slave interests; and that, as we now know, led to the Civil War. He thought them to be imprudent, they simply were not paying attention, attention to election results and to what that would mean.

Prudence and justice lay the ground work for a larger vision. The absence of what we call moralistic narcissism lays the ground work for the Grail King. The Grail king is alert and is, particularly, the one who serves the whole and not the self. While he attends to his own proper personal behavior he is not thinking about himself. He attends to himself so that he can keep his clear vision on the wider community. It is whimsically interesting that a spontaneous youth movement erupted in support of Lincoln's first campaign for the Presidency, a corps of youth across the North who called themselves the "Wide Awakes."

When Moore and Gillette write of the steps in "accessing the king," they mean having the psychological powers of the archetype available to the person. It begins, they state, in having a cognitive distance between oneself and the kingly role one is in. This is the spiritual step of dis-identifying the ego with the role. We see this distance in Lincoln from the very first. When he play-acts and mimics preachers as a boy he shows the distance an actor has from the role he plays. He was the youthful jester showing the preacher-kings something about themselves that they perhaps could not see. When he captures his melon-stealing friends he is not ego-invested in showing them who is boss. He wrestles with Clary's Grove boys' leader, Jack Armstrong, and he either wins or creates a draw, reports differ. But all agree that he shakes his foe's hands, making him an equal in the fight and not a loser or a cheater, which Armstrong may have been. It was never Lincoln's desire to make anyone feel less than him. Lincoln was never on an ego-trip, so he didn't need to become the bully that replaced the bully. Lincoln wanted to be the President, but he did not want to become a President. It was an office not an identity. He says to his young law partner "Billy" Herndon that when this is all over he will return and they will put out their shingle and practice law as if nothing had ever happened. Lincoln is NOT a man who has identified his ego with his office.

What then is the source of a king's or president's greatness if not ego strength? It is, both psychologists and spiritual leaders tell us, a relationship to a greater source. Gillette and Moore say, "That proper relationship is like that of a planet to the star it is orbiting. The planet is not the center of the star system; the star is…. The planet derives its life from the star…. to use another image, the Ego of the mature man needs to think of itself—no matter what status or power it has temporarily achieved—as the servant of a transpersonal Will, or Cause…not for the benefit of itself, but for the benefit of those within its 'realm,' whatever that may be."

That relationship of the individual ruler to a greater power is the theme of the Fisher King myth. Coming to us from the early medieval ages, it is the source of our King Arthur stories, but it is not complete. It is an unfinished myth. Parsifal, the central figure, comes to a kingdom that is in devastation, as did Lincoln. This "innocent fool" is from Wales, the outer lands; Lincoln is from the frontier. He is a rube, not a civilized gentleman or prince. Lincoln was seen by the New England elite as a Parsifal. Parsifal's charge is to complete a spiritual quest that takes him from following the violence and glory of the Red Knight, who ends up destroying life at will, to finding out what has wounded the king. Lincoln was a War President on his way to becoming a Peace President. He, too, by the end, had to ask and find the answer to an important question. It is a spiritual question: "Whom does the Grail serve?" We shall look into that mysterious query. What is the purpose of all this near endless suffering and my role in it, Lincoln asked.

The wounded land—according to that "superstition" we have already named—lies in ruin as a consequence of the king's wound. That is why he is called the Fisher King. The story had seemingly been one of Parsifal searching for the Grail. It ends, not with gaining the Grail, but with gaining an insight into what the Grail is all about, and it is not about having it. It is about learning that it, itself, the Grail, serves the Grail King. What that means is that the Grail and the Grail King are in an I-Thou relationship with each other. They live for each other.

"The Grail King is the image of God, the earthly representation of the divine. The myth is telling us that our task is to learn that the Grail serves the Grail King, not that the Grail serves us," says Robert A. Johnson. An application of this spiritual idea would be to know that Mother Nature is not here to serve us, but that we are here to serve Mother Nature. That reorientation is what cures the wounded Fisher King and brings abundant life back to the realm. The healing is to learn that life is not about us, but we are about life. To Lincoln that was a deep learning that took his life-time and his life. He came to believe that he was a servant of God. He believed that the war, rooted in injustice and inequality, was in the service of God's sovereignty and justice, and that his role and power was to bring order and union back to the nation, charity to those who suffered, and freeing equality to all who lived here.

Not unlike the Ring in *The Lord of the Rings,* power in this myth is not self-power. Power is other-power, power for others. The Grail King is the man for others; the king for others imitates the Grail who serves the Grail King. It is in living the truth of the servant king that the orderly, integrated, self-less king becomes a spiritual leader. If, the myth tells us, we serve our reality, we will be flooded with happiness. What then, in this story, do we live for? If it is ourselves we will be at war, if it is for others and each other, we will suffer, but we will not be wounded, but whole. We will be blessed.

The king, in this spiritual world, is not at the top of the mountain. He is in an inner chamber. But the king is in touch with some high power that is so great that, once upon a time, his original touch with that power had left him wounded, vulnerable. In other words, he feels that from his boyhood on there is a great gulf between himself, his ego-self, and the role he knows he can play as king. Unless he finds a greater vessel than his ego to hold this power he will not bring health and well-being, or peace and prosperity, to the kingdom. Lincoln as a boy felt some call to some greatness. As a middle-aged man that call was his story. Beginning in the 1850s Lincoln was awakened to the increased danger of the spread of slavery from the Dred Scott Supreme Court ruling and an ideology in the words of Stephen A. Douglas of an immoral popular sovereignty ideology. Lincoln had yet to find the larger vessel for his huge talent and ambition, but one vessel he re-discovered in his devotion to the American idea and union. He is Parsifal searching. He is the Fisher King wounded. He will become the Grail King in communion with the Grail.

That grail will be the vessel large enough to hold his powers of being king, of ruling. But, and here's the rub, to grab the Grail is not the way out of the diminished health of the wounded king. Service, not achievement, salves the wound to the boy ego. Why? Because the Grail will not serve us, the Grail will not serve the ego, the Grail will not be put in the service of the kingdom. The kingdom needs to be, like the Grail King, in the service of the Grail. This is the underlying spiritual logic of Lincoln's Second Inaugural Address. He said himself after the address, to Thurlow Weed the political leader, that he knew people did not like to be reminded that their purposes and the Almighty's could be, and were in this case of the long, long war, at odds.

The grail, Robert A. Johnson tells us, is like nature itself, "this great cornucopia...this great feminine outpouring, all the material of the world—the air, the sea, the animals, the oil, the forests, and all the productivity of the world—we assume that it should serve us. The lesson that we have to learn is that this cornucopia of nature does not serve us: it serves God."

The answer to healing the Fisher King's ego wound and the unhealthy kingdom is then that the Grail serves, not us, but the

Grail King, God. As the vessel it is the icon of the feminine, feminine outpouring. The Grail and the Grail King are locked in deep and reciprocal mutuality. Lincoln, as a spiritual being, knew this. Mutual service was both the pragmatic and the spiritual dialectic of his way of being. His language is one way he reveals to us his tacit knowledge of the outpouring feminine in the ground of our being. We see this in the metaphors of the *Gettysburg Address*. Matter and spirit are reciprocal in him and seem, ever since his boyhood at Pigeon Creek, to have been so. While he hated working the plough he was formed turning over the earth to help his mother and father and sister to live. When his mother died he helped his father make the wooden box to put her into the ground on the small hill just over from where they had their cabin. His sister died in child-birth.

So when he comes to Gettysburg to dedicate the grounds as a sacred place—a burial ground and a birthing place—he knows deeply what this means. Even though it was four score and seven years ago that our fathers did what they did, what they did was feminine. Like mother earth herself they "brought forth," they gave birth. That is what Mary does in Luke's Gospel. She brings forth Jesus, as Lincoln would have read in the King James Bible. The Woman in the West in Revelations also "brings forth." Lincoln was ridiculed in the papers for his gynecological imagery. It was not lost on people what he was saying. These founders of a nation had given birth to something that was conceived, conceived in a spiritual place. That place is called the idea of Liberty. When a child is born in the Bible they are taken to the Temple, as was Jesus taken to the Temple, to be dedicated on the eighth day. The creation of a nation so conceived then also has been dedicated, dedicated to a great idea, and taken to that temple: the idea that all men are created equal. We have here images, his nouns and his verbs, of birth and words that echo baptism and Biblical consecration. But, says Lincoln, we cannot dedicate, consecrate, or hallow this place where this re-birthing has happened. Why? The birthing blood has been brought by the men who died on the ground. The fragile nation and its ideal have almost died, and much death has come. Death and birth are deeply connected here, as they were in Lincoln's life history. The killing blood and the blood of the dying have changed the goal of the warriors' journey, the warriors' goal of winning. Something more sacred than winning has happened. The power of sacrificial love makes a rebirth, a rebirth of freedom, possible. Sacrifice has done this, and the value of the idea that has held. The original order, the conception of the nation, has held. Liberty and the proposition of equality have held. We can assume that the sacrifice of both sides has done this, because it is for something greater than either side. Those who lost their part in this battle are, in Lincoln's vision, still part of the testimony of America. By failing to make their vision hold, the larger vision, the Union, does hold. In Lincoln's vision, and it is the vision that has held, it was neither southerners nor northerners who died in Pennsylvania, it was Americans who died in America and ultimately for America. The fragile child called Liberty could so easily perish from the earth, but it has been, like the Fisher King himself, restored by the Grail, the generative outpouring, serving the Grail King, God. The fragile life and frequent death of the child, as John Burt points out in *Lincoln's Tragic Pragmatism*, was a major 19th century literary and cultural motif, often seen as the transforming event in the parent's life and the re-creation of their spiritual worthiness. This was in the air in Lincoln's time.

This is all, of course, a mystical vision. For all his distancing of himself from Christianity, Lincoln has expressed himself, in these most crucial words of his, in the symbolic language of the penultimate Christian experience, rebirth. Of course Jesus himself took the images of birth and rebirth from the sacred feminine. Lincoln could have chosen words for that paramount Christians idea, resurrection. We remember that Lincoln is a secular spiritual person. The natural and the feminine imagery are represented in his secular mind and give his words meaning beyond the Christian community and its doctrines associated with the resurrection of Jesus.

It is a vision that is incarnational, the world of matter and the world of spirit are incorporated. In such a vision things are not simply as they seem but rather are seen for their spiritual reality. Life serving God is the same kind of reciprocal mystical vision we find in the Hebrew Bible, in the Prophets, in the Psalms, even in the Prophet Muhammed when he saw all of nature and all of life, even the ships passing on the sea, as serving God and God alone.

How Lincoln expressed his version and his vision of what happened at Gettysburg comes in a language of image and symbol. As John Henry Cardinal Newman believed, such expressions come from an imagination held within the capacities of reason. But it is a language not based solely on sense perception, but on what is imagined. This of course is the deep capacity of Yonder that we have seen in Lincoln. It explains his remarkable ability to hold together paradoxical opposites. As Christopher Pramuk points out in his book *Sophia,* this is the heart of the kind of wisdom that the contemporary religious writer Thomas Merton saw in "the hidden attunement of opposite tensions." Opposites even to the highest degree, of evil and good, have a unity in such a vision and the words that express that unity are imaginal, poetic, and religious.

We have seen the role of imagination that John Keats saw in poetic expression. His contemporary, Samuel Taylor Coleridge, with whom Keats had differences, also understood imagination to be a mode of perception. "It dissolves, diffuses, dissipates, in order to recreate," creating an order of reason that enlarges and reorders perception through creating and mediating words. Hence the poetry of the

Gettysburg Address, and it has been scanned and read as sheer poetry, serves the role of religious symbol. Life and even these deaths are the outpouring of the Grail and they consecrate the earth and serve the Grail King. Lincoln's vision is broad here. It can be seen to say that all the men who died at Gettysburg, all those who died in the Civil War, were serving God. Of course their ideologies were different, the sides they took. Yet we see that Lincoln never took ideology as his final view, nor do spiritual visions take ideologies as the ultimate truth. There is something about human beings, north and south, black and white, that Lincoln valued, held sacred.

In this spiritual view the king is never the redeemer, the Grail is never the object to the kingdom, the Grail is to serve God and God is the redeemer. The Biblical tradition, in the voice of the prophets, always makes this distinction between king and redemption. It is why King David has to answer to the Prophet Nathan. In the story of Jesus it is why Jesus does not take the secular crown at the beginning of his ministry or at the end. The king can never be the Grail King, and this Lincoln knew. He was to serve the Grail, and for him the Grail was the conception of democracy. When the freed blacks in Richmond tried to kneel before him he quickly made them rise and told them only God is knelt to. He meant it. Both in Richmond and on the "River Queen" returning Lincoln was not the Grail King, not God, only a good king.

The King Archetype

As I Would Not Be a Master

This was one boy who would not be king. Lincoln did not have much hate in him, but one thing he hated, as he hated slavery, was the idea of the king. "Medieval despotism" became the code for all that was wrong with civilization in Lincoln's mind. Yet what was the biggest, strongest, smartest boy in any neighborhood to feel but that he was destined to be great. In the patriarchal Old World the greatest one was, of course, the king. However, what flowed through Lincoln's veins more than any other thing was that this was a New World.

It was not the sword "Excalibur" that young Abe would pull from a rock to anoint his fate, but the axe. Even at the age of seven that was the instrument to make this new civilization grow. Only the rifle vied for that role. Lincoln always chose the more creative instruments, the axe and then the pen, over the weapons of rifle and sword. Although it was a broad sword he chose in his infamous near-duel. Recall he got out of that lethal ritual by extending his long arm, with its broad sword, and suggestively lopping off a limb of a tree as he and his short opponent marched to the dueling grounds. His short opponent saw his fate when he saw the tree limb fall. Comic irony often proved Lincoln's strong suit. He became America's king as much as jester as by warrior.

To the American Founders "the King" was also the root of all evil. Lincoln drank deeply from their Enlightenment cup. More than Caesar or Arthur, it was Cicero and Washington that shaped Lincoln's mind, even while Aesop's fables, the Psalms of David, Shakespeare, and the Parables of Jesus shaped his heart. Almost all the roles in Shakespeare defined his social world and his inner landscape. As a true Shakespearean believer Lincoln saw that all roles made the play. He became adroit at playing with his own identity from a whole cast of characters. Psychological agility made him a most successful king. King he had to become. Archetypes, like The King, work as fate as much as instinct. The Founders, after the failed Articles of Confederation, put much of the king's power back into the Constitution. Lincoln was to put the legitimacy of that power more into the hands of the people.

King He Had to Become

A girl from Lincoln's Indiana youth remembered him saying that he would become President. It was during those years that Lincoln shamelessly imitated the local preachers by standing on a tree stump and mimicking them, to the hand-clapping joy of his many young friends. Lincoln was his full six feet four inches as a young teenager. He was a tower. Boys of his ilk recalled being "captured" by him as they stole family melons from the fields. Lincoln was a dominate person, tallest one in his family and exuberant in his fun making and flawless in his helpful obedience to his powerful stepmother Sarah. He was a born leader, much to the competitive fury of his short, stolid father.

He was of the stuff male legends are made. He could have been Young Arthur, or in the cohort of Beowulf, a friend of Gilgamesh, or one of those giants who travelled in American tall talk, Pecos Bill or Paul Bunyan. Lincoln was not only a nearly mythic being in real life, he was shaped by the myths of history and myths of culture even unknown to him. He was big and America was big and getting bigger. He was a born ruler and Shakespeare's plays were full of rulers, good and bad, mostly tragic.

Lincoln had physical courage and he took initiative. When his little dog landed in the river as the family was migrating to Illinois in Lincoln's 20th year he quickly jumped into the water and swam to save his beloved fife dog. In Illinois he was chosen by the other young men as the natural wrestling-match challenger to Jack Armstrong the powerful leader of the tough Clary's Grove Boys. When a flatboat he was taking down the Sangamon River ran aground on a sand bar he quickly moved barrels, drilled a hole in the bottom of the boat, releasing the water flow and rebalancing the boat off of the sand bar—all to the astonishment of the neighbors watching this on shore.

He had mental courage. In New Salem he wrote a treatise on his religious, his anti-religious, views and he actively debated in the prestigious local men's intellectual club founded by a Dartmouth doctor. Of course he read, read, and read. Ideas did not scare him and not knowing something made him furious.

He was bold in his shy approach to older women, seeking maternal-like relationships. He was bold, as we have seen, in his leadership of young men in the Black Hawk war. He was a psychologically and socially strong person. He was not depressive, he had great agonies and ecstasies. He was essentially motivated by spiritual forces like love, equality, the desire to rise, and the idea of America. He knew how to make friends, earn respect, and enjoy life.

Lincoln was then an abundant young man who would, despite himself, become a king. He also had a deep desire to please people and to be worthy of their trust and esteem. He would go to the ends of the earth—usually long miles of walking—to repay a favor, earn the right to a job, or to respond to another human being's need. He was a young man who would be the Good King because he was incorruptible.

By the time the "little engine," of his ambition, as his law partner Herndon called it, got him into elected politics he used intuitive humor, sarcasm, and wily ways to win at the minor political tussles of the day, tussles that really contained the major political issues and divisions of the growing American country. In his Young Men's Lyceum speech, as we have seen, in his thirties Lincoln psychologically expressed his dark knowledge of ambition and its ruthless qualities. Only Reason and his natural humility kept his inner King in check. But still he would be as much a king as his beloved democracy would allow him to be. It was idealism—his conviction that the expansion of slavery would ruin America—that made him the challenger of the great Stephen A. Douglas in their famous debates. But it was not ambition to rule that made him challenge the most powerful man around. Moral passion stoked the firebox of his inner King, making the little engine of ambition a great locomotive of executive power.

The political figure whose ideology Lincoln most opposed was Andrew Jackson. Lincoln believed in the new economy of wage-earning individuals and in national improvement through capital investment, including government investment and tariff protection for manufacturing. Jackson's political mythology was of the old agrarian South. He fiercely opposed a national bank that would regulate and fund the national improvements that Lincoln and the Whig Party sponsored. Yet Jackson became the target of those who thought he abused executive power. Cartoons of "King Andrew" were aplenty.

We know that enemies become alike in ways that are not visible to them, as they wrestle with each other. How then did Lincoln become like "King Andrew?" How is it that in another generation political cartoons pictured "King Abraham, the Despot?" How is it that a local Maine newspaper editor would liken Lincoln to Genghis Khan, building an empire with the skulls of his conquered foes? In the unconscious, where archetypes are held, images of good and evil, icons of black and white, can be seen as mirrors of each other.

Any close reading of Lincoln's life reveals him to be intuitively, even spiritually, aware of the fundamental mix of opposites. His joking shows us this. The dark side, the unconscious side, is initially accessed in humor. Humor brings up the opposite of conscious expectation. It is in Lincoln's quick wit that we first see how deeply he could see into opposites and expose the pretenses of conscious cloaking. He would, for example, rather puncture the pretentiousness of his General McClellan with a joke than with an angry assault.

Down in the murky soup of the unconscious there is also the profane and the obscene. One of Lincoln's jokes about McClellan, about his infamous delays in battle, was because he had, said Lincoln, a bad case of the "slows" Lincoln's pun off of a bad case of the "runs." Lincoln shows his ability to shape a clear insight with the rough and shady edges of bawdy humor.

He is at home in the ethereal upper and earthy lower worlds of Shakespeare. He is able to outwit the blunt and dangerous, like General Fremont's impolitic wife, as well as the disciples of rectitude and righteousness that surrounded him, such as his Malvolio-like Secretary of the Treasury, Salmon Chase.

Early in his career Lincoln was able to be cynical and satirical to a lethal degree. As President he softened his tongue into humor and irony, but he never lost his insight into a dark character who was all dressed up in acceptable clothing. He could always see a pure soul dressed in dishevelment.

Nowhere do we see Lincoln's mind playing with dark opposites more than in his Lyceum speech of 1838, so revealing of the Shadow Warrior. We have seen how he pictures, in what seems almost to be a dreamscape, the unrestrained ambitions of a man who would be excellent, who would stand out from the crowd. Clearly this would have been a trait Lincoln would have had a dim awareness of in himself. The expansion of his ego as a Shadow Warrior would then move darkly toward the role of the Tyrant King, "an Alexander, a Caesar, or a Napoleon."

Lincoln sees how, in the darkness of the shadow ego, right or wrong makes little difference to the ambition that would rise. The scholar and literary critique, author of the Civil War and Lincoln book *Patriotic Gore*, Edmund O. Wilson compared Lincoln to Napoleon and Bismarck. In this speech Lincoln's sees both the potential for an evil king and for a civil war lurking in the future.

Recall that Lincoln is the grandson and namesake of a Captain from the American Revolution. We talked, in our discussion of his warrior archetype, how much being chosen "Captain Abraham Lincoln" was a singular thrill in his life, by his own account. No such glory awaits him now, he fears. The Warrior archetype has run its course for him. Only the King is left. Lincoln's thinking here is not unlike the real life haunting reveries of another nineteenth century figure, Herman Melville, whose grandfathers too were Revolutionary War officers and luminaries of real distinction. Melville places this curse of former greatness on his benighted hero, Pierre Glendenning, in his novel *Pierre, or The Ambiguities*. We see then two men in the same generation, Lincoln and Melville, both haunted not only by Calvinist determinism and melancholy, but by shame over the lack of glory since the Revolutionary War.

The point here is to see how close Lincoln, in this speech, was to feeling and knowing, even if unintentionally, how the unredeemed warrior can lead to the Shadow Warrior or the Tyrant King in both his psyche and his generation. The only good "king" over Lincoln at that time was Washington. His father, Thomas, had almost always been a tyrant. He solved the king's identity for himself with an absolute worship for the positive good king, George Washington. Lincoln held the icon of Washington as his shield against his own potential of ruthless ambition. Washington, he seems to scream, is one whose grave we will never desecrate with our feet and with whom—he intimates—we will arise when the "last trump" shall awaken Washington from his long sleep. This resurrection faith in

Reason and Washington is Lincoln's psychological guard again the dark identities that he is aware of in a person of genius who, like himself, has ambitions for esteem and greatness.

Lincoln, a quarter of a century later, ruminates over the king and the kingdom of darkness once again. This time he is aboard a steamship coming back from seeing the horrors of the defeated Richmond, a capital he has indeed torn down. He is also completely humble at this point. The suddenly freed blacks in Richmond want to kneel before him as he walks in the rubble. He bids them rise immediately and says only God deserves such worship, praise, and gratitude. He walks neither as a king or a god. He is totally sincere about that. There were blacks singing a hymn that had these words: "No force the mighty power withstands of God, the universal King." There was a soldier from Connecticut who said they were greeted more as Roman Emperors. It was also said that there was a rifle pointed at him out of an upstairs window as he walked the streets. Did he see it?

Back on board the "River Queen," he shares with his fellow passengers as they return upriver to Washington long recitations and reveries on the death of a king, King Duncan in *Macbeth*. Lincoln holds forth on the guilt that would attend such regicide. He understands both sides, all roles, in this story. Even, as John Wilkes Booth is approaching, he believes in a divine order that assigns guilt and glory as it will. One feels that he is satisfied, in a deep if troubled way, over his own journey, fulfilling what would become the legacy of, yes, a good king.

Lincoln as Spiritual Poet

"This was like a sacred poem. No American President had ever spoken words like these to the American people. America never had a President who found such words in the depth of his heart."
- Carl Schurz, on the *Gettysburg Address*

He was the heartbroken lover of Anne Rutledge. His unbearable grief at her death spilled out in this image: rain and snow falling on the mound of her grave. He could not stand the thought of it raining on her ground-covered body, he said. But, we must see, his heart did gravitate to the image his mind had made. Lincoln was, whether he liked it or not, a poet. Let us look at Lincoln the poet.

Poets, we know, live in a world of words. As a boy he was taken with his hand-written name "Abe," and was said to have remarked, "Don't look a blamed bit like me." Also as a boy he wrote, "Abraham Lincoln, his hand and pen, / He will be good but God knows when."

Scan it. Is that a poem? Yes, iambic tetrameter. The poet's mind reflects on the mystery of language, such as one's name, and the tenuous relation those letters have with the body one lives in. That is the stuff of poetic thinking, and it is the first language we know of from Abraham. He liked his long name.

This poem also comes to us from his early youth. "Abraham Lincoln his hand and pen, he will be good but god knows when." He did not capitalize god.

We see his unusual psyche, this boy struggling with many things, the role of language to life, the relationship of his personal identity, "Abraham," to reality and even to morality. He makes unusual references to himself in the third person. This is something we know of as a spiritual practice in Hinduism. It is also a mind-body skill for centering and calming the self.

Huston Smith in his classic book originally entitled "The Religions of Man" on world religions says, "If the yogi is able and diligent, such reflections will in due time build up a lively sense of the abiding Self that underlies his phenomenal personality. The two will be distinct in his mind, related as oil and water, not milk and water as formerly. He is then ready for the third step which consists in shifting his self-identification from the passing to the eternal part of his being. The most direct way of doing this, of course, is simply to meditate as profoundly as possible on one's identity with the Eternal Spirit, trying to think of oneself as such even while going about the tasks of the day. This, however, is not easy; it is a high, exacting art.... An effective way to do this is to think of one's finite self in the third person. Walking down the street, the yogi, instead of thinking 'I am doing this' should say to himself, 'There goes Jones down Fifth Avenue.'" He should even try to visualize himself as seen from a distance.

This self-distancing consciousness is evident in Lincoln even as a youth in his very first recorded handwritten words. It is the same "witnessing" consciousness that leads him to be able to conceive of the rain falling on his beloved's grave. The mind is both separate from so-called reality, but is ironically able to enter into the reality of The Other in deeply aware and self-identifying ways.

The technique of third-person self-dialogue is not only a mystic skill in Hinduism, it is a skill taught in Cognitive Behavioral therapy, in Mindfulness Meditation and even in sports psychology as a motivator. The professional basketball player Larry Bird (also, like Lincoln, from southern Indiana) was able to see himself and the whole court all at the same time and into the next moment.[8] This is mystical vision and it is the essence both of a spiritual being and a poetic being.

Easily overlooked as just cute or whimsical, this consciousness in the young Lincoln is remarkable and a step in his increasingly spiritual and poetic consciousness. He is beginning to see himself objectively. He grasps the mystic sense that his persona and the reality of the world around him are both somehow separate and yet connected to his life. He is Abraham and there is the world of what things look like. Are they the same from the same material nature? Is he just the thing he looks like, or is there something else about him that is true? Does he look like his name? There also is morality. What does it have to do with him? Does his humor, self-irony, say yes or no, or maybe, or both? His dialogue between his inner self and the outer world ponders it all.

Poets are touched with this ambiguous connection to the world and themselves. But they also use the world of words to write about it. As a young Whig Party campaigner in 1844, visiting back in his "unpoetical" (by his terms) southern Indiana, he was inspired to write a long and well-crafted poem on his favorite topic: a melancholy reflection on the passage of time and the futility of human effort.

In the very poem he sees his childhood home. He ranges the fields with "pensive tread," the woods and fields where he once was with the "playmates that he loved so well."

This outer world that he loves is held in memory, and in the woods and fields. It is the loss of people that most grips his heart,

---

[8]   A great musician plays himself rather than the instrument, and the skillful soccer player plays the entity of himself, the other players, and the internalised and embodied field, instead of merely kicking the ball. The player understands where the goals is in a way that is lived rather than known. The mind does not inhabit the playing field but the field is inhabited by a "knowing body," writes Richard Lang when commenting on Merleau-Ponty's views on the skills of playing soccer. Pallasmaa, Juhani, *The Eyes of the Skin: Architecture and the Senses,* pg. 71.

and yet the containing presence of the fields and land sets the context for his poetic expression. The ocean-like land swells and dips, and to him it was a bleak place. Much of the land was thick virgin forest when he came to it at the age of seven.

How does thickly forested land work upon the consciousness? Is there a spirit and poetry there?

We have talked of Rabindranath Tagore and his book *Sadhana, The Realization of Life*. He starts with the history of the Indian land as the origin of the spirit and the poetry of India. The primeval forests that he describes could just as well be that other Indian land we know in America, the millions of acres that had been ceded by the defeated American Indians to General William Henry Harrison and the new Republic. Soon the Lincolns would come to Indiana, in 1816. That was the year Indiana became a state and thick dark woods began to be cleared. Was there spirit and poetry in that primeval forest as well?

About spirit and land Tagore writes, "When the first Aryan invaders appeared in India it was a vast land of forests, and the new-comers rapidly took advantage of them. These forests afforded them shelter from the fierce heat of the sun and the ravages of tropical storms, pastures for cattle, fuel for sacrificial fire, and materials for building cottages."

One thinks of the four Lincolns sheltered under huge trees in the thick forests of southern Indiana living in their three-sided lean-to and then a log home. Southern Indiana is near the same latitude as Madrid, Spain. It is hot and at that time there were tropical-like birds everywhere, although not so near the Equator as India.

"Thus," and we have stressed, Tagore concludes, "in India it was in the forests that our civilization had its birth, and took a distinct character from its origins and environment." Once again a poet reminds us of the connection we have from the land to our spirit and to our words. As civilizations are born in a land and poets speak of the spirit of that land so Lincoln's Yonder vision is rooted in the forest land of Indiana and the prairies of Illinois. From the point of view of the land his poetry and his moral political vision are of one spirit.

Tagore states that the early aim of these settlers was not to expand control over the land but to expand their consciousness into it. This is the goal that we see working in the young and growing Lincoln. He was certainly a part of the secular mode extending civilization. But Lincoln adds to the American spirit of expansion and control a spirit of expanded consciousness as well. We see this in his desire to limit how, the way, America grew. We see another spirit at play. Consciousness of a certain value was more important than sovereignty over new land. This was a spiritual insight first before it became his political and moral position against the extension of slavery into the Nebraska Territories. His was not the mind of Senator Douglas, who simply wanted to find the best way forward into expansion. Lincoln wanted to find the better way forward in time, the moral way forward into the land. We can feel his spiritual roots in the land at work in his spirit. Land without expanded human consciousness is not worth having. Lincoln didn't love the land; he loved how people could be on it and with it. To Lincoln the American land was a new and awesome possibility. It formed his language, poetically and politically.

We see the spirit that Tagore celebrated in his Indian history echoed in Lincoln. Tagore says, "To realize this great harmony between man's spirit and the spirit of the world was the endeavor of the forest-dwelling sages of ancient India." When you are alone in the forests and on the prairies you have a need to think about the spirit of life and how you might live in harmony with the greater spirit of the world, or not. The size of such wilderness itself accomplishes one of the initial stages of spiritual formation, the annihilation of the ego, a holy sense, an awe, of the finite person in the infinite world.

We don't think of Lincoln having been a forest-dwelling sage, but, miraculously he was both that and someone who could become the nation's leader.

Yes, says Tagore, kingdoms came to India, but even in material prosperity "...the heart of India ever looked back with adoration upon the early ideal of strenuous self-realization, and the dignity of the simple life of the forest heritage...." Domination was not the goal, but rather a harmony with nature so that thoughts can flow, power be expressed, in a spirit that is in sympathy with the world.

Lincoln continues to hold echoes of this consciousness throughout his life, even into his presidency. His instinct for harmony, his modesty of spirit, his deep desire to include, not exclude, these have no necessary book-learning origins. We can look to his poetic spirit and his life with the land for such inspiration, and Tagore is one who can make explicit how this happens.

He goes on more fully to say, "The first invasion of India has its exact parallel in the invasion of America by the European settlers. They also were confronted with primeval forest and a fierce struggle with aboriginal races. But his struggle between man and man, and man and nature lasted till the every end; they never came to any terms. In India the forests which were the habitation of barbarians became the sanctuary of sages, but in America these great living cathedrals of nature had no deeper significance to man. They never acquired a sacred association in the hearts of men as the site of some great spiritual reconcilement where man's soul had its meeting-place with the soul of the world." Except, we say about America, in some of our better poets and thinkers and in the rare political man, Lincoln.

"In the making of him, the element of silence was immense," says Carl Sandburg in his "Prairie Years" volume of Lincoln's biography. Sandburg, recall, is the one who gives us the crucial word "yonder" for the sense he perceives in Lincoln, a sense we can find at home in the expanded consciousness that Tagore finds in his Indian ancestry. There was, deep in the culture of the early settlers, a sense of the Sabbath as much as there was a sense of the struggle to exist with and from nature. Sandburg gave voice to that Sabbath and Yonder spirit of people on the frontier and the prairie. Sandburg, often scorned for this, uses intuitive imagination to find the images that explain the spiritual context of Lincoln, the kind of rooted context Tagore finds in India, its land, formation, and early history. What he imagines is consistent with the spirit we find in the many biographies of Lincoln. What we see here are spiritual roots. Words we used about Lincoln's mother now tell us about the land, and time itself. Sandburg writes,

> Beyond Indiana was something else; beyond the timber and underbrush, the malaria, milk sick, blood, sweat, tears, hands hard and crooked as the roots of walnut trees, there must be something else.
>
> After a day of plowing corn, watching crop pests, whittling bean poles, capturing strayed cattle and fixing up a hole in a snake-rail fence, while the housewife made a kettle of soap, hoed the radishes and cabbages, milked the cows, and washed the baby, there was a consolation leading to easy slumber in the beatitudes: 'Blessed are the meek: for they shall inherit the earth…Blessed are the peacemakers: for they shall be called the children of God.'
>
> The footsteps of death, silent as the moving sundial of a tall sycamore, were a presence. Time and death, the partners who operate leaving no more track than mist, had to be reckoned in the scheme of life. A day is a shooting star.

Sandburg, of course, is reading back into Lincoln's origins, and he is reading from the evidences we have from Lincoln's life. One such evidence is the poetry Lincoln wrote as a boy. It is here that we find some of the images that Sandburg would use to reconstruct the atmosphere of Lincoln's early life. Here we see young Lincoln had copied a rhyme:

> Time! What an empty vapor 'tis!
> And days how swift they are:
> Swift as an Indian arrow—
> Fly on like a shooting star.

In poetry Lincoln found a way to know what he was silently learning. He would know time and the mercilessness of its means. The Indian arrow, he would learn, had taken his Grandfather. And the Milk Sick his mother. Childbirth would take his sister. Lincoln was becoming a sage in the forests.

Not all historians and biographers of Lincoln pay as much attention to land and spirit and how they shaped the language and mind of Lincoln as does Ronald C. White. In his award-winning biography he takes us deep into the prairie time of Lincoln in his mid-career life. In the circuit riding years of 1849-54 he shows Lincoln reconnected deeply to his inner life, his solitude and his emersion in the land. This time it is not the hills of Indiana and the woods, but the prairie. Lincoln spent months of each year riding in his solitary buggy over a court circuit of 15,000 square miles, the size of Connecticut. Here the law was still practiced with argument as much as citation, and the wisdom of the judgments was directed by three books: Blackstone's legal commentary, but also the Bible and Shakespeare. Those were the works found in Judge's offices and in Lincoln's saddle bags. And, then too, it was a time for him to go more deeply into poetry. Ronald C. White:

> After his failed political career, Lincoln often pondered the question of the purpose and the meaning of his life. Returning to his law practice he looked forward to traveling alone for hours, or even a whole day, on the open prairies, well-worn edi-

tions of Shakespeare and the Bible his traveling companions. He found mental refreshment in the poetry of Lord Byron and Robert Burns, whose rhyming stanzas he always read aloud. At the end of each carnival-like day in court, Lincoln always found time for solitude and reflection.

Spring and Fall on the Eight Circuit Court of Illinois, a five hundred mile circle for him, was not just a practice of work, it was a practice of reflection. Hours alone in his buggy, this was what Lincoln would see:

Lincoln had grown up in the forests of Indiana, but he became enthralled by the endless prairies of Illinois. The prairies were a striking mixture of blue stem, Indian, and Canadian white rye grasses. By summers end, they were a foot higher than Lincoln's head. As the Indian summer of late September gave way to October's cooler nights, the prairies turned from green to tawny and vermilion. Black-eyed Susans, goldenrod, and sawtooth sunflowers came into final bloom, thriving not simply from the fall rains, but also from the rich subsoil beneath the prairies. In the woodlands, the foliage of red and white oaks blazed orange and dark purple in the last days of October and early November. The prairies were wondrously silent, with only the voice of an owl, or a fox to break Lincoln's solitude.

Lincoln was becoming as much a sage as forests and open lands can conceive. Soon he would be speaking poetic wisdom, such as in his acceptance speech for the Senate run in 1858, "If we could first know WHERE we are, and WHITHER we are tending, we could then better judge WHAT to do, and HOW to do it."

Is this legal logic, a Euclidian Geometric proposition, or just plain poetically worded wisdom coming from one who followed rutted roads for miles?

As President he spoke to Congress in 1861 of the entanglements of our journey through history.

> The fiery trials through which we pass will light us down in honor or dishonor to the latest generation. No personal significance nor insignificance can spare one or another of us. We must disenthrall ourselves, and then we shall save our country.

His 1858 speech had gone on with the iconic image: A house divided against itself cannot stand, this image he had read in his boyhood readers from secular sources and from the New Testament as well.

Poets gravitate to poets and in our time Sandburg has been one who gravitated to Lincoln. In Lincoln's time Walt Whitman was such a poet. He wrote a Civil War poem that echoes Lincoln for us and melds their voices into a poetry that moves toward prophecy. The American radio voice for poetry, Garrison Keillor, read the second half of the *Gettysburg Address* on the "Writer's Almanac" recently at the 151st anniversary of the *Gettysburg Address*. He read it as a poem.

Walt Whitman's poem is entitled, "Over the carnage rose prophetic a voice." That voice in our minds is not just Whitman's but also the voice of Lincoln's prophetic spirit. Whitman was not thinking of Lincoln in the poem, but Lincoln's spirit—which Whitman glorifies elsewhere—is the spiritual force within this poem. What is the prophecy? That love and mutual relations of affection shall solve the problems of freedom, if not now, soon.

> Over the carnage rose prophetic a voice,
> Be not disheharten'd, affection shall solve the problems of freedom
> Yet,
> Those who love each other shall become invincible,
> They shall yet make Columbia victorious.

Whitman addresses the rest of the poem to the sons of the "Mother of All," and gives us compelling special states and men who will be the dependable ones for Liberty and the continuing ones for Equality. Such lovers and comrades will be the ones who tie and band us stronger than hoops of iron. He, the ecstatic poet, will, with the love of lovers tie us, partners and lands.

Whitman was one ecstatic poetic lover of America and its people. Lincoln was another.

Whitman ends with humor and parenthetical irony, a kind of Lincolnesque tone of voice saying:

> Were you looking to be held together by lawyers?
> Or by an agreement on a paper? Or by arms?
> Nay, nor the world, nor any living thing, will so cohere.

This is where poetry takes on the voice of prophecy, where the yonder vision of Equality and Liberty become the spirit of the people of the land. Prophecy is not a prediction; it is vision and a moral spirit about a direction and a call, the just and merciful fate of a people.

To say that Lincoln is a poet requires some definition of poets and poetry. A poet is one who lives in that second kingdom, language, as well as the immediate kingdom of what the rest of world calls reality. Lincoln, as we have seen, was enthralled with language and its mysterious relation to reality from the very first. A poet is one who plays with language and moves back and forth between the two worlds with intriguing if not also entertaining rapidity. Lincoln's youthful imitation of the local preachers showed his ability to get inside the language of the preacher and then with exact mimicry play with and re-display the drama of the worship service's language event. Born into mystery, playing within reality, the poet then also is one who reads poetry for necessary sustenance, and writes poetry as necessary creation. Lincoln wrote and read. He was religious in his hands-on life with poetry, especially his small volume of Burns and his larger one of Shakespeare. These were well-worn tools for the implementation of his life. Poets, whether they write little or a lot are writers and speakers who respect the structures of language, the roots and grammars, and who revere the rhythm of written and spoken expressions. Here we see examples of Lincoln and the structures and the poetry of language:

> The flow of the *Gettysburg Address*, "... a new birth of freedom... government of the people, by the people, for the people, shall not perish...."

> The ending of his 1861 address to Congress, "...the dogmas of the quiet past, are inadequate to the stormy present.... The occasion is piled high with difficulty, and we must rise—with the occasion....the fiery trial through which we pass, will light us down, in honor or dishonor, to the latest generation...."

> The ending of his Cooper Union lecture, "Neither let us be slandered from our duty...nor frightened from it by menaces...of dungeons to ourselves. Let us have faith that right makes might..."

> The ending of his First Inaugural, "The mystic chords of memory, stretching from every battlefield, and patriot grave, to every living heart and hearth-stone, all over this broad land, will yet swell the chorus of the Union, when again touched, as surely they will be, by the better angles of our nature."

> The entirety of his Second Inaugural and its closing, "With malice toward none; with charity for all; with firmness in the right, as God gives us to see the right, let us strive on to finish the work we are in; to bind up the nation's wounds; to care for him who shall have borne the battle, and for his widow; and his orphan..."

All these move in muscular rhythms to the heat beat of poetic expression. The poetry of this language, the new turns of phrase and the moral vision, compose the voice that Whitman also raised in his poem "Over the carnage rose prophetic a voice." Lincoln's voice is the one calling us not to be "dishearten'd" and to know that "affection shall solve the problem of freedom yet...."

The poet also is one who finds new words, new phrases, and new images for bringing to life old or mysterious realities. It is in the metaphorical linking of language to insight and vision that the poet begins to move from a master of language to a prophet.

The poet Lincoln is also the prophet in his vision. Lincoln's constant and Yonder vision was of the higher good of God's "almost chosen people" as he called Americans, a people experimenting with a self-government energized by equality and directed toward freedom. The prophetic vision of the good implied for Lincoln that the hopes were also held in judgment. It was possible for the people to fail the vision. The work then of the poet prophet was also the work of the politician. Politics was the ephemeral movement of the eternal good. As a politician, the poet and prophet is the actor who acts in the same spiritual attitude of the empty self, that Keatsian aptitude of the self that can become one with all that it sees and knows.

This capacity, as we have noted, of Negative Capability is what John Keats asserted makes the poet a poet. The best poet is the one who knows and loves what he or she sees so to represent it in its fullest. The poet is not present in the poem, says Keats, but rather what the poet lifts up is what is in the poem. So too for the self-absenting Lincoln. He, as a politician, is the man for others. Lincoln had the same kind of de-personalized objectivity that allowed him to fully understand the subjectivity of others. That is what made him humble. That is what kept him moving ahead. That is what gave him the wisdom of compassion and mercy when it was needed, and the ability to administer war when it was the only way to cut the knot of slavery that had plagued the new nation from the start. For Lincoln the greatest poetic metaphor was "The Instrument." As the axe was his instrument from youth to young adulthood so he became the instrument of God from then on.

This empty place is an endless place of profound creativity because life keeps pouring into the beholder. It is, of course, a spiritual place and it becomes one of the hallmarks of Lincoln's spiritual life. He was the poet in two significant and spiritual ways: he was bringing the noble truth of the Good, especially equality and freedom, into the world by word and deed; and he was doing it from the place that Meister Eckhart called "pure nothingness," what Keats called Negative Capability, what the Christian theologian and martyr Dietrich Bonhoeffer called being "a man for others," self-emptying kenosis.

This approach to poetry, rooted in the aesthetic of John Keats, is also comprehensively rationalistic in the Enlightenment mode. This is not poetry as spiritualism, nor as aesthetic emotion, and certainly not as personal self-expression. Keats and Lincoln both had starting points of strong anti-clericalism. Both rejected church authority and emotional religious superstitions, although Lincoln remained superstitious in a folk way. The English-born Keats was fourteen years older than Lincoln and the two shared time on Earth as well as the origins of English liberal democratic culture and romantic idealism. In the democratic English liberal tradition Lincoln would say "as I would not be a master so I would not be a slave." Keats would say, "'Tis the man who with a man/ Is equal, be he king, / Or poorest of the beggar-clan" Both were progressive in the modern sense of life being evolutionary. Life is for the soul's evolution and progress not the tragic vale of tears of medieval Christianity. For both, also, life is tragic in its seeming lack of eternal salvation but liberating in its drive to free the mind of clannish irrationalities. All this is a shared spirituality that Lincoln, unknowingly, had with Keats at the beginning of the 19th century.

But it was in his folk and rustic Western ways that Lincoln brings his poetic mind to the tasks of politics. He is more like Robert Burns in his tales and poems than like Keats or Ralph Waldo Emerson in his poems and essays. When as a politician was Lincoln most metaphorical like the poet? When he was constantly reminded of the stories of his past as illustrations of the truth of the present.

When Lincoln burst upon the national scene and became the unlikely President, the literate people, especially of the northeast, as well as the south, thought him a foolish story teller. Westerners understood him better, by and large. Lincoln was weaving a web of poetic metaphors around his argumentative and ideological adversaries and friends. When he was reminded of legislation, or an army maneuver, stuck like the cow that couldn't jump the fence and could go neither forward nor backward, he was making a rustic image that made a teaching point. The original skill of the poet to find the image that links two disparate truths is a skill that Lincoln honed as a court room lawyer telling stories. His tales told in essence that this is really like that. As he would show how these two are similar he would reveal a deeper and a felt truth. Lincoln ran circles around his colleagues and adversaries because he really thought like a poet. He did much of his best politicking that way. Lincoln's rustic and seemingly endless stories of how "this here" reminded him of "that there," that was him doing the basic work of poetry: establishing metaphors for the purpose of insight and revelation of the underlying unities of life.

The poet in Lincoln is made obvious when we contrast the ego-centered lives of the generals and the politicians that so be-deviled and surrounded his noble quest for saving the Union. Not all poets follow John Keats' views of Negative Capability. The traditional and florid poetry and prose of the professor of rhetoric, and Gettysburg hero, Joshua Lawrence Chamberlain is written unaware of John Keats' self-emptying style. But those who do, including Whitman, whose loving self is assumed into the larger national Self, come closer to linking this world with the next. Lincoln saw that as his Yonder task as well.

The role of poet and prophet in Lincoln's words was noted years ago by Daniel Kilham Dodge, the founding chair of the English Department as the University of Illinois in the 1880s. Dodge was another student of words and history who had fallen under the spell of a love for Lincoln. He confessed in his books that his students and readers would accuse him of being like the professor in *David Copperfield* who makes all occasions ones in which he can talk about his beloved English monarch George, about whom he is writing a great book! In 1924 Dodge published a 176-page volume entitled *Abraham Lincoln: Master of Words.* In his summary of the Second Inaugural he concludes, as we have, that poetry and prophecy have come together in Lincoln. He cites how many local, national, and English newspapers failed to see the literary and philosophical excellence of Lincoln, but for a few.

One such editor was a Carl Schurz who, as we have quoted, says of the Second Inaugural, "This was like a sacred poem. No American President had ever spoken words like this to the American people. America never had a President who found such words in the depth of his heart."

An English source of appreciation for Lincoln after his death is found in London's "Spectator," as quoted by Ronald C. White:

> For ourselves we cannot read his last inaugural address, delivered only five weeks before his assassination, without a renewed conviction that it is the noblest political document known to history, and should have, for the nation and the statesmen he

left behind him, something of sacred and almost prophetic authority. Surely none was ever written under a stronger sense of
God's government.

This character of a man who opened himself to wider life and
so emptied himself was recognized by Lord Gladstone, the towering
speaker and leader of Victorian England, writing, "It is by cruel suffering that nations are sometimes born to a better life." So it is with
individual men. Lincoln's words show that upon him anxiety and
sorrow have wrought their full effect."

The quality of a poet who has been shaped by the reading
of great poetry is noted by an English biographer of Lincoln, Lord
Charnwood, seeing in Lincoln the traces of Shakespeare. "The com-
parative rank of his oratory need not be discussed, for, at any rate, it
was individual and unlike that of most other great speakers in history, though perhaps more like that of some great speeches in drama."

Lincoln and Revelation

We expect a President to do things, and even to name what those actions are and what they may mean. We expect and need some words, even explanations, for governmental actions. What we do not expect, but what we find in Lincoln, are words from time to time that are so deeply embedded in the action that they become a necessary part of the meaning of what has been done. We call that art. When the deeds of a President become a part of the idea of America then the art of the language itself takes on a new dimension. When, as in the case of some of Lincoln's speeches, the very idea of America is invested with deep personal value and broad world significance, then language has come to the boundary between the secular and the sacred categories of meaning.

By following the trail of Lincoln's language we can find places where battlefields have been turned into sanctuaries, and acts can be remembered and live on as present and eternal values. To follow this trail there are markers that tell us that some words are sense-based and some words are spirit-based. Like blazes to mark trees, some pathways lead to explanations and others lead to revelations. When, for example, Lincoln uses his meticulous and mighty mental focus to define the specific terms for the Emancipation Proclamation, he explains exactly in detailed, sense-based words. As a lawyer who has hand-written many documents for court proceedings Lincoln is keen and astute to define legally and strategically where what slaves can be free and where not. He knows the kind of language that finds the devil in the details. But then just as specifically, at the last minute, he throws in a clause that will allow black men to become Union soldiers. That clause produces, eventually, 200,000 black troops, 40,000 of whom die, and who all make a huge difference in the outcome of the war and the definition of the future of the races in this country. A transforming value, equality, is named in specific explanatory language; it is an angel in the detail.

We eventually come to feel and assent to the life-changing values that Lincoln enshrines in words, words that we read in marble at the Lincoln Memorial. It is important to remember that Lincoln was a master of detailed and specific empirical realities. He taught himself surveying. He waded out into the Sangamon River to measure the depths of the channel at various turns and twists so that he could sponsor the idea of steamboat traffic up the river and eventually, for one day, become the chief pilot of a steamboat trying to do just that. Lincoln taught himself the six books of Euclid because he wanted to understand logic, and no great speech he gives is far from the rigid framework of logical thought. For example in the Second Inaugural Address he says, "Both read the same Bible, and pray to the same God; and each invokes His aide against the other…The prayers of both could not be answered; that of neither has been answered fully." In a paragraph earlier he has logically parsed this: "Both parties deprecated war; but one of them would make war rather than let the nation survive; and the other would accept war rather than let it perish. And the war came."

When Lincoln releases the full creative power of his poetic genius he did not sacrifice clear and logical sense awareness and thought. The near side of Yonder is seen in known specifics. Lincoln was, as a young boy, enthralled with the mysteries of language, including the appearance, in hand-written letters, of his own name. He was intrigued and gripped by the workings of the factual world, including his creation of a long and nearly infinite version of the multiplication tables. As a kind of sexton in the local church he kept detailed accounts of the numbers of candles available, and there is a hand-written note found in a crevice of some timbers in the old church, signed by A. Lincoln to that effect. Lincoln did not have his head in the clouds even as he has long and dreamy-eyed visions of life, death, and human values. We find the marks of these abilities in his words, both specific and poetic.

Language is more than a way to represent reality but it is not less. In the more than two hours of his memorized address at Gettysburg, the famed and able Edward Everett gave a crowd-thrilling and specific account of the very battle whose dead were being commemorated. His was realistic representational history at its best, scholars tell us. His famed compliment to Lincoln tells us that language has other uses. He asserted that he would have counted himself fortunate if he could have in two hours captured the essence and the meaning of the battle as well as Lincoln did in two minutes. What kind of language, then was Lincoln using?

Lincoln was not a philosopher. But he does ponder our experience, including what we call history. The philosopher Suzanne K. Langer opened a new field of understanding the psychology of language in her 1942 ground-breaking book, *Philosophy in a New Key: A Study in the Symbolism of Reason, Rite, and Art*. We are the language-making animal, with an urge to symbolically express reality. Language itself, she says, helps us attain assent to value and belief. Lincoln does this largely at first with logic and reason and then increasingly with symbol and emotion.

The startling rise of Lincoln's political life is parallel to the dramatic changes he undergoes personally, as his changing language shows. Historians mark his huge ability to master new tasks and rise to new and ever harder situations. For example, he had never administered anything before he became President; he had no executive experience whatsoever. Yet he becomes a master presider. His Black

Hawk Indian War Captaincy hardly equipped him for building and marshaling the largest army America had to that time. His steadiness of character obscures the facile ability he shows for changing who he is and how he will talk and act. The changing language of Lincoln, the way his diction, rhetoric, style and tone changes, all show how deep are his transformations. His changed verbal tone and word choice, from the bombastic Lyceum Speech of 1838 to his tender Farewell remarks in 1850, show in language his changed heart.

The rhetorical markers from his First Inaugural Address to the *Gettysburg Address* show a similar yet more rapid change. The spiritual journey between these two speeches is as startling and deep as are his personal changes in capability and point of view. Lincoln is the paramount lawyer in his First Inaugural, and his tribunal is the courthouse of America. In his view the South is on trial as the law-breaking party. Reading that speech today any fair-minded jury would have awarded Lincoln the victory. Calling for patience, rationality, and humane common sense, he makes a brilliant, logical and persuasive speech. And it is to no avail. At that moment, people were simply not rational enough to be guided by Lincoln's supreme appeals to rationality and virtue. Even his personal appeal at the end, "I am loath to close" is a court-winning, heart-breaking, but not crowd-pleasing, rhetorical statement. Nobody in the country was moved an inch by this magnificent address. The North probably was solidified by it in important ways, but his goal to avert war was not even close to being reached. Why? Because it is all about being reasonable and law-abiding, and that is just too thin spiritually.

By the time he gets to the *Gettysburg Address* Lincoln will speak from a wholly changed spirit. He is no longer the rational leader, he is the national poet. He is no longer the political power broker, he is the spiritual psalmist. He shows this change in spirit in several important linguistic ways.

First of all, time is removed from the *Gettysburg Address*. We are not in historical time, we are in eternal time. In the First Inaugural time is marching on, and the days are ticking down. It is merely historical time. It is newspaper editorial time. It is a time-bound crisis speech.

When language changes from logical narrative to spiritual poetry the first ingredient to change is time. The rhetorical device for this in much of scripture is to tell the religious truth through story. The Prophets often told dramatic illustrations, such as the Prophet Nathan telling King David the story of the man who killed the poor man's only lamb, making David aware of his own similar guilt with Bathsheba. Jesus does the same transformation of time within his parables. For children it is done with "Once upon a time." When those magical words are spoken the teller and the audience are transported out of day-by-day time into a sphere of timeless time, a no-time place where the imagination is free to go places and see things and feel things and think things not allowed in timely time. Lincoln does this, as the theologian H. Richard Niebuhr pointed out years ago, with the Biblically reminiscent, "Four Score and seven years ago." This changes the time in which the audience exists. No longer is it November 19th 1863, it is once upon a time when America started. It is vague about then but it is especially not now. It is in a time-place where Lincoln can then begin to tell people about things they feel and know and value in a trans-historical way. That is what all scriptures eventually do; they tell people values and realities that exist in spiritual time, not chronological time. History is changed into a holy story, a revelation.

Of course historically Lincoln is re-starting America from the Declaration of Independence, not from the Constitutional Convention. That is a crucial values move on Lincoln's part. But more than that he has taken people into the spiritual plane wherein he will tell them things they need to know and will value forever.

Time had always been mysterious for Lincoln. Death and the fleetingness of life had captured Lincoln and made him a melancholy person from boyhood on. The poem "Mortality" by William Knox, with its opening line, "Oh! Why should the spirit of mortal be proud?" was a mantra to young Lincoln. People even assumed he wrote it. His own extended poem on memory, "My Childhood Home I See Again," written after his mid-career return visit to southern Indiana, is full of the images of time eclipsed, leaving him "'twixt earth and paradise."

The other spiritual maneuver in Lincoln's language at Gettysburg is his removal of himself. While it was powerful at the end of his First Inaugural to say "I am loath to close," he makes no first person statements at Gettysburg at all. In fact he does not exist inside this speech. You cannot find Abraham Lincoln in his language. It is the ultimate expression of John Keats' Negative Capability, wherein the poet removes himself from the thing presented. This is so that the thing presented can be fully seen, known, felt, and understood. Keats does this in his poems. He celebrated Shakespeare for doing this. And Lincoln does this in the *Gettysburg Address*.

In the spiritual language of Martin Buber, the renowned Jewish theologian and philosopher, the place of the eternal is found when the personal as an object disappears and the personal as part of relationship appears. Buber calls the personal as an object the "It", and a person living in this objective way is in an I-It relationship with the world and with him or herself. We know this category when we say someone is using someone, when a person is a means to something else, not an end in themselves. Time is flat and not eternal in this way of being. But time takes on the spiritual quality of the eternal when one is in relationship with oneself and the world through complete participation. This is when the world is a place of Thou, and one's relationship with it is called, in Buber's terms, an "I-Thou" relationship. Lincoln effects this transition from It-self to Thou-self and from It-history to Thou-history by removing himself from this speech.

What takes over is the communion of himself with the audience, in a relationship with each other within the history that began
four score and seven years ago. Now we are in the world of a communal time. Community is the ultimate form of reference in this
speech. Spiritual language establishes community and Lincoln does
that. Not only does he not ever say "I," he refers to *us* many times:
he says the plural pronoun "we" nine times, "us" or "our" four times,
and he says the plural nouns "men" and "people" five times, and
"they" three times. Twenty-one times then he frames his references
to the community, and never to any one person, or even any one
group. Soldiers who died are only "the dead." People who survived,
whether soldiers or not, are only "the living." No one is a northerner
or a southerner or even an American. They are only We, only people,
living and dead, in the world.

The location of meaning in this speech could not be more
abstract, yet it is not abstractly impersonal; it is supremely personal.
This is our story and we are in the midst of living it, together. We are
not only bound by the idea of democracy, we the people are bonded
by the reality of a blood community. These are our fathers who have
started this proposition and it is in blood that it has been brought
forth, and it is in blood that it has been tested. Whatever issues we
may now have with the glorification of war, there is no disputing that
human glory, personal birth and communal survival are all brought
about and bought in blood. It is to the living that the sacred bonds
are reborn and lived. There is no religious scripture that does not use
the image and the reality of blood to make its values known, except
perhaps in Buddhism. Breath more than blood is the central physical
aspect of Buddhism,

Niebuhr says that sacred history is one in which the inner lives
of people are shared communally. In sacred history, time is lived as
duration. Revelation is language that awakens assent to this inner

communion of value. What Lincoln does in the Address at Gettysburg is to set the stage for a profound metaphorical shift in the national consciousness, for the people present and for all who ever read and felt this speech. He has dramatically altered the nature of time and the personas on the stage, including himself. All are transformed into symbolic not personal beings. Lincoln then does the most powerful thing a poet can do: he changes the nature of the reality presented. If the simple poet says that love is like the red rose, the spiritual poet, Lincoln, now says that this killing field is a birthing place. This transformation is more than a poetical move it, is a symbolic transformation of reality. His words cannot be separated from the deed being commemorated, and his words become deeds; they make a new reality for the consciousness of this community. He does this through language, but the result is beyond language. He does it with his consistent use of verbs and nouns of birth and conception and dedication. All these words evoke, semi-consciously, but not lost on the newspaper editors who objected, images of women and childbirth as well as religious temple dedication. Lincoln has given up trying to argue and to logically persuade Americans of this American reality. He had moved into the language of spiritual time and place and to a method of expression that is sheer beauty. The prophets, too, spoke in beautiful language.

Where and when do great ideas enter our minds and motivation? That is a question that historians of religion as well as philosophers of language try to answer. The Christian historian Sidney Mead once asked this question, wondering what "compulsive power," often called a revelation, is it that, over time, creates in people a "critical discontent" with the reality of their lives, a reality that falls short of their ideals and great ideas. It comes to Lincoln to speak to the tension that exists in American history between our ideals and our reality.

The third speech in the transition of his language is the Second Inaugural, his last great public speech. His voice returns not as a personal voice but one of pronouncement, the voice we find in much of the Hebrew Prophets, and in many of the words of Jesus. It is the Old Testament tone that Lincoln most strikes when he decries the critical distance between our ideals and our reality. Lincoln now adds the reality of God to his political address. The American idea is freedom but the reality has included slavery. This he terms an "offense," a word he had read in his schoolbook readers long ago. Logically for Lincoln the offense is against God as well as humanity, and his pronouncement is that God's judgment and justice was to rebalance those two opposites. Again it is human blood that is the sacrifice for the instrumentality of God's justice, and Lincoln's language is based on a spiritual discontent, not a Euclidean logic.

There had always been in the air in Lincoln's life the idea of God's providence, God's sovereignty, even the Kingdom of God in America. Thomas Jefferson famously said that his own statements on human equality in the Declaration of Independence were not his creation but were ideas that were simply "in the air" of his time. Similarly Lincoln, after his great Job-like questioning of God and the war, and his Jacob-like wrestling with the very idea of God, reveals to the American people that the will of God has been to balance the blood of slavery by the cost of the blood of Americans who were all complicit in this great offence.

Of this aspect of the speech Lincoln said, "Men are not flattered by being shown that there has been a difference of purpose between the Almighty and them." But that had been his purpose, and his language is based on spiritual principles—justice, human equality—and on spiritual assumptions—divine will and the shaping of human motivations—and it is delivered in religious language. His Christ-like words of mercy and care for the casualties of the war and his appeal to human brotherhood complete the spiritual language and the sacred call of this secular speech. Lincoln is no longer the lawyer in the tribunal of American civilization as he was in his First Inaugural. He is not the mystic poet of a transformational image of reality that he was in the *Gettysburg Address*. He is now the revealer of the meaning of history, and he has transposed history from the halls and battlefields of civilization to the temple of the sacred where the divine will rules and people are called to come forth with the better angels of their nature once again and to care for the victims of their guilt.

What had been the language of his political religion in the Lyceum Speech of 1838 has become the language of a sacred history in 1865. In his First Inaugural Lincoln had asked "Why should there not be a patient confidence in the ultimate justice of the people?" The Almighty ruler of the nations, with eternal truth and justice, will prevail by means of God's judgment, but the outcome will be enacted in this "great tribunal, the America people." Lincoln is following the categories that the theologian Paul Tillich would define in the 20th century when he said that religion is the substance of culture and culture is the form of religion. In other words, God, and the religion that knows God, makes up the stuff of history. But culture and the forms of human creativity make up the forms of religion. In the *Gettysburg Address* and the Second Inaugural, Lincoln is acting in a cultural form, a humanly created act of language. But he is expressing the very stuff, the substance of religion—God's life—as it is known in the history that is being addressed. The sacred that is in this history is being spoken of and made real by the living secular words of Lincoln in the cultural form of a speech. This is how he is able to be both a secular person and a sacred being. By the end of the great suffering of the war, it is not so much that the people's struggle has revealed God's will but that God's will has been the very anvil and altar of the people's suffering. So-called secular events have had sacred meaning.

Revelation in sacred traditions is not the interjection of something miraculous into the historical account of life and nature. It is rather a discovery in the very inner meaning of events. The human heart knows the divine purposes, and the ideals of the human mind are transformed. The miracle of revelation is not that magic trumps reality but that reality transcends history, and that reality is spiritual and is made known in human words and deeds. The words and deeds of Lincoln belong to that indivisible union.

The Future of Lincoln

"Abraham Lincoln was really one of those characters, the best of which is the result of long trains of cause and effect—needing a certain spaciousness of time, and perhaps even remoteness, to properly enclose them—having unequal'd influence on the shaping of this Republic (and therefore the world) as today, and then far more important in the future. Thus the time has by no means yet come for a thorough measurement of him. Nevertheless, we who live in his era—who have seen him, and heard him, face to face, and are in the midst of, or just parting from, the strong and strange events which he and we have had to do with—can in some respects bear valuable, perhaps indispensable testimony concerning him."   - Walt Whitman

This chapter could be entitled "Lincoln and the Future," as if there is a knowable future and even "a" Lincoln in it. The birth of this book, however, is that Lincoln is present. Recall my felt sense of Lincoln and his good spirit in the air and among the trees and fences of his Indiana boyhood home. The point of view is that Lincoln is an historical figure who may or may not be relevant to aspects of the future. Unlike most historical figures but very much like many religious ones, Lincoln is not just a kind of person we might want in the future. He is a present and enduring constellation of ideas and values in our history and as our history unfolds. The question is not then how would Lincoln fit or not fit into the future, as if he were a peg for some future hole. Rather the entailments of his whole being, the intensity of his actions, his ideas, his spirit, are ongoing forces.

The question really is: What is the future of the Lincoln that we are still in conversation with?

There are several reasons to counter the argument of this book and to say that Lincoln's future with us will not be great, that he has had his day.

One counter argument is the limits of nationalism. While Lincoln saw the American experiment as one of crucial importance to the universal hopes of humanity, the nationalistic trapping of that hope may not allow his Yonder vision to speak to rising peoples around the world in this century. Is there, then, a way to distinguish Lincoln from America?

Dostoyevsky once said, "For what else is the strength of the Russian national spirit than the aspiration, in its ultimate goal, for universality and all-embracing humanitarianism?" This was in an address on Pushkin he gave in June of 1880 as quoted in *The American Conservative*, September/October 2014.[9] The article addresses a review of a book on Solzhenitsyn saying, "...a burning love for one's motherland (is) compatible with humility before God and deference to a universal moral order." (D. Mahoney)

This universal goal would be Lincoln's Yonder view, his hope. But is it true and is it possible? Can a spirit be separated out from a national spirit? More specifically can both "God" and "Nation" be untangled enough from each other, and from the sad tale of their embedded history, to carry forward universal humanitarian aspirations and moral hopes?

A second question plaguing Lincoln's future with us is war itself. If war is an every-present necessity to the human story—as it clearly was in Lincoln's time and life—then his ability to manage war with both deadly efficiency and rare mercy might be a crucial reason to

---

9   Congdon, Lee. "Solzhenitsyn Wasn't Western." *The American Conservative* 3.5 (2014).

have him be a part of our future. But, on the other hand, the cry for peace, the role of non-violent social change, the possible history of pacific matriarchies that pre-date our Iliad-driven history, all these might argue that his very grip on the sword disqualifies him from our future.

A third potential limit to Lincoln and our future is his apparent psychological limitation when it comes to emotions and irrational passions in human nature. The emotions and passions which limited Lincoln are, at first sight, those culturally identified with the archetypes of the feminine. The role those archetypes played in the emotions of his life seemed to stump him. In many ways Lincoln is the ideal 19th Century male. He is Father Abraham. He calls his wife, "Mother." He is distant from his eldest son and overly identified and indulgent with his younger boys. He is powerful with men in scores of astonishing ways, and yet he is like the King on the chess board, the Queen can run circles around him. He was bullied by his future wife Mary's ambitions into writing a newspaper column that foolishly almost landed him in a duel. He was enchanted by Mary's beauty, wit, charm, learning, and spunky spirit, but he could barely form a contract with her for marriage. He avoided his home life and her needs, feelings and increasing temper, and for years went months on the road riding the legal circuit and deeply enjoying the camaraderie of men. He increasingly took the Victorian high road of reason in his marriage, and with the country, leaving the passions that pulled the country into war and his wife into insanity unaddressed. His First Inaugural Address for all its intelligence and clarity was spoken on a plane that did not acknowledge or address the power of the irrational feelings underlying the south and the north. Perhaps there was nothing more he could have done, but his appeals to good sense and rational and moral restraint are delivered in a way that seem not to acknowledge the impotence of his argument. My belief, however, is that Lincoln had a huge and powerful inner feminine and emotional side to him. More than most men and most all of the men surrounding him Lincoln was, as we would say, in touch with his feminine side. He looks completely natural, and yet still powerfully masculine, wearing his keep-my-shoulders warm shawl. He was incredibly sweet, often exquisitely gentle, and almost always deeply compassionate. But for our day and our future he seems to lack a language that can reform our own less rational natures, the "worser devils of our nature." And Lincoln rarely ever knew what to do directly with his passions. Passions in others he could eventually out-fox, but is that enough?

Clearly if men had been as reasonable as Lincoln was in his First Inaugural Address the Civil War could have been prevented. But passions ruled the Abolitionists and the Secessionists. Lincoln was simply blind-sided by their emotional passions, as well as often by his own life and his wife's. His less reasonable countrymen and his beloved Mary were beyond his reason.

A fourth limitation to Lincoln being a wise and useful guide and force in our future is the crux of this book—his secular religious views. He could, like his North-South country, lose to each side of this secular religious issue by the objection of the other. Secularists now may not abide his appeals to God and the spiritual and moral order he knew from the Bible. Religionists may not be able to tolerate his lack of allegiance to the forms of faith that faith seems to require. If God is a necessary part of a civilization's future, as Toynbee has argued, then Lincoln may not be Godly enough. If, however, it is the forms of faith that may destroy us with religious wars and intolerance, then his very appeal to religion itself might make the secularist throw this President out with the holy water.

Having lived with these issues for decades and with him as well, my belief is that his ability to generate life from the center of each of these paradoxes—God-nation, war-peace, reason-emotion—

is what recommends him as the necessary person for our future's guidance and direction.

What role can Lincoln, his life and words, indeed his spirit, play in the real world of the state and the spirit today? We live in a time of multiple secular nation states and alliances, and even more evident multiple faith allegiances. What could possibly be the role of a white male political leader from a Christian context, the secular head of a nation state, in either the secular world's strategic games or the global religion's claims?

There are only two or three basic issues at stake in the complexities of our post-modern secular and religious life. Lincoln's grasp of those two or three issues is what propels him to our view and can even compel us to embrace him.

There is the issue of the relation of the state to the institutions of religion. There is the issue of whether these two institutions have overlapping or divergent goals.

A subsequent issue in the definitions of state and religion is the potential superiority of one or the other. Which one serves which? If it is the state what is its ultimate role with religion? If it is religion what does religion have to say to the state? There is the issue of how religion may inform the definition of the secular state actions. What does religion have to say to how the wars and the laws of the state are defined?

Ultimately what is the goal of the religious view and what did Lincoln do or say that fit or did not fit, that goal?

In our time the state and religion have made one of two choices. There is the trend to merge the state with religion and to institute a theocracy. We see that even in liberal democracies in the polity of Israel, in the claims of the Religious Right in America, but more so, in the fundamentalist and even violent manifestations of radical Islam.

Contrary to the effort to have the state wear the robes of religion has been the more radically secular efforts to strip the state
of any and all religious connotations or denotations. The French
Revolutions was clearly an extreme reaction to separating the right
of the divine from the might of the king. The secular revolution of
Communism in Russia has been another example. The similar secular state established in China, the various military dictators and government throughout Latin America, Africa and Asia also have been
efforts at secular military power asserted over religious mandates.

The dangers of conflating religious passion with state power
have been abundantly clear to us in terms of the underlying languages and belief in our wars none more so than World War I. We
see this conflation in the various theocratic take overs in recent years.
But historically the manifest destiny idea of America can be seen as
an expression of this infusion of religious passion into state expansion. The God, Glory and Gold expansion of the Spanish empires
into Latin America is another example of how easily religion and
state can mix.

Lincoln's lesson to us is clear. Unlike most nation states that
have anything to do with religion he came close to religion but did not
let religion take over. Never was America to him the Kingdom of God
in America. The American experience was perhaps humanity's last best
hope as he saw history. We were engaged in a pivotal enterprise but it
was both for what he always called God's "almost chosen people" but
it was also for the world as he saw the world. The line he drew was
important and the difference crucial and unique in world history.

Yet Lincoln did not use this line of separation and limitation
as a way of subtracting religion from the life of the people in the nation state. Both the chastising judgments of God, as he knew God
from the Biblical traditions, and the mercy of God's love, as he knew
mercy from the Christian religion, were deep resources for the spiri-

tual life in his mind for the American people. He appealed to these spiritual pillars often, intensely so in 1863 with the *Gettysburg Address* and *Thanksgiving Day Proclamation*, and again in 1865 in his Second Inaugural.

Less overt in his words, but clear from his life, Lincoln expressed the message of religion in his willing sacrifice to serve the wellbeing of others. Both personally and communally Lincoln lived his life increasingly as a sacrifice, a sacrifice we understand as basic to the ethics and the rituals of the world's religions in their various forms. Particularly important in this aspect of religious embodiment is the role of the spilling of blood. Lincoln's ethical and spiritual sense was not that violence was redemptive but that sacrifice was necessary. Sacrifice was the first of all the Classical Virtues of a loyalty to the community as it had been founded. In the hands of Lincoln that virtue feels elevated into a hope for the life of others, something we could call love of the beloved community.

The Civil War for Lincoln was not an exaggerated version of the Christian doctrine of Atonement, the sacrifice of Jesus for our sins. It was rather a just chastening for our ungodly injustice, slavery. It was not a glorious redemption that Lincoln saw, but a meaningful and harsh expression of God's will. The blood was not unlike labor, a bloody rebirthing in anguish.

Perhaps secondary only to his embodiment of sacrificial love, was Lincoln's humility. In the gift of humility, both in person and in policy, Lincoln connected spiritual life and national life. He did so with various degrees of success and failure. This was an aspect of a personal life not easily built into state power but one that is necessary to religious power. Lincoln's legendary mercy in his Second Inaugural was not just an expression of a spiritual teaching of mercy toward the bereft, but a necessary consequence of his way of looking at people, and the peoples, of his country. Unlike almost everyone else in this era of our history he did not look at the other as the enemy. He did not have a Northerner's view of the Southerner. As a Western man deeply rooted in the south, with a southern wife, a southerner best friend, and a southern mother, he also did not view the North as somehow an enemy. Lincoln's compassionate heart informed his mental views, and in his mind he could see each side as the other saw it. He would say to the Northerner who hated slavery that we, he and the Northerners would be and do just as the Southerner were we living in their in their circumstances.

Lincoln had learned then the most important lesson facing this nation now: How to be able to see America as the rest of the world sees America. He knew objective self –insight. Remember one of his favorite poets was Robert Burns; and "the gift to see ourselves as others see us" is one of Burns' most lingering lines. The expansion of the Western world, Arnold Toynbee argues, has made the whole world necessarily have to see themselves differently. Each Kingdom of God on Earth, from the Chinese, the Japanese, the Germans, the Russian, the Ottomans, the Semites, have had to lose their crown and their blinders when the Western world confronted them with our technological and economic power. The whole world has been chastened if not also indeed resentful, but humbled, to now be able to see themselves as Americans see them, and no longer to be only seeing themselves as they once, gloriously, did. All the world but we ourselves have learned this. But we are about to have to, and Lincoln knew how to, how to see himself as others saw him and how to see each side as the other saw the other side.

This is of course the nearly God's-eye view of the people of the world, and Lincoln's closeness to that kind of benevolent omni-science—along with his self-emptying sacrifice—that is what recommends him to our age. It is, Toynbee, says the goal of religious life to have each person, each personality, become as God-like as possible during their earthly journey from birth to death.

It might also be, Toynbee pictures, that the rise and fall of civilizations is for the religious purposes of such personal salvation. If so, the wheels of the chariot of religion, he imagines, might just be the empires that we build. Eventually they fall off, but the chariot continues to rise.

The array of complexities and paradoxes in Lincoln as we have known him gives rise to the question: how did he find living ways through so many apparent irreconcilable opposites? Of course, here we have looked at the spiritual life versus the life of secular civilization as the polarity that has come to the surface for us. It is impossible to conceive that Lincoln had some moderating calculus that added up opposites and divided by two to find a middle path. While he was a superb logician, the agility required of his resolutions required something more dynamic than moderating calculations. But neither did he have some one deep principle, some core ideology, that resolved all differences to some operational principle, some party platform or ideological conviction or truth. His triumph seems to be the victory of no single idea that emerges the winner at the end.

What then was it about him that cut the Gordian Knots, took the rich man's camel through the eye of the needle, and braided the multiple threads of life into a Celtic-like weave even now to be circles and spirals in a direction worth going, even calling us forward?

Underneath Lincoln's characteristic allegiance is to Greco-Roman Enlightenment ideals, such as loyalty to the commonwealth as the mark of the virtuous person, was the rule of law versus the passions or wills of either aristocracies or mobocracies. However, inside Lincoln's rational allegiance to the Greek Revival ethos of his frontier experience was the charity of his spirit born of his early suffering and the grace that came to his nature from that suffering, what has been called his anguish.

Arnold Toynbee reminds us that one of the deepest spiritual laws comes to us from the Greek tradition of Aeschylus' two Greek words translated as "it is through suffering that learning comes."

Lincoln, as a boy, leaves an Eden-like Kentucky childhood of seemingly stable cabin homes, beautiful rolling hills and clear water streams to a beyond-the-pale wilderness. Crossing the Ohio at age seven he entered a baseline of suffering. Physical hardship that was nearly pre-historic, hard and ungenerous treatment was at the hands of his father, and the impending death of his beacon of life mother, all three weave into an inescapable cloak of human and spiritual pain. Within that dark and thick forest only his wit and his humor opened clearings for shafts of light. But always, always, he was at the most basic level simply coping. Compassionate-while-coping is the mechanism of Lincoln's spiritual genius. This would be Lincoln's version of John Keats' definition of Negative Capability. Lincoln did not try to escape his suffering through loyalty to one polarity of paradox or the other. He did not, for example, subsume his love of the American national enterprise to some Kingdom of God or Christ in America. Nor, however, did he forsake his knowledge of the spirit of the Almighty in history as freedom for the people and life for the person. The spiritual pilgrim was an ideal that, while expressed in poets like Burns, was rooted for him in the Christian ideal of *Pilgrim's Progress*.

BIBLIOGRAPHY

Bate, Walter Jackson. *Negative Capability—The Intuitive Approach in Keats,* ContraMundum Press, 2012

Beveridge, Albert J. *Abraham Lincoln, 1809-1858.* Boston: Houghton Mifflin Co., 1928.

Bodichon, Barbara Leigh Smith. "A Brief Summary in Plain Language of the Most Important Laws Concerning Women (1854)" *University of Indiana: The Victorian Women Writers Project* 2005.

Boorstin, Daniel. *The Americans—The Democratic Experience,* Random House, 1974.

Burt, John. *Lincoln's Tragic Pragmatism: Lincoln, Douglas, and Moral Conflict.* Belknap Press, 2013.

Caputo, John D. *The Prayers And Tears Of Jacques Derrida.* Bloomington, Ind.: Indiana University Press, 1997.

Chambrun, Adolphe de Pineton. *Personal Recollections Of Mr. Lincoln.* [New York]: [Scribner's], 1893.

Charnwood, Godfrey Rathbone Benson. *Abraham Lincoln.* Garden City, N.Y.: Garden City Pub. Co, 1938.

Dickens, Charles. *David Copperfield.* [Waiheke Island]: Floating Press, 2008.

Dodge, Daniel Kilham. *Abraham Lincoln: The Evolution of His Literary Style.* Urbana: University of Illinois Press, 2000.

Dodge, Daniel Kilham. *Abraham Lincoln: Master of Words.* D. Appleton And Company Inc.; First Edition, (1924)

Donald, David Herbert. *Lincoln.* Simon & Schuster; 1st Touchstone Ed edition, 1996.

Eckhart, Meister, C. De B. Evans, and Franz Pfeiffer. *Meister Eckhart.* London: J. M. Watkins, 1952.

Emerson, Ralph Waldo, and Edward Waldo Emerson. *The Complete Works Of Ralph Waldo Emerson.* Boston: Houghton, Mifflin and Co., 1903.

Guelzo, Allen C. *Abraham Lincoln*. Grand Rapids, Mich.: W. B. Eerdmans, 1999.

James, William. *The Moral Equivalent of War, and Other Essays: And Selections from Some Problems of Philosophy*. New York: Harper & Row, 1971.

Johnson, Robert A. *He: Understanding Masculine Psychology, Based on the Legend of Parsifal and His Search for the Grail, Using Jungian Psychological Concepts*. New York: Perennial Library, 1977.

Jung, C. G, and Marie-Luise von Franz. *Man And His Symbols*. Garden City, N.Y.: Doubleday, 1964.

Kaplan, Fred. *Lincoln—The Biography of a Writer*. New York: Harper-Collins Publishers, 2008.

Keller, Helen. *The Story Of My Life*. Garden City, N.Y.: Doubleday, 1954.

Kierkegaard, Søren. *Fear And Trembling*. Garden City, N.Y.: Doubleday, 1954.

Langer, Susanne Katherina Knauth. *Philosophy In A New Key*. Cambridge (Mass.): Harvard university press, 1979.

Lincoln, Abraham. *Great Speeches*. New York: Dover Publications, 1991.

Lincoln, Abraham, and Roy P Basler. *The Collected Works Of Abraham Lincoln*. New Brunswick, N.J.: Rutgers University Press, 1953.

Melville, Herman. *Moby Dick*. Irvine: Saddleback Educational Pub., 2005.

Melville, Herman, and Robert Penn Warren. *Selected Poems Of Herman Melville*. New York: Random House, 1970.

Miller, William Lee. *Lincoln's Virtues*. New York: Alfred A. Knopf, 2002.

Moore, Robert L., and Douglas Gillette. *King, Warrior, Magician, Lover: Rediscovering the Archetypes of the Mature Masculine*. San Francisco: Harper San Francisco, 2001.

Murray, Lindley. *The English Reader: Or, Pieces In Prose And Poetry, Selected From The Best Writers*. Philadelphia: Printed for Benjamin Johnson, no. 31, and Jacob Johnson, no. 147, High-Street, 1804. (Murray's Reader)

Newell, J. Philip. *Shakespeare and The Human Mystery*. New York: Paulist Press, 2003.

Niebuhr, H. Richard. *The Meaning of Revelation*. New York: Macmillan Co., 1941.

Pallasmaa, Juhani. *The Eyes of the Skin: Architecture and the Senses.* Chichester: Wiley, 2014.

Peck, M. Scott. *The Road Less Travelled.* London: Rider, 2008.

Pramuk, Christopher. *Sophia.* Collegeville, Minn.: Liturgical Press, 2009.

Ricoeur, Paul. *Time And Narrative.* Chicago: University of Chicago Press, 1985.

Sandburg, Carl. *Abraham Lincoln.* New York: Harcourt, Brace & Co, 1939.

Sandburg, Carl, and Michael Hague. *Rootabaga Stories.* San Diego: Harcourt Brace Jovanovich, 1988.

Scheibe, Karl E. *Self Studies.* Westport, Conn.: Praeger, 1995.

Schurz, Carl. *Abraham Lincoln, An Essay.* Boston: Houghton, Mifflin and Company, 1891.

Shenk, Joshua Wolf. *Lincoln's Melancholy How Depression Challenged a President and Fueled His Greatness.* Paw Prints, 2008.

Slotkin, Richard. *Abe.* New York: H. Holt and Co., 2000.

Smith, James. *The Christian's Defense.* Classic Reprint, 2014 reprint of 1843 original.

Smith, Huston. *The Religions of Man.* New York: Harper Colophon, 1958.

Tagore, Rabindranath, *Sadhana. The Realisation Of Life,* New York, The Macmillan Company, 1916

Thomas, Benjamin P. *Abraham Lincoln—A Biography.* New York, Barnes & Noble Books, 1994.

Tolkien, J. R. R. *The Lord of the Rings.* Boston: Houghton Mifflin, 1967.

Twain, Mark. *Joan Of Arc.* New York: Harper and Bros, 1924.

Warren, Louis A. *Lincoln Lore. Titles Of Bulletins And Indexes For Bulletins One To Fifteen Hundred, April 15, 1929 To February 1963.* Fort, Wayne, Ind.: Lincoln National Life Foundation, 1967.

Warren, Rosanna. *Fables Of The Self.* New York: W.W. Norton, 2008.

White, Ronald C. *The Eloquent President.* New York: Random House, 2005.

Whitman, Walt. *Complete Poetry And Collected Prose.* New York, N.Y.: Literary Classics of the United States, 1982.

Whitman, Walt. *Prose Works.* Philadelphia: David McKay, 1892; Bartleby.com, 2000. www.bartleby.com/229/. 2/24/2017.

Whyte, David. *Where Many Rivers Meet: Poems.* Langley, WA: Many
     Rivers, 1996.

Wilson, Edmund. *Patriotic Gore.* New York: Oxford University Press,
     1962.

Winkle, Kenneth J. *The Young Eagle.* Dallas, Tex.: Taylor Trade Pub.,
     2001.